ABOUT ROB COUTEAU:

Rob Couteau is a writer and visual artist from Brooklyn. He's the author of the novel *Doctor Pluss*, the literary anthology *Collected Couteau*, the epistolary memoir *Letters from Paris*, and the poetry collection *The Sleeping Mermaid*. In 1985 he won the North American Essay Award, a competition open to North American writers and sponsored by the American Humanist Association. After living in Paris for twelve years, he now resides in the Mid-Hudson Valley in New York, where he writes and paints.

His work as a literary critic, interviewer, and social commentator has been featured in books such as *Gabriel Garcia Marquez's Love in the Time of Cholera: A Reader's Guide*, by Thomas Fahy, *Conversations with Ray Bradbury*, ed. Steven Aggelis, and David Cohen's *Forgotten Millions*, a book about the homeless mentally ill. Couteau's poetry, fiction, essays, and reviews have appeared in over thirty-five magazines, newspapers, and literary journals, and his interviews with other authors include conversations with Christopher Sawyer-Lauçanno, Ray Bradbury, Hubert Selby, Dr. Albert Hofmann, Michael Korda, Jeffrey H. Jackson, Robert Roper, Justin Kaplan, and James Dempsey.

more
Collected Couteau

ROB COUTEAU

more
Collected Couteau:
Essays and Interviews

Introduction by
James Dempsey

DOMINANTSTAR

Dominantstar, New York.

ISBN 978-0-9966888-1-9
First edition. 1 2 3 4 5 6 7 8 9 10 01

Essays and interviews from this collection have previously appeared in a slightly altered, abridged form in the following publications: *Emerging Civil War, Evergreen Review, Open Road Integrated Media,* and *Rain Taxi Review of Books.*

Thanks to James Dempsey, Mary Larkin, and Amanda Levin.

Cover: Photo of Walt Whitman © 1887 by George C. Cox. Restoration by Adam Cuerden.

www.robcouteau.com

For my brother,
Thomas Keith Couteau

CONTENTS

Introduction by James Dempsey

An introduction to a book is a kind of upscale sales pitch, a blurb in a suit and tie, as it were. I myself am not particularly fond of such business attire, but I greatly enjoyed reading this collection of pieces from the prolific keyboard of Rob Couteau, and I'm happy to take on the role of introducing this work to the reader, perhaps like the wedding usher at the door of a church. On second thought, though, my job here is not to show visitors to their seats, but simply to welcome them inside. So maybe I'm less of an usher and more of a greeter. Have a smiley-face sticker, sir and madam, and welcome.

But since formal attire often causes the wearer not thus sartorially accustomed to exercise a concomitant and awkward stiffness, perhaps the author won't be too chagrined if I execute my literary duties in something a little more comfortable. And so if the reader will politely fail to remark a little literary shitkickerism on my part, let us turn to the matter at hand.

Good luck trying to pin down Rob Couteau. Name the genre, and Couteau has almost certainly been there and done that. Poet, novelist, essayist, critic, journalist, memoirist, and travel writer, Couteau is not one to be hampered by constraints. He passes easily from one form of literature to another as if the borders between them did not exist for him. Perhaps they don't.

Couteau has been called a "literary enthusiast," and although he certainly is enthusiastic about literature (and indeed all art), the phrase carries the smack of the amateur about it, and Couteau is anything but. He is, in fact, an undeniably consummate professional. He is an independent scholar in every meaning of the word – unaligned with any institution except for the literary and artistic canon he so loves, and a thinker who comes to his own conclusions.

I discovered Couteau when his essay on Marion Morehouse came to my attention via a group of E. E. Cummings scholars and readers with whom I correspond. Morehouse was Cummings' muse/companion and a much-sought-after model who pioneered modeling as a career in the 1920s. But along with her beauty came a desire to shun a public life, and she covered her tracks so successfully that Cummings's biographers, Richard Kennedy and Christopher Sawyer-Lauçanno, were greatly frustrated in their efforts to collect the kind of details a biographer needs to bring a subject to life.

Couteau took on the case with the doggedness of an investigative journalist, and managed not only to piece together a solid biography of this accomplished model and actress but also to discover that she had been born out of wedlock, which may have caused her wariness of publicity.

From there I read more of Couteau's writing with admiration, so discovering his ability to turn his hand to so many forms of literature. This collection gives the reader a good sampling of Couteau's literary and scholarly talents, not the least of which are his interviews with writers he admires. Having spent many years as a journalist, I believe I have some ability to recognize and admire an artful interviewer, and Couteau is a master. His preparation is comprehensive, meticulous, and profound. His understanding of the process of writing in so many genres allows him insights into the particular problems faced by the writers he interviews. His style is conversational and relaxed, but deceptively so; he is always in control of the interview. This said, however, when a sudden fact or insight takes the interview down unexpected pathways, Couteau has the aesthetic nimbleness to recognize the opening and to follow it.

This collection features interviews with biographers, memoirists, historians, an inner-city antiviolence activist, and the creator of LSD. You'll also find herein Couteau's writings on literature, which I hesitate to call criticism since they lack the worst features of much literary criticism, which can be clogged with so much pretentiousness, cant, and philosophical obfuscation that it would take a plunger of Brobdingnagian proportions to restore a healthy flow. Couteau's essays are often rhapsodic appreciations and evocations of the work under study, and are stuffed with both insights and joy. Consider this, from the essay on Miller:

> And one of the great powers that surges forth from *Cancer* is the wit that explodes like a minefield beneath the reader when he least expects it. Again, at this stage of his career, since Miller had nothing to lose and only himself to please, he didn't give a rat's ass whether you'd be horrified, amused, or both. As is well known among the poor, humor is the one thing you cannot take away from a man who has been stripped of everything else. And humor is also the medium through which you will be reborn.

Couteau shares two things with Miller – love for Paris and birth in another place that crops up often in this collection, and which, as you would no doubt recognize, the moment Couteau (or Miller, for that matter), opened his mouth and spoke, as Brooklyn. Three of the pieces here are about a trinity of writers beloved by Couteau and closely associated with that famous borough – Walt Whitman, Henry Miller, and Hubert Selby. It is perhaps that each of these men shared in common an obsessive desire to produce something new and revolutionary with their words, something that was based not only on a powerful sense of self but also on closely-observed and unflinching descriptions of their outer and the inner worlds in all their ugliness and wonder. Lucky for us, Couteau is doing much the same.

And so my little sales pitch is done, and all that remains is for you, reader, to dig in. Get busy.

An award-winning journalist and a professor of literature at Worcester Polytechnic Institute, James Dempsey is the author of *The Tortured Life of Scofield Thayer* (Gainesville, FL: University Press of Florida, 2014) and *The Court Poetry of Geoffrey Chaucer: A Facing-page Translation in Modern English* (Lampeter, Wales: The Edwin Mellon Press, 2007).

Essays

Hubert Selby:
The Counterpoint to the Demon is Love*

I remember, when I was eight or ten years old, making a decision
   that I was going to find a way to stop the suffering in the
world…. I guess I had, by that time, seen enough suffering. And
I just wanted people to stop hurting each other. – Hubert Selby.*

It would be difficult to think of an American writer who
suffered a greater amount of physical and mental pain and
anguish than Hubert Selby Jr., or one who depicts rage and
brutality on such a raw, maniacal, sociopathic level.

Oddly enough, it never occurred to me to ask Selby about
the role of violence in his work. Reading him now, I realize
it's not just the characters in his stories who are assaulted;
the reader is a victim of the greatest and most inhuman assault of all. No matter how monstrous or horrific his depictions of abject brutality are, Selby always ups the ante and
makes them worse, pushing the limits until, by the end of
the tale, he manages to rape our imagination once again, to
puncture yet another hole in our innocence.

Selby was not only a victim of the violence done to him
by terrific illnesses and endless surgeries. He grew up in a
neighborhood where it was taken for granted that you could
have your head handed to you for the slightest infraction,
but only after it was stomped on, bloodied to a pulp, burnt
with cigarettes, kicked like a soccer ball, and sliced like an
onion. It didn't occur to me to dwell on this aspect of his
work because I grew up not far from Selby's Bay Ridge,
less than thirty years after Selby, and not much had

changed there during those decades. Indeed, when I raised this with him, he said: "Yeah, Bay Ridge, I think, is the same for the last eighty years. With a few physical exceptions." With its tree-lined sidewalks and miniature backyards where you could plant a garden and pretend you were in the midst of a natural world, with its gemütlich block parties and ecstatic games of stoop ball and stick ball and box ball, with its sunny summer days – the fire hydrants open full blast and the radios from parked convertibles blaring pop music – you could imagine for a moment that you were in some strange man-made heaven. But then, a carload of kids comes screeching down the block at sixty-miles an hour, swerves to a halt, and baseball bats in hand they go chasing someone up an alley because he made the mistake of trying to steal a bicycle.

Violence, vengeance, terror and torture for the fun of it: this was all a "normal" part of our everyday world. What made Selby different was that, while he was a part of that world, he was simultaneously endowed with a large measure of empathy, compassion, and artistry with which to portray it. Of the many incredible things in his life, the fact that he was blessed with this talent is perhaps the most miraculous thing of all. There was no one to mentor or guide him, or to pass along such gifts, or even to suggest such a calling.

That he managed to develop, hone, and refine his talent and plug away at it day after day – mocking the palpable presence of death even after the doctors said he would not live much longer – is the one thing that doesn't surprise me. Selby was a graduate from the Brooklyn School of Hard Knocks, which taught us that, if you put your will to it, anything was possible. Once you survived that time and place, the rest was a piece of cake. This was the mentality and approach Selby fostered, and it paid off. In his own humble words:

> See, you must remember that I have no natural talents or abilities in any area of life. I'm not a natural writer or a natural reader. I'm not an exceptional mechanic; I'm not an exceptional athlete; I'm not a draftsman at all; I can't draw or ... Absolutely no natural talent. But I had an obsession to do something with my life before I died. And I just sat in front of that typewriter every day, for six years, until I learned how to write. Now, I can't say that the ability *wasn't* there, obviously. I guess it was there, and I just had to fight like hell to activate it, to animate it ... It was a lot, a lot of work.*

In each of his books, there's an ever-increasing arc of suffering, inhumanity, and pointless pain. Yet there's something else that stands in shocking contrast to all this: the appearance of characters who, in the midst of a loveless, godless, twisted universe, nurture an alternative vision. Even while surrounded by such hopelessness and anguish, they yearn for something gentler. Something that would allow a reprieve, or a bit of love, or even a chance at greatness.

No matter how awful her treatment is at the hands of Vinnie and his pals, Georgette – the "hip queer" of *Last Exit* – still imagines that Vinnie will eventually offer his affection and make everything OK. Even the most sociopathic figures in Selby's demented cosmos hold out for experiences that will make them feel, if not more human, then at least more alive. Harry, the murderer in *The Demon*, is lured by antisocial acts because at least they allow him to feel *something* and to escape the numbing, deadening milieu of a soulless, corporate lifestyle. The nameless prisoner of *The Room* is driven to fantasies of torture because they serve as a compensation for the endless humiliations and mental distress he has survived. No matter how "bad" these characters are, this sliver of humanity, this urge of self-transformation grips us and draws us to their plight.

Selby once said: "There is no light in my stories, so the reader is forced to turn to his own inner light" to make it through this journey. I now realize this is only partially true. The great beacon in his demonic oeuvre is that of the artfully crafted line and the immense vision of wholeness and transcendence that lurks behind it. Selby's empathy is there, omnipresent, even while recording the darkest hues of black. The utmost depravity is portrayed with the noblest verse.

I've always considered Hubert Selby to be not just a novelist but a poet as well. Only the most refined lyrical genius could have crafted sentences that, had they been presented with traditional line breaks, would read as the best that poetry can offer. The transcendental vision of the bard is right there, in the forefront of his "prose," and it's the contrast of this highest thing that humanity can accomplish – creation – with the lowest that it often succumbs to that makes Selby a great artist and makes his work what it is: some of the most powerful literature of our times.

---

* An earlier version of this essay was featured in a Critical Symposium on Hubert Selby sponsored by his e-book publisher, *Open Road Integrated Media*, and published in January 2012.
* From Couteau's 1999 interview with Hubert Selby.
* Ibid.

Abandoning Hope to Discover Life:
Commemorating the 51st Anniversary of the
Grove Press Edition of *Tropic of Cancer*,
with a Special Tribute to Barney Rosset

"A world without hope, but no despair.
It's as though I had been converted to a new religion."
– Henry Miller, *Tropic of Cancer*

In the politically correct university village where I currently reside, each year both the town and campus libraries host a banned books exhibit. Yet I've never once seen any mention of Henry Miller or *Tropic of Cancer* in these displays, despite the fact that the 1964 Supreme Court decision to allow for its distribution represents the most important censorship case in modern publishing history. Since Miller is often labeled as a misogynist, the cause célèbre of *Tropic of Cancer* has been conveniently ignored in this and in many other "liberal" college communities.

To mark the fifty-first anniversary of the Grove Press publication of this modern masterpiece, I decided to reread the novel – for at least the fourth time – and to see if I could get not only at the core of the book but also at what so many readers find disturbing, obscene, and censorable about it. And, more importantly, I wanted to relish once again the music, the vitality, the eloquence, the unparalleled stylistic genius and love of language itself that weaves like a symphony through a landscape littered with icons of hopelessness, despair, ennui.

The leitmotif of the work may be that "the cancer of time is eating us away," yet this theme, which runs like an open sewer throughout the text, exposing us to the slime and stink of human "civilization" at every turn, is counterbalanced by an even stranger one: that despite this – in fact, *because* of this – we must celebrate life and meet it with even more joy, ecstasy, and rapture. The way to kindle this rapturous, hallucinated, visionary state is through the senses: being open fully to the pleasure of the moment. To do so, we must annihilate the overly rational, vaporous dogmas and abstract notions of traditional wisdom and replace them with a sagacity that is at one with the knowledge of the body, which knows what it needs and directs us to it without hesitation, via impulse and desire.

Ultimately, this is an Epicurean message, not only for its acknowledgement of the importance of pleasure but also because Miller realized that only when one abandons hope of anything that might lie beyond this immediate existence and accepts the extinction that death brings in its wake will we be able to truly live.

For those who remain blind to the miracle of life and to the wonder that confronts us at every turn, *Tropic of Cancer* must remain a most perplexing, irritating novel. Here is a man reduced to penury, living hand to mouth, surviving off the kindness of friends or thankless minimum-wage jobs that barely leave him with enough to eat; yet this fellow has not only the gall to celebrate life but to do so while he caricatures, critiques, lampoons, and vulgarizes everything and everyone around him. He despises conventionality and spits upon all forms of propriety. Worst of all, he views the vast social, institutional, and collective efforts of our nations and cultures as laughable, and he prophesizes they will lead nowhere and end in apocalypse, for the simple reason that the actions of most men are committed without purpose, meaning, or passion. Without wonder. And even beyond what must already seem like the ultimate cynical viewpoint, he sets the stakes a notch higher by asking if it isn't the universe itself that may be out of kilter: that there may be something fundamentally wrong with creation itself.

Yet, *Tropic of Cancer* certainly doesn't read like a bleak tract of Sartrean existentialism. Neither a missive of hollow, wooden prose nor a linear, literal discourse of grim cynicism, *Cancer* is a live wire that burns in your hand and sets you afire. If you are open to it, you realize that a great literary torch is being passed along here; if your mind is closed or offended by the author's "bad words" and unpalatable notions, your hands are scorched by this hot potato cooked in the abandoned Brooklyn lot of his terrifying imagination.

Some of Miller's most vivid descriptions of Paris were first conceived in letters written to his Brooklyn pal, Emil Schnellock. As Miller's editor George Wickes points out, often, these "were not letters in the ordinary sense but rough drafts of feature articles that Miller intended to revise for eventual publication in a book about Paris." Besides being able to focus his voice upon an "audience of one" who would appreciate its distinctive tone and phrasing, this notion of a helter-skelter guidebook with a surrealistic, Milleresque undertow – a form much less constricting than the traditional novel – helped to liberate the author's imaginative, lyrical prose. In a passage from one such "rough draft" letter of April 1930, he writes:

> I climb up instead of down to take the Metro, at Jean Juarès. Twilight hour, Indian blue, water of glass, trees glistening and liquescent. Juarès station itself gives me a kick. The rails fall away into the canal, the long caterpillar with sides lacquered in Chinese red dips like a

roller coaster. It is not Paris, it is not Coney Island – it is crepuscular mélange of all the cities of Europe and Central America. Railroad yards spread out below me, the tracks looking black, webby, not ordered by engineers but cataclysmic in design, like those gaunt fissures in the Polar ice which the camera registers in degrees of black. I have gotten into the first-class compartment by mistake….

This is reworked, condensed, and crystallized, in *Cancer*, into:

Twilight hour. Indian blue, water of glass, trees glistening and liquescent. The rails fall away into the canal at Juarès. The long caterpillar with lacquered sides dips like a roller coaster. It is not Paris. It is not Coney Island. It is crepuscular mélange of all the cities of Europe and Central America. The railroad yards below me, the tracks black, webby, not ordered by the engineer but cataclysmic in design, like those gaunt fissures in the polar ice which the camera registers in degrees of black.

Composing only for himself and a small circle of friends, for the first time in his life he was able to create without reservation and without any preconceived idea of what a novel or work of literature should be. Unimpeded, the river flowed. But this also meant that he'd write without caring much about whether what he was saying might offend, alienate, or disturb the reader. Therefore, this is an honest book, and therein lies its power – and its power to provoke.

Here, two of Picasso's most lucid aphorisms come to mind:

> Painting is not made to decorate apartments. It's an offensive and defensive weapon against the enemy.
>
> To me there is no past or future in art. If a work of art cannot live always in the present it must not be considered at all. The art of the Greeks, of the Egyptians, of the great painters who lived in other times, is not an art of the past; perhaps it is more alive today than it ever was.

Tropic of Cancer fits quite neatly into this definition of art as provocation and of great art as eternally modern regardless of its chronological date of birth, because it's made of the stuff that will never cease to piss people off – and for all the right reasons.

On the surface, the protagonist – called "Henry Miller" but not synonymous with the actual Henry Miller – is a hardened, often cold, calculating, ego-driven man: one with almost no sentimentality who looks out primarily for himself, and who never fails to dissect the person or situation in front of him and reveal the most disquieting details about what's really making this person tick or this situation unfold. There's an unerring Machiavellian insight behind everything, coupled with an eccentric yet penetrating psychological analysis that highlights a person's worst foibles, shortcomings, neuroses, and limitations. And that not only reveals all this but also revels in the tragicomic quality of it.

A third Picasso aphorism serves to explain why *Cancer* transcends a merely cynical, dreary, nihilist point of view:

> You must always work not just within but below your means. If you can handle three elements, handle only two. If you can handle ten, then handle only five. In that way the ones you do handle, you handle with more ease,

more mastery, and you can create a feeling of strength in reserve.

The "third element" that Miller held "in reserve" was his innate gentleness and tenderness, what might be called the gentleman in him. (As Anaïs Nin wrote in her journal: "Will anyone ever be as tender ...") For the astute reader, this quality shines forth in a variety of nearly inexplicable and subtle manners. For one thing, there's the narrator's ability to provoke a sense of transcendental awe as a result of his lush vocabulary and the way he reacts to certain events. Only a man propelled by a refined sensibility and a reverence for the exquisite mystery of existence could con-struct something as evocative as this:

A wagon from the Galeries Lafayette was rumbling over the bridge. The rain had stopped and the sun breaking through the soapy clouds touched the glistening rubble of roofs with a cold fire. I recall now how the driver leaned out and looked up the river toward Passy way. Such a healthy, simple, approving glance, as if he were saying to himself: "Ah, spring is coming!" And God knows, when spring comes to Paris the humblest mortal alive must feel that he dwells in paradise. But it was not only this – it was the intimacy with which his eye rested upon the scene. It was *his* Paris. A man does not need to be rich, nor even a citizen, to feel this way about Paris. Paris is filled with poor people – the proudest and filthiest lot of beggars that ever walked the earth, it seems to me. And yet they give the illusion of being at home. It is that which distinguishes the Parisian from all other metropolitan souls.

Or this:

> The day opens in milky whiteness, streaks of salmon-pink sky, snails leaving their shells. Paris. Paris. Everything happens here. Old, crumbling walls and the pleasant sound of water running in the urinals. Men licking their mustaches at the bar. Shutters going up with a bang and little streams purling in the gutters.

And regardless of the gangsterlike façade he commits himself or his "protagonist" to in *Cancer*, Miller's bark was always worse than his bite. In reminiscing about the author, the renowned First Amendment lawyer Stanley Fleishman once said: "He was a funny guy. Very gentle. I remember we were over at his house once. And we were talking about his kids, and our kids, and he was saying things like, 'When Tony had to go doo-doo, or pee-pee ...' *That* was Henry Miller!"

This is just one example of what I mean by considering carefully how the fictional Miller and the actual Miller react to events. Of course, it might be argued that Fleishman was remembering an older, more mature Miller. Yet we also have the testimony of Samuel Putnam, who knew Henry from his earliest Parisian days and who published his short story, "Mademoiselle Claude," in the *New Review*. In Putnam's memoir, *Paris Was Our Mistress*, we learn that, in the early '30s, before most of Henry's companions were even aware that he aspired to being a writer, "To us he was a good drinking companion, a nice guy to run into at Jimmy's or the Coupole or in those desolate shivering hours at the Dôme as we watched the dawn come creeping down the boulevard du Montparnasse to awaken M. Potin's grocer boys across the way and send the 'artists' home to bed. We found him humorous, affable, generous, somewhat reserved with those who did not know him well, and with a certain timidity behind it all."

Most significant of all, Putnam composed this warm and balanced homage even after Miller had utilized his memory of Putnam to fashion the ridiculous figure of Marlowe, a drunken magazine editor who's lampooned in the fourth chapter of *Cancer*. So, despite his acerbic wit, something about Henry must have endeared him to his cronics. Although he attempts to mask his empathy and to promote a roguish fictional persona, Miller was usually held in high regard by his friends and was valued as a caring companion by many of the women in his life. A hardened, bitter, pathological narcissist could not have developed the kind of friendships, or elicited the everlasting devotion, that remain the hallmarks of his biography. Lawrence Durrell best exemplified this when he wrote Miller: "I think you know I love you more than any man I ever met." In addition, in the years to come, Henry was deeply loved by his children and never deprived them of his attention, even when they burst into his studio and interrupted his writing.

Of course, there remains an unquestionable strain of narcissism running throughout Miller's life and work: one that was surely imprinted upon him by his emotionally distant, self-centered mother, whom he portrays as being either icy cold or raging and wrathful. But while she was clearly a narcissist in the most pathological sense of the word, Henry is more accurately described merely by the adjective, *narcissistic*. As is well known among clinicians, there can be both a healthy and an unhealthy aspect to the narcissistic function in a person's life. The dividing line is whether one is capable of extending empathy toward others, and this Henry was not only capable of but at times almost obsessed with, perhaps as a compensation for what he never received as a child. One of the joys of reading *Tropic of Cancer* stems from the manner in which this seemingly ruthless individual cares about the downtrodden, forgotten dregs of humanity. Miller commemorates them in a series of portraits that extend throughout his oeuvre, and the impulse to do so can be traced back to his early days as employment manager for Western Union, when he dreamed of writing a novel based on the "lost boys" who served as messengers for what he called the Cosmodemonic Telegraph Company. Part of the narrator's rage and resentment in *Cancer* is linked to this sense of injustice suffered by the anonymous, unknown, silent souls who make the world go round and who never receive the credit or the paychecks they so sorely deserve. (In Walt Whitman's words: "the absentees, the forgotten, the shy nobodies who in the end are best of all.") In a 1956 interview with Ben Grauer, he again touched on this theme:

> It's true, "the folks," "the people," are what supports us … the people who do the dirty work. Who are without name, without honor…. It's they who are doing the work of the world.

And in chapter seven of *Tropic of Cancer*, he fondly recalls his Hindu messengers from New York:

> Two of them were saints, if I know what a saint is; particularly Gupte who was found one morning with his throat cut from ear to ear. In a little boarding house in Greenwich Village he was found one morning stretched out stark naked on the bed, his flute beside him, and his throat gashed, as I say, from ear to ear. It was never dis-

covered whether he had been murdered or whether he had committed suicide. But that's neither here nor there....

This urge to, if not immortalize, then at least pay his respects to such men closely resembles that of another Brooklyn-born author, one who also held his profound empathy "in reserve." In recalling the inspiration behind his first novel and its unforgettable drag queen, Georgette, Hubert Selby said: "I met someone from the old neighborhood and they said Georgie had been found dead in the street, evidently an O.D. He was only about twenty years old when he died.... I guess I felt Georgie needed more than a death in the street. He needed a memorial.... Thus, in a very real way, Georgie is responsible for the book *Last Exit to Brooklyn.*"

While briefly working as a language instructor at Dijon, in one of his early letters to Anaïs Nin, Miller wrote:

> God, it is maddening to think that even one day must pass without writing. I shall never, never catch up. It is why, no doubt, I write with such vehemence, such distortion. It is despair.... And with it grows a certain hard selfishness – or self-interest. I don't know whether I am becoming a solipsist or a narcissist. Certainly, more and more the world revolves around me, in me.

When I reread this the other day, it struck a most discordant note. I realized that, like other children of narcissistic parents, Miller's own needs were unjustly deferred; the authentic self had long remained under the shadow of a domineering mother who always expected nothing but conventionality from her son. And this letter to Nin reminded me that it was only when he expatriated to Paris and escaped both the narcissistic demands of his mother as well as those of his second wife, June, that his own needs could finally be attended to.

More than anything, this explains the self-centered, self-obsessed nature of the protagonist of *Tropic of Cancer*. It also explains the naive surprise with which Miller frames this revelation of perhaps being egoistic. Deep in his gut, he felt an obligation to nurture his *daemon*, no matter how unpalatable this might appear to others. Part of this unbolting of the floodgates involved allowing himself to serve himself, to feed his soul on the most profound psychic level, to tend to the self whose needs had been eclipsed for so long, and which is nourished in normal development in the early and adolescent years but which was not properly succored in that period of Henry's life. Food of all kinds, exotic and mundane, and rhapsodies to hunger and to sustenance appear like fragments of an ancient opera in *Tropic of Cancer*. Yes, he was literally starved, but he was also emotionally famished; and he needed to engorge, no matter how unsavory that appetite might appear to a well-heeled politically correct graduate student skimming over the novel fifty years later. Again, this is an honest book, and the world does not always appreciate honesty. As Miller would clarify in a letter to Nin a few months later: "Really, I can't consider myself an egotist … No, I feel merely like a force which must express itself, at any cost."

The author Norman Mailer thought he'd detected a narcissistic pattern in Miller's work and tried to explore it in *Genius and Lust*, but lacking any real understanding of the clinical definition of the disorder and, more importantly, being a full-blown narcissist himself, he possessed no way of seeing with any clarity into its deeper implications. A bully who thought nothing of intimidating and physically attacking people with whom he disagreed, he was perhaps not the person best suited for this task.

Another reason that Mailer was thrown off track is that, in popular usage, the meaning of the term "narcissist" has been distorted to simply imply self-centeredness or self-aggrandizement: symptoms of the illness, but certainly not the core of the problem. Instead of being based on love, the narcissist's relationships are focused on gaining control over others. A thirst for power obliterates any possibility of empathy or tenderness. The pathological narcissist is interested only in abusing others for material or emotional gain. To the extent that he lacks empathy, to the same degree does he revel in disempowering, tormenting, or torturing others. When the need to torture increases to the point of fearlessly breaking serious laws in order to do so, we enter the realm of the sociopath: just a step beyond the narcissist in the spectrum of personality disorders.

Again, although Miller wasn't a pathological narcissist, he was narcissistic in that he preferred to pursue romantic obsessions and infatuations rather than authentic love based on commonality and reality. He could state unequivocally "I don't want the truth, I *want* illusion, mystery, intrigue" because only illusion fuels the drug of infatuation and promotes its joys. But the modest love of spiritual union is grounded through truth, takes roots in reality, and blossoms only there.

Of course, infatuation can lead to love and even spark and ignite it. And what would life be without such delicious obsessions? Miller's oeuvre is, in many ways, an epic poem celebrating an infatuation with every aspect of life: even with its "cancer" or, at least, with the *acceptance* of it. That he refused to complete the epic with a realistic or convincing portrayal of love, however, is what so many readers find unbearable and obscene. They may focus upon and object to his "dirty" words, but, whether they're aware of it or not, this is the real reason Miller alienates a certain kind of reader: both the überfeminist puritans of today or the post-Victorian prudes of the Thirties. And, as H. L. Mencken might remark, this alienation becomes a moral condemnation. Rather than accepting the novel for what it is and valuing the truth of its portrait, we as Americans feel compelled to render a moral judgment upon the work – and then upon its author. The reaction is typical since, as Mencken reminds us, "There has never been any question before the nation, whether political or economic, religious or military, diplomatic or sociological, which did not resolve itself, soon or late, into a purely moral question."

One of the most effective tools against what Mencken calls the "dirty-mindedness of Puritanism" is humor. And one of the great powers that surges forth from *Cancer* is the wit that explodes like a minefield beneath the reader when he least expects it. Again, at this stage of his career, since Miller had nothing to lose and only himself to please, he didn't give a rat's ass whether you'd be horrified, amused, or both. As is well known among the poor, humor is the one thing you cannot take away from a man who has been stripped of everything else. And humor is also the medium through which you will be reborn. Thus, *Tropic of Cancer* is nothing if not a *renaissance* document – a testament of *naissance* and a manual for how to effect it. But only if you are truly free of the manacles of propriety can you laugh so heartily – or even laugh at all – at the wit and wisdom of this diabolical tract.

Like any renaissance man worth his salt, Miller was also moved by the power of beauty in art. Entwined in the substrate of *Cancer*, there is a perennial root and vine that surfaces here and there: sometimes in no more than a passing phrase, or an ode of a few sentences or paragraphs, or even as a keynote around which everything harmonizes and resounds into a major chord. I'm speaking of Miller's awareness of and respect for the antique Parisian Muses, and his attempt to return something to them in the creation he titles *Tropic of Cancer*. The most significant form this embodies is his continual homage to the "soul of Paris": la Seine. Here are two such examples:

> After everything had quietly sifted through my head a great peace came over me. Here, where the river gently winds through the girdle of hills, lies a soil so saturated with the past that however far back the mind roams one can never detach it from its human background. Christ, before my eyes there shimmered such a golden peace that only a neurotic could dream of turning his head away. So quietly flows the Seine that one hardly notices its presence. It is always there, quiet and unobtrusive, like a great artery running through the human body. […]

> The sun is setting. I feel this river flowing through me – its past, its ancient soil, the changing climate. The hills gently girdle it about: its course is fixed.

———

> For the moment I can think of nothing – except that I am a sentient being stabbed by the miracle of these waters that reflect a forgotten world. All along the banks the

trees lean heavily over the tarnished mirror; when the
wind rises and fills them with a rustling murmur they
will shed a few tears and shiver as the water swirls by. I
am suffocated by it. No one to whom I can communicate
even a fraction of my feelings....

This last hauntingly beautiful passage is just a paragraph
away from a more vaudevillian and censorable one made
famous by Lenny Bruce, who would read it to audiences as
part of his comedic routine: the section where Miller tells
Tania, "I will make your ovaries incandescent" and "After
me you can take on stallions, bulls, rams, drakes, St. Ber-
nards." One has the impression that the comic, like so many
others – including the lusty American GIs who smuggled
the book back from Paris and made it a cause célèbre –
never bothered to carefully read the adjacent paragraph.
And, if they had, one wonders who among them would
have understood or appreciated it, regardless of the fact that
it contains the real message of *Tropic of Cancer*.

And then, in a nod to the splendors of the antique Medi-
terranean world, Miller composes a eulogy to a nameless
veilleur de nuit (night watchman) employed at a lycée in
Dijon. The narrator informs us that he "is the only human
being in the whole institution with whom I feel a kinship.
He is a nobody." Yet something about him, particularly the
way he imbibes his bottle of wine, fascinates the author:
"To me it's like he's pouring rubies down his gullet.
Something about this gesture which seizes me by the hair.
It's almost as if he were drinking down the dregs of human
sympathy." Then, two pages later comes a proclamation
that completely distinguishes Miller from a typical American author:

> The whole Mediterranean seemed to be buried inside him – the orange groves, the cypress trees, the winged statues, the wooden temples, the blue sea, the stiff masks, the mystic numbers, the mythological birds, the sapphire skies, the eaglets, the sunny coves, the blind bards, the bearded heroes.

Although *Cancer* unfolds almost entirely within the crucible of Paris, the two main adventures that take place outside the city also occur in the vicinity of the Seine: at its culmination at la Havre; and in Dijon, near the river's source. Thus, the chronicle is framed between the beginning, middle, and end of this historic, mythic, and majestic river.

In August 1932, the manuscript was shown to the book agent William Bradley, along with Miller's more traditional novel, *Crazy Cock*. Yet, when Bradley offered to represent *Cancer* and to send it to the publisher Jack Kahane, Miller made little of the gesture and instead tried to convince Bradley to take on the far-inferior *Crazy Cock*.

Biographer Jay Martin regards this "curious" reaction as a "backpedaling loss of confidence exactly at the moment of his triumph." Was Miller's hesitation due to a sudden realization that, if it were published, the unwavering provocations in the text would open him to a variety of attacks for which he was not yet prepared? A more likely explanation is that, to the end, there remained something in Henry that refused to take seriously the prospect of its success, and those very doubts had allowed him to hold nothing back in the actual composing of it.* (And, in fact, it wasn't until Anaïs Nin helped him to whittle it down to its present form that its success would become inevitable.) In April

1932, he even asked Nin: "Are you sure I am not crazy? I mean, is all this personal narration justifiable? [...] I begin to think even you will balk. But I have said to myself 'there must be no limits.' I must be the one person in the world to risk everything, tell everything." As late as July 18 – a few weeks before Bradley agreed to represent the book – Miller added: "Yes, I am going completely nuts these days, not knowing whether I have failed again or not, but feeling as I wrote certain passages that they were fine, splendid, the best I ever wrote, only nobody will take the pains to read them."

Put another way, Henry's hyperconscious approach to *Crazy Cock* – agonizing over it for years in an attempt to create a saleable novel – had yielded nothing of value; while the playful, intuitive approach to *Cancer*'s creation yielded a success that surprised even Miller, since it was the product not merely of his conscious efforts but also of an instinctive urge to give free rein to his unconscious, his *daemon*.

Perhaps as a result of holding nothing back, *Cancer* remains more didactic than Miller's other novels, in that he repeatedly returns to an overt message of hopelessness and destruction in the narrative (due to the influence of Spengler's *Decline of the West*), even though it's the dramatized, humorous, and vaudevillian scenes that remain more firmly planted in the reader's memory. But despite the directness of their message, these more didactic passages represent some of the most lyrical ones in the book (and I use the word *didactic* simply to describe their nature and purpose and not to imply any shortcoming):

If at intervals of centuries there does appear a man with a desperate, hungry look in his eye, a man who would turn the world upside down in order to create a new race, the love that he brings to the world is turned to bile and he becomes a scourge. If now and then we encounter pages that explode, pages that would wound and sear, that wring groans and tears and curses, know that they come from a man with his back up, a man whose only defenses left are his words and his words are always stronger than the lying, crushing weight of the world, stronger than all the racks and wheels which the cowardly invent to crush out the miracle of personality. If any man ever dared to translate all that is in his heart, to put down what is really his experience, what is truly the truth, I think then the world would go to smash, that it would be blown to smithereens and no god, no accident, no will could ever again assemble the pieces, the atoms, the indestructible elements that have gone to make up the world.

Once *Tropic of Cancer* was published in Paris and a small but significant readership began to respond (drawing accolades from the likes of H. L. Mencken, Marcel Duchamp, and Blaise Cendrars), the novelistic character of "Henry Miller" began to shift a bit closer to the man Henry Miller in one subtle way. As someone once remarked in comparing Miller and Céline, the difference between them was that Miller wanted to be liked while Céline went out of his way not to be liked. (In the single correspondence that he allotted him, Céline warned Miller: "Learn how to be wrong – the world is full of people who are right – that's why it is so *revolting*.") In his major novels that followed *Cancer*, even when Henry portrays himself at his "worst," there's a cunning sleight of hand that warms up the reader to the protagonist and shows him in a redeeming light sooner or later; or that evokes our pity or concern; or that encourages us to forgive him simply because he's so witty, bright, naive, and human. To put it in the context of our earlier discussion: we're reminded of the narcissist's need to be liked, while the sociopath doesn't care whether you like him or not. Henry was deeply wounded by his mother's callous denial of love, and he spoke of it repeatedly throughout his life and work. Like anyone suffering under such circumstances, he tried to replace this loss of fundamental emotional sustenance with the attention and approval he gained from others.

While Miller has been accused of creating a book filled with hatred, the careful reader will discern that it's actually rage against the injustice and futility of the world that propel him, both in *Cancer* and in his subsequent work. In the case of Céline, one of our greatest novelists despite his personal faults, it is, sadly enough, a real and unadulterated hatred – which often crosses over to the sociopathic – that burns in his heart, as evidenced by his joining anti-Semitic groups in the 1930s and his racist, inflammatory pamphlets, published during the Occupation, in which he calls for "urns for the Jews" and other such niceties. After the war, Céline spoke of "the magical gas chambers," feeding revisionist doubts that it ever happened. As biographer Nicholas Hewitt informs us in his definitive *Life of Céline*, the French author chose "to adapt a position which is in a minority even among anti-Semites, that of racism." And it was "part of an integral racism extending from his disparagement of the Blacks in Africa to later paranoia at a possible Chinese invasion of the West after the Second World War." Indeed, in this context, Miller's declaration that "it never occurred to me that I was a sinful man – selfish, yes, but not sinful" takes on new light.

In the winsome documentary, *Henry Miller Asleep and Awake*, Henry points to a German poster advertising the cinematic adaptation of *Tropic of Cancer*, and he translates the caption: "Without love, we're nothing." Then, with a laugh and a sparkle in his eye, he adds: "But of course, the *Tropic of Cancer* wasn't very much about love!" Yet, one could argue that this is one of the marvelous things about it. For here is a character who lives not only without proper employment, or regular meals, or the propriety and respect that one is expected to accord social and cultural institutions, but he also lives without what we'd normally define as romantic love. In its place are obsessions, infatuations, and what one might call a love of the universe itself: an openness to and continual embrace of the Epicurean sense of cosmic awe, carefully counterbalanced by an unceasing acknowledgment of the horror and futility of life as it's ordinarily lived. Yet, the author has conceived of a protagonist who not only finds peace; he prospers and flowers as few men do. And for this to happen, we suspect that the author himself, although perhaps not identical with his creation, shares this essential aspect of it.

In his book, *The Swerve*, Stephen Greenblatt describes how

> Christian polemicists had to find a way to turn the current of mockery against Epicurus and his followers. Ridiculing the pagan pantheon did not work in this case, since Epicureanism eloquently dismantled the whole sacrificial worship of the gods and dismissed the ancient stories. What had to be done was to refashion the account of the founder Epicurus so that he appeared no longer as an apostle of moderation in the service of reasonable pleasure but instead as a Falstaffian figure of ri-

otous excess. He was a fool, a pig, a madman. And his principle Roman disciple, Lucretius, had to be comparably made over.

I see an identical strategy at work in besmirching modern Epicureans such as Henry Miller, and one that ran a similar course against his predecessor, Walt Whitman. Like Epicurus and Lucretius, they, too, were accused of exactly the same thing. Thus, it comes as no surprise that critics continue to attack the author of *Tropic of Cancer* with as much vehemence as they excoriate its hero.

Toward the end of his life, Miller confessed to his housekeeper Twinka Thiebaud: "Looking back, I realize that my loves were, in actuality, obsessions." And he added: "I don't want the truth, I *want* illusion, mystery, intrigue. That is why women have been able to take advantage of me so often." When I read this, I see evidence of the wound that Miller suffered at the hands of his mother, Louise Marie Neiting, and how it bit into him like a slowly burning acid all his life. And when I hear him proclaiming to Twinka, "Love is the be-all, end-all, and cure-all," I harbor lasting doubts about whether Henry, even at the age of eighty-eight, really knew what love was. I see this limitation reflected throughout his work, yet I also see that, despite this, he created not one but several masterpieces to the human spirit. Like a tree trunk forced to grow round an obstacle blocking its path, he grew round this impediment and was simultaneously shaped by it.

This lack of authentic love in his novels is certainly linked to the accusation of misogyny. Yet, rather than simply a case of misogyny, I see in *Cancer* a man who thumbs his nose at men and women alike, who has decided for once in his life to enjoy himself even if it means being a bit selfish, rakish, and callous. I see a character who's living on so few material resources that he cannot always afford to be honest, caring, or sincere. And I see a fellow who is desperately trying to understand himself and define himself: one who's ever aware of a fecund, creative power surging within but who hasn't yet learned enough about how to channel it, or where to direct it, or what forces to train upon it, or how to balance it with the merely human and profane needs that comprise quotidian life. I see a silhouette bobbing along the quai de la Seine, admiring each gleaming cobblestone while the dismal clouds of violence, war, and chaos swell ever larger over the Continent. And this man is also aware of the coming catastrophe and weaves that too into his prose:

> If you want bread you've got to get in harness, get in lock step. Over the earth a gray desert, a carpet of steel and cement. Production! More nuts and bolts, more barbed wire, more dog biscuits, more lawn mowers, more ball bearings, more high explosives, more tanks, more poison gas, more soap, more toothpaste, more newspapers, more education, more churches, more libraries, more museums. *Forward!*

And I see an American who was even more horrified by the acultural life that drove him into a deep anguish in New York; and now, this same soul is reborn, and he walks electrified, surrounded by a mystery and beauty he can hardly find words for. But find them he does, and with these words – admittedly, "dictated" by an inner voice that wells up from a completely transpersonal source – he succeeds in handing back to the Parisian Muses what they've been giving him all along.

A word as loaded as *misogyny* has come to have all sorts of subjective and unintended meanings. And now, it's casually tossed about, just as the word *witch* or *communist* was bandied about in earlier epochs. If misogynist means someone who uses the word *cunt* to describe part of a woman's anatomy, then Miller is guilty, and if you need to crucify him for that, so be it. But if, as Merriam-Webster's defines it, it means someone who hates women, then Miller is not guilty, because, no matter how the protagonist of *Cancer* behaves toward others, it's never with actual hatred, and the same can be said, with an even greater emphasis, for Henry himself.

Instead, I would argue that the key figure of this novel has one goal, and that is to make fun of everyone – and everything – he encounters, including himself. And, in so doing, to create not only a new world but also a new self, a new raison d'être. *Tropic of Cancer* caricatures, analyzes, dissects, and bemoans of everything – and yet it also rejoices in everything. Whether one agrees with this treatment or with the conclusions drawn by its fictional hero, it remains one of the great books. Therefore, I have no ultimate interest in judging the morality of the author or his protagonist. But I do wish to commend both: for what they are and for what they accomplished.

And I would offer a final proviso: that we'd be better served when appreciating literature if we took heed of the words of a critic who was an early supporter of Miller's work (calling it "one of the most beautiful prose styles today"). Almost a hundred years ago, in his essay "Puritanism as a Literary Force," H. L. Mencken warned:

> the prevailing American view of the world and its mysteries is still a moral one, and no other human

concern gets half the attention that is endlessly lavished upon the problem of conduct, particularly of the other fellow.... The American, save in moments of conscious and swiftly lamented deviltry, casts up all ponderable values, including even the values of beauty, in terms of right and wrong. He is beyond all things else, a judge and a policeman; he believes firmly that there is a mysterious power in law; he supports and embellishes its operation with a fanatical vigilance.

Even more to the point, he goes on to say: "the American, try as he will, can never imagine a work of the imagination as wholly devoid of moral content. It must either tend toward the promotion of virtue, or be suspect and abominable." It's also in this essay, published in book form in 1917, that Mencken coins the terms "the new Puritanism" and "neo-Puritanism," phrases that are often utilized today, and he concludes:

Any questioning of the moral ideas that prevail – the principal business, it must be plain, of the novelist, the serious dramatist, the professed inquirer into human motives and acts – is received with the utmost hostility. To attempt such an enterprise is to disturb the peace – and the disturber of the peace, in the national view, quickly passes over into the downright criminal.

In other words, don't throw the baby out with the bathwater. Even if it involves as unsympathetic a person as Céline, we must judge the work itself primarily on its own merit. The witch hunt that has commenced to either accept or condemn the labors of an artist based on whether he fits into our current notion of what is politically correct is, at heart, no different from the puritanical hypocrisy that has always assailed the so-called land of the free. As Mencken says, in America, eventually every inquiry turns into a moral question. Miller's key contribution is that he revealed what it was like to be a particular man, an American, floating like a cork through the human wasteland of the underclass of Paris in the early 1930s. He didn't lie about the thoughts and fantasies that riveted his mind and body; instead, he unveiled them, and, as Whitman did in the previous century, he celebrated them.

In his Preface to *Tropic of Cancer* – signed by Anaïs Nin but obviously composed by Miller himself – he calls it a "naked book" (a remark bearing a prophetic resonance to the title of William Burroughs's *Naked Lunch*). There, you may be sure, he wasn't stretching the truth. He unabashedly exposes himself and demands – if you are to be as honest a reader as he is a writer – that you do the same, even if it causes quite a bit of discomfit.

In a country in which it's all right for a woman to call a man a *prick* but akin to heresy for a man to call a woman a *cunt*, this has created a bit of a ticklish problem for old Henry. And when every thirteen-year-old hipster considers herself a "Goddess," what dear me are we to do about an author who uses the vagina as a symbol and metaphor with which to promulgate various disturbing images from the *Decline of the West*? In *Tropic of Cancer*, the cunt is a crack through which the meaningless pursuits of modern "progress" are seen as null and void; the cunt is the acme and nadir of emptiness and ennui; the cunt is as "fucked out" and "pooped out" as the universe itself. And, on the microcosmic level, the cunt, in the character Van Norden's words, doesn't even contain a harmonica or a calendar: there's not a thing inside, nothing that would redeem us, and Van Norden knows this because he's carefully trained a flashlight upon its barren walls. Worse still, Fillmore (such a fitting name, since his cock is gargantuan!) is so cunt struck that he's lost in the abysm of a loveless marriage ruled over by a vicious, conniving, thieving cunt, and he only escapes by the cunt hairs thanks to Henry, who sees right through this venereal illusion and ships him off to bloody England. The cunt is a trapdoor through which we may fall thanks to syphilis and gonorrhea, and so the walls of every Métro station are plastered with posters bearing the sign of Cancer, the crab: its claws outstretched like two chancre-ridden grasping cunt lips. Yet, this only raises the stakes, because if you brave the dangers the rewards seem that much sweeter, and thus we have that mighty blast of sperm-ridden ecstasy that heralds the coming of a new literature in *Cancer*'s opening pages, when Henry pays homage to the emotionally unfettered joys of ejaculatory male sex by proclaiming that he will ream out every wrinkle in Tanya's twat, set her ovaries ablaze, and yank "toads, bats, lizards" from her juicy little cubbyhole.

This, more than anything, is what gets people steamed about Miller. Too much cunt. And without the proper reverence, without the "appropriate" wrappings with which we're supposed to deliver it. In his own words: *"Tropic of Cancer* wasn't very much about love!"

* * *

In one of those strange twists of personal fate, in the moments after I completed this tribute to a man and a book I love, I learned of the passing of Barney Rosset, who was also one of the great men of our time. In the words of

Miller-biographer Frederick Turner: "Even in 1961, the year of its American publication, [*Tropic of Cancer*] still looked amazingly avant-garde, enough so that its appearance through Barney Rosset's Grove Press was a cultural sensation felt far beyond the realm of arts and letters. It was in truth one of the first major shots fired in what were to become the cultural wars of that remarkable decade."

If Barney hadn't decided to publish *Cancer*, and if he hadn't so doggedly persisted in convincing Miller of the need to do so – cutting through each of the author's fears and hesitations about finally introducing the book to a potentially hostile Cold-War America – our lives would have been substantially different.* Not only because of *Tropic of Cancer*, but also because many of the gems that followed it – such as *Naked Lunch*, *Last Exit to Brooklyn*, and the works of the Marquis de Sade – would have remained hidden away from our collective consciousness for who knows how long. After *Tropic of Cancer*, anything seemed possible, and the publishing world was indeed forever altered.

"Everything is possible" – the battle cry of the Sixties counterculture – may have seen its truest expression in the list of titles that Barney courageously brought forth. Many of those in my generation, who came of age in the Sixties and Seventies, grew up studying these works as if they were Holy Scripture. We fashioned our style after them, expanded our vocabulary through them, molded our ideas upon them. Even more important than having long hair or wearing blue jeans, if you encountered a stranger with one of these titles tucked under his arm, it was something akin to the ancient Christians, under the Roman Empire, who recognized each other by drawing the sign of the fish on the arid sand. Conversations commenced, relationships formed or dissolved, friendships expanded or deflated based upon how you reacted to characters such as Dr. Benway in *Naked Lunch*, Vanessa in *Tropic of Capricorn*, or Harry in *Requiem for a Dream*. Behind it all was the éminence grise of Barney Rosset, polluting our minds with such wonderful "filth and smut" and turning us all into "angelheaded hipsters."

In *Tropic of Cancer*, in one of his hyperbolic invectives against the air-conditioned nightmare, Miller writes: "America is the very incarnation of doom. She will drag the whole world down to the bottomless pit." So true. And truer now, perhaps, than ever. Yet, as the ultimate counterpoint to such unredeeming malefic forces, we have the likes of Barney Rosset, who lives on in so many ways but especially as an example of how one real man – "who would turn the world upside down" – makes a difference.

---

* Originally featured in the *Rain Taxi Review of Books* (online), August 2012.

* "In writing it … I had almost no hope of its ever being accepted by a publisher. It was something I had to do in order to preserve my own integrity. It was a case of do or die. Certainly the last thing I ever dreamed of was that it would one day be published in my own country." Henry Miller, letter to Stanley Fleishman from December 26, 1962, as quoted by Edward de Grazia, *Girls Lean Back Everywhere. The Law of Obscenity and the Assault on Genius*, New York: Random House, 1992, p. 367.

* I once asked Barney Rosset if Miller appreciated the enormous personal sacrifice that Rosset underwent: selling his beachfront properties, worth millions of dollars, to finance the trials of *Tropic of Cancer*. With a straight face and a tone of utmost sincerity, he replied, "Oh, yes. He was very nice to us. He even gave me some of his watercolors"!

A Review of *Kerouac Ascending: Memorabilia of the Decade of 'On the Road'* by Elbert Lenrow*

In Gerald Nicosia's panoramic Jack Kerouac biography, *Memory Babe*, the author recounts an electrifying exchange between Jack's creative writing professor, the New School's Brom Weber, and Allen Ginsberg, the latter a visitor to the class. In his delightfully histrionic manner, Allen demands that Weber be more like Professor Mark Van Doren, who, Ginsberg claims, expresses "love" for the students as well as for their work. Meanwhile, Jack, who was profoundly shy unless he was drunk, at first merely agrees with everything Allen says but then enters into the argument and concludes that criticism is worthless since writing is a "prayer to God." This encounter, remembered long afterward by fellow students such as Mario Puzo and George Mandel, appears like a dramatic foreshadowing of many far more confrontational scenes that would serve as high-water marks in the culture clashes of the late Fifties and early Sixties, culminating in social movements that Ginsberg and Kerouac wittingly and unwittingly prophesized and personified.

When I first encountered this passage, I wondered if Jack had ever been blessed with a more sympathetic academic mentor and, if so, what such a relationship might have entailed. The answer is to be found here, in this collection of literary scraps and miscellany, which in its brevity and heterogeneity resembles a time capsule reflecting key moments of Beat history.

Taking advantage of the G. I. Bill, in the fall of 1948 Kerouac signed up for courses at the New School and enrolled in Professor Elbert Lenrow's class, "The 20th-Century Novel in America" (and reenrolled with him the following semester). Shortly after they met, Jack invited Lenrow for drinks at a Sixth Avenue bar, where, along with Ginsberg, they conducted the first of many congenial, informal discussions about life and literature. The following year, Jack wrote Lenrow several letters from out West and reported on his latest progress with *On the Road* (the correspondence is included here and contains long passages from a draft of the manuscript).

Besides featuring postcards and letters from Kerouac and Ginsberg, first and foremost in this "memorabilia" collection we have two term papers authored by Jack and commented on by this genteel, ever-supportive mentor. Jack struggles to enumerate his thoughts on figures such as Dreiser, Sinclair Lewis, Thomas Wolfe, and Céline, all the while attempting to follow as rigorous an academic form as possible (something that clearly goes against his grain). In Lenrow's words, Jack displays an "easy command of the conventions" yet "regularly and consistently introduces insights that prove quite pleasing and give the writing a stamp of authenticity." For example, in his paper on Dreiser and Lewis, Kerouac concludes: "Dreiser is calm and his people are cautious, and the whole is overlaid with the mild grace of Classical tragedy; but the Lewis tragedy is a Dionysian, crazy, Faustian tragedy. Even Babbitt is 'wild,' he goes on sprees." In his study of Thomas Wolfe, Jack describes how, in the eyes of social realists, Wolfe was viewed as a politically incorrect author because of his focus on transcendental "wonder." But for Jack, Wolfe's writing "sometimes achieves a quality of awesome revelation that is reminiscent of the old and sacred writings, and all great poetry."

The other gem in this collection is a story told by the professor himself. One evening, Ginsberg and Kerouac drop by Lenrow's Richmond Hill flat accompanied by Neal Cassady, who meets the professor for the first time. Cassady, he tell us, appears with the same bandaged thumb that makes a dramatic appearance in *On the Road*, after Neal takes a swing at his girlfriend LuAnne, and, instead of hurting her, his hand deflects off her head and the bones of his thumb are shattered, leading to a serious infection (osteomyelitis) and forcing Cassady to deal with the physical limits and demands of the body.

After entering Lenrow's apartment, Neal excuses himself, supposedly to use the bathroom to soak his sore thumb but actually to case the joint. (He disappears for so long that Ginsberg even goes to check up on him.) A week later, while Lenrow is teaching at the New School, someone gains entry to his flat by smashing open a wooden panel on the back door and steals several gold rings, a gold watch, and money, all from the professor's bedroom bureau.

The police inform Lenrow that it appears to be a robbery by someone who was familiar with the apartment. It was committed in a rush; after scooping up the booty, the perp failed to search the rest of the flat, and he even missed some cash in a partitioned billfold. (They call it a "hit-and-run": a resonant metaphor considering Cassady's role behind the wheel in *On the Road*.)

Besides forming a telling portrait of Neal, who was ever the callous hood, the episode neatly reveals Ginsberg's endless naïveté. Despite the obvious, he remains doubtful that the burglary was accomplished by his pal. As Katherine Burkman notes in her Introduction: "Lenrow had known Thomas Wolfe, a significant connection for Kerouac … and kept a collection of Wolfe memorabilia." Lenrow's digs were a sacred grotto to Kerouac, in that he was able to examine Wolfe's manuscripts and handwritten notes, connecting to Wolfe through the intercessor of Lenrow. Yet, Neal thought nothing of befouling such a special retreat and taking advantage of this modest, self-effacing man's hospitality.

Lenrow's commentary also provides insightful comments about a key conflict within Kerouac's life. Although Jack was a gifted raconteur who, for a time, remained at the forefront of innovative literary prose, he was also a maladapted, eternal child – childish rather than merely childlike – who couldn't handle the celebrity role foisted upon him and who increasingly withdrew into an alcoholic stupor: both to numb his pain and to ease his way into a more extroverted facade. Commenting on one of Jack's letters that is included here, Lenrow remarks: "When upset by negative criticism, he became confused, childish, maudlin, and sentimental." According to Lenrow, Jack "had glimpses of an earlier self that had shown intelligence and coherence, and here he was wasting himself on 'twaddle' [quoting Jack himself]. In the next year or two, having achieved fame (or notoriety) as 'King of the Beats' … Jack was taken less and less seriously as a literary artist. He could not resolve his growing dilemma except through increasing withdrawal via his mother and drink."

In *On the Road*, Kerouac recounts a reoccurring nightmare he has of traveling across a parched desert toward "the Protective City" while being pursued by a shrouded figure. As Gerald Nicosia paraphrases it, in the dream, "while other men struggled diligently across the desert to the Protective City, he wandered about looking for the soft repose of an oasis." Indeed, Jack remains in a shelter for so long that he never reaches his goal.

In retrospect, one cannot help but wonder at the all-too-obvious connection between this dream and Jack's later life. His addiction to alcohol and his emotional dependence upon his mother were the primary toxins that were served in such oases, and they derailed him from the manly struggle to endure – and even to treasure – the hardship that molds us along the way. Ginsberg and Lenrow each commented upon this in their own way: Lenrow, in the above quote, and Allen in a letter to Lenrow from the summer of 1968: "Kerouac's been taking care of his mother all these years & also seeing ashes and sorrow deeper than anyone I know, & he drinks too much for his body to stand ..."

This slim but engrossing volume also features a warm, personal Preface by Lenrow's cousin Katherine Burkman (a Professor Emeritus of English); a brief essay by Barbara Phillips, Lenrow's niece; and an Introduction by Howard Cunnell (editor of *On the Road: The Original Scroll*), who provides a broader literary context for what follows. (For example, Cunnell points out that Kerouac, "in preparatory notes" for his Wolfe paper, "writes that he is concerned with Wolfe as a 'writer of the 'soul' – a soul-worker – in the tradition of 'sacred letters.'") Although the collection has a somewhat fragmentary feel to it, it also possesses the charm of a personal scrapbook, containing memories of a time long gone and one that ultimately remains accessible only through the imagination.

---

* Published in *Evergreen Review*, February 2013.

* Apparently the shrouded figure was a reoccurring motif. In one of his journals he writes: "Dream of the grownup man chasing me, I'm a little boy in some town somewhere, homeless, I've done some prank or vandalism and he's mad and wants to catch me, wears white shirt like Shrouded Traveler in the Hall ..." The notion of a split-off maturity (the "grownup") attempting to unite with a *puer* sensibility (the little boy) could not be made any plainer. Jack Kerouac, *Book of Dreams* (San Francisco: City Lights Books, 1981), p. 154.

On the Trail of the 'Elusive'
Lillian and Marion Morehouse

While preparing to interview the E. E. Cummings's biographer Christopher Sawyer-Lauçanno, I became intrigued
by the figure of Marion Morehouse (the poet's lifelong
companion), or perhaps I should say by her *nebulousness*.
In the late Twenties and early Thirties, before meeting
Cummings in 1932, Marion was one of the most widely
recognized fashion models of the day, appearing in both
Vogue and *Vanity Fair*. The renowned photographer Edward Steichen called her "the greatest fashion model I ever
shot," adding: "Miss Morehouse was no more interested in
fashions as fashions than I was. But when she put on the
clothes that were to be photographed, she transformed herself into a woman who really would wear that gown or that
riding habit or whatever the outfit." She was also a favorite
of the photographers Cecil Beaton and Baron George
Hoyningen-Huene. Two years before her death, Beaton
wrote:

> It was not until Miss Marion Morehouse was discovered
> by Steichen that photographic models became so well
> known that they exerted an influence on the public. The
> aim of models at this time was to be grand ladies, and
> Marion Morehouse, with her particularly personal ways
> of twisting her neck, her fingers and feet, was at home in
> the grandest circumstances.

These quotations were each included in Marion's ample,
two-column *New York Times* obit, "Marion Morehouse
Cummings, Poet's Widow, Top Model, Dies." The title of
the obit could just as easily have been phrased, "*First* Top

Model." In the words of Tobia Bezzola, a curator at the
Kunsthaus Zürich, Steichen's "mannequins – even if they
were not stars of stage and screen – became recognizable
personalities. In his collaboration with Marion Morehouse,
he in effect laid the groundwork for the idea of an identifi-
able supermodel."*

In *The Model as Muse: Embodying Fashion*, Harold
Koda, the Curator in Charge at New York's Metropolitan
Museum of Art, places the careers of Morehouse and Stei-
chen in a broader cultural context:

> Cultural awareness of modeling as a respectable, stand-
> alone profession was slow in coming…. [and] it was not
> until the mid-1920s that the fashion model began to
> emerge as a fully formed social and professional entity.
> One event in particular – a model search organized in
> New York by *Vogue* in 1924 for the visiting French
> couturier Jean Patou – signaled, perhaps, that society had
> finally recognized that fashion presentations featuring
> live models not only advanced the agenda of the
> industry, but also provided women with viable career
> opportunities. Among those discovered in the process of
> selecting from more than 500 applicants hoping to join
> Patou's *cabine* were Miriam Hopkins, Ann Andrews,
> Dorothy Smoller, Lily Tosch, and Marion Morehouse –
> the latter, though not selected by Patou, was certainly
> noticed by *Vogue* and would appear to have been chosen
> by fate. With Morehouse's meteoric ascent, America
> witnessed the beginning of the model's rise to interna-
> tional fame and eventual influence upon feminine beauty
> and popular culture. Confident, emancipated, and
> unapologetically liberated, Morehouse's image was as
> fresh and exciting to the young sophisticates of the
> 1920s as it was alarming to the old establishment. When

Edward Steichen was hired at *Vogue* in 1923 to replace [Adolphe] de Meyer, his innovative modernist photographic style ripped through twentieth-century visual culture like a searing knife. Almost overnight, de Meyer's painterly pictorialist images were thrust into the past as Steichen introduced the twentieth century to the modern woman by way of unerring clarity and his favorite model – Marion Morehouse.

Corsetless and carefree, wholesome – but still somehow racy – Morehouse had all of the glamour of the ubiquitous Hollywood starlets but none of the stagey self-consciousness. The perfect model for Gabrielle "Coco" Chanel's highly innovative form-liberating designs, Morehouse's on-camera look and off-camera lifestyle were a pronounced departure from the demure, decorative females of the Belle Époque. In her sensational early sittings for *Vogue*, Morehouse heralded the triumph of the cool, sleek modernist style that would prove enormously influential upon American photography, fashion, graphic design, and female archetypes alike. [....]

Embodying the adventurous and self-directed lifestyles celebrated in magazine and novels of the era, [model Lee] Miller and Morehouse in many ways symbolized the fully realized, progressive attitudes of the 1920s. Living examples of the newly liberated modern American woman, they put a face on a generation intent upon turning their backs once and for all on still-lingering Victorian sexism and the last gasps of Edwardian propriety – sentiments that fashion (no matter how high hemlines might rise) could only hint at. Doing much to temper the more frivolous connotations of the out-all-night, free-spirited flapper, Marion Morehouse and Lee Miller – with their cool, nonchalant elegance and confident, unaffected smiles directed right into the lens – projected refreshingly frank and fearlessly modern attitudes, and heralded not only changes in fashion, but also a new way of living for American women.*

Koda's book was published in 2009 to coincide with the exhibit "The Model as Muse," featured at the Metropolitan Museum of Art. More recently, a September 2010 article by Robin Muir in *FirstFT* magazine, "Vogue's Earliest Celebrity Models," expanded on this theme:

> That models became so recognizable that they began to fascinate the public is often traced back to Marion Morehouse. And with justification. She was not an actress or a society figure but something new entirely, a dedicated model, and *Vogue* began to use her name in credit lines.*

Yet Marion had managed to cloak so many details of her personal life for so many decades that Cummings's previous biographer, Richard Kennedy, had at times clearly thrown his hands up in exasperation. In an essay titled "The Elusive Marion Morehouse," he complained of "a great many obstacles" that were placed in his way while working on his thirty-year project, adding: "The principal obstacle was Marion Morehouse herself." This was the case even more so when the subject was Marion instead of Cummings: "Whenever I would ask her a specific question about some feature of her life, she would raise a warning finger against my inquiry…. It was not until after her death that I was able to begin my real biographical research." Kennedy adds: "My gathering of information about her had to start with the facts set down in her obituary, a course that gradually raised questions in my mind about the persona she had created for herself during her lifetime." Indeed, one glance at her *Times* obituary reveals several key errors that took root as a result of these obfuscations, the biggest one being the year of her birth. Kennedy himself was suspicious on this score: "In Edward Steichen's photograph of her, made for *Vogue* magazine in 1925, she was supposedly only nineteen years old; yet she looks much older."* Unable to track down a March 9, 1906 birth certificate for Marion in South Bend, Indiana, Kennedy also failed to find one for 1905 or 1904. As I would soon discover, even if he'd gone back another year, to 1903 – the actual date of her birth, according to census records I eventually unearthed – he still would have come up empty handed, at least in South Bend. A county clerk with whom I recently spoke said that birth certificates were not legally required in Indiana until about 1906 or 1907, so most of the "home births" (the majority of births in the state, at that time) remained unrecorded. Marion's obit also erroneously reports that she and Edward Estlin Cummings were married and that Marion attended St. Anne's Academy in Hartford: a school that, according to Kennedy, never even existed.

Almost twenty-five years had passed since Kennedy's *Dreams in the Mirror: Biography of E. E. Cummings* had first appeared. As an avid genealogist, I realized that online resources for family research had snowballed into tremendous proportions in just the last ten years. Thus, when Christopher Sawyer-Lauçanno's *E. E. Cummings: A Biography* was published in 2004 – a lyrical and informative work that successfully builds upon Kennedy's foundation – much of this genealogical material still remained unavailable. When I contacted Christopher in July of 2014 and raised the possibility of finding something new, he enthusiastically gave me his blessing to start digging.

What followed in just the next few hours was one of those uncanny serendipities that resonate with the allure of a Sherlock Holmes episode. First, I had a look at the obit that had sent Kennedy on a trip down the rabbit hole. As a genealogist, my eye instinctively lingered on the names of the other family members mentioned therein: a sister, Lillian, who had refused to speak with Kennedy after Marion's death, leading him to "wonder about what family secrets were being protected," and a brother, Benjamin.

Logging into "Ancestry.com," after a search for a family tree on Marion yielded nothing of note, I tried to find something on Lillian. (Although Marion was included in most of the E. E. Cummings pedigrees, none revealed the names of her parents or anything of interest about her background.) Then I stumbled upon a lodestone. A listing for "Lillian Morehouse Cox" appeared on Ancestry, and it was cross-linked to a web site that I'd found helpful in the past.

"Find-a-Grave.com" revealed that Lillian was buried in a cemetery in Bloomfield, Connecticut, along with several other Morehouses. (The site allows members to erect online memorials for the deceased, including vital statistics and photographs.) And a memorial for Lillian contained three amazing portraits. One was a snapshot taken of Lillian, her brother Benjamin, and her mother, who appeared to be in her seventies. The other two photos were professionally composed. One was captioned, "Lillian modeling circa 1920s," and it featured a tall, slender, willowy figure wearing a satin dress with a matching cape, with her bobbed hair cut short in the style of the flappers. The last picture was the most amazing of all: the bust of an beguiling young woman, perhaps eighteen to twenty years old, with pale, opalescent skin, an oval face, full lips, a prominent nose, long flowing hair, and an utterly entrancing expression as she gazes off, into the distance. The caption reads: "Actress Lillian Morehouse Cox."

None of these intriguing images had ever appeared in print. In addition, Lillian's birth was listed as March 31, 1906: the same month and year that her sister, Marion, claimed to have been born. Although Richard Kennedy had expressed doubts about the family actually hailing from South Bend, the memorial states that Lillian was indeed born there – and that she was the "daughter of Benjamin and Anna Morehouse." When I shared this information with Christopher Sawyer-Lauçanno, he excitedly confirmed that the names of Marion's parents had never been known to any of Cummings's biographers. And there was no doubt the memorial was referencing the same family. A bio on Lillian said she was

> The sister of Marion Morehouse Cummings, the wife of poet e. e. cummings. Also a brother Benjamin Morehouse. Lillian was a model and stage actress. Lillian was married on August 3, 1928 to Alan B. Cox in New Jersey. They divorced in June 8, 1942 in Miami, Florida, St. Joseph County.

An additional note indicated that the memorial was created by one Tony Ungaro on February 16, 2009. Just as I'd suspected, all this was relatively new information.

With these crucial facts in hand, I returned to Ancestry and began to dig up additional data. Most importantly, I located Lillian and Marion in a 1910 U. S. Federal Census taken in Connecticut, which shows that Marion was then seven years old and was born in Indiana to "Annie" More- house. Lillian's age was off by a year: on April 15, 1910, she was actually four years old, but the enumerator has written "3." (Her birth in 1906 was later confirmed by her death certificate.) The census also includes their brother, Benjamin, who was two, thus born in 1908. The family was then living at 20 Centre Street, in Hartford. Although it said Anna was married, her husband wasn't listed along with the rest of the family. Instead, "Benjamin I. Morehouse" ap- pears in the 1910 census recorded in South Bend, living at 810 North Lafayette Street with his seventy-four-year-old father, John Morehouse, his sixty-four year old mother, Elizabeth, and three of his younger siblings. According to this document, he's married; and under a column headed "Number of Years of Present Marriage," the enumerator has written "7."*

I next contacted a clerk named "Chuck" at the Mount Saint Benedict Cemetery. A brief telephone conversation confirmed the accuracy of the memorial data and revealed that Lillian was buried in the same plot as her brother, Benjamin Jr, and Anna Shortell Morehouse, their mother, who died in 1965. Anna's husband died first, in 1954, and he was buried with Anna Halpin, Anna Shortell's mother, in another part of the cemetery.

An obituary in the online *Hartford Courant* newspaper states that "Lillian (Morehouse) Cox, of Hartford, died Tuesday (May 31, 1994) in Hartford Hospital. She was born in Hartford, daughter of the late Isaac and Anna (Shortell) Morehouse." Another edition of the paper, pub- lished on May 28, 2000, featured an article about local ce- lebrities and people of note who are interred in the vicinity.

Titled "The Sweet Hereafter," it features these consecutive paragraphs:

> Isaac Benjamin Morehouse (1870-1954), Mount St. Benedict Cemetery, Bloomfield. He was an actor on the vaudeville stage.
> Lillian M. Morehouse (1906-1994), Mount St. Benedict Cemetery, Bloomfield. She was an actress and model, and the sister-in-law of e. e. cummings.

As I would eventually discover, the reversal of Mr. Morehouse's first and middle name appears throughout his life, and on several key documents, such as his first marriage certificate and his death certificate (the latter lists Lillian as the "informant"). On his son's birth certificate, under "Father's Name," the clerk had initially typed "Isaac," but then he crossed it out and replaced it with "Benjamin."

After spending the next few days collecting additional information and constructing a basic family tree, I contacted Tony Ungaro via e-mail. I explained that I was preparing to interview Professor Sawyer-Lauçanno, and that I hoped we could speak. A genial former executive from Hartford, Tony telephoned the following day, on August 5, 2014. And he had quite a story to tell.

Tony was formerly employed as an executive for the Heublein Corporation in Hartford, where Lillian Morehouse worked in a clerical position. ("We manufactured A1 Steak Sauce, Smirnoff Vodka, and Grey Poupon mustard.") During this period, Tony had no idea that Lillian was related to the wife of E. E. Cummings. Although they didn't know each other that well, he would occasionally "help her out with a ride home from work," for which she was quite grateful.

After thirty-four years at Heublein, Tony retired in March 1994, his last position being Manager of Period Cost Control. ("I developed and managed ninety-million dollars in budgets.") Four months later, he moved with his wife to Sarasota, Florida. After Lillian passed away in May of that year, he received a probate letter from her lawyer in West Hartford, which informed him that Lillian had remembered him in her will. Quite surprised by all this, Tony replied that he didn't want any money – but that he would be happy to receive some mementos.

Shortly afterward, a UPS truck delivered three large boxes containing letters, photographs, and divorce papers. There were also "photo albums going back to the 1800s, and many very personal letters," including some that had been exchanged between Lillian's parents. As we spoke, Mr. Ungaro remained eminently discreet about the contents of some of these letters. "The mother and father experienced serious difficulties and were separated for a time," he said, but he didn't get anymore specific than that regarding the contents of these missives – and I didn't press the matter. He added that many of the letters exchanged between Anna and Benjamin were so personal that he decided to destroy them. When we spoke a second time, about seven months later, he was more specific: the letters concerned great financial hardship, and the separation he was referring to occurred in the Thirties, when Lillian was in a hospital in New York. (More on this later.) This dovetails with the contents of the 1930 U. S. Federal Census, which shows that Benjamin was married and living with his mother, Elizabeth, at 302 Hawthorne Drive, in South Bend. Anna doesn't appear in the census, although a city directory from this period says that she officially resided at the same address. Therefore, she may have been in the hospital during this period.

Retaining only a small file of mementoes for himself, the remainder he forwarded to a relative of Lillian's that he tracked down in Indiana. Tony constructed a pedigree based on what he'd found in the family documents, which he emailed me that same day. This allowed me make rapid progress in assembling an even broader genealogy.

When I asked if there was anything else of note in the boxes, Tony said there were a few small pieces of artwork, including pastels, which were created by Cummings and which he also sent to Lillian's relative. (Early in his career, Cummings was a well-respected visual artist; and besides composing portraits of Marion he continued to dabble in the arts later in his life.)

Attached to the pedigree that Tony had shared with me were a handful of photos of Marion and her family that have never appeared in public before. The first was a head shot of Lillian's father, Benjamin I. Morehouse, whom Tony referred to as "Isaac." Tony said that the letters and memorabilia also revealed that "Isaac was a vaudeville actor who was "known for his ability to go from 'black face' to white in just minutes." An oval-shaped portrait, the photo appeared to be printed on a flier or publicity sheet of some sort, with lettering embossed on the paper beside it. (Although the image I received was cropped, the letters "BE" – perhaps the first two letters of his name – appear to the right of the picture). Tony's photo archive also gives us an intimate look at the other members of the Morehouse family, and it includes the only known image of Marion posing with her sister, which appears to be the earliest extent photo of Marion.

In the family tree that Tony created, there was also a note regarding a nuptial ceremony of some sort that had occurred between Benjamin and Anna in a church in the Bronx. When I remarked that this was "well after the birth of their children," Tony said it "may have been after the fact," but that, given the difficulties experienced by Anna and Benjamin, "nothing would surprise me." I later contacted the church and obtained a record of this event, which proved to be a marriage. I should add that there was no other record of their marriage in any online database, and the church's files from this period were not digitalized. If Tony hadn't inherited Lillian's papers, I doubt anyone would have found a trace of this event, especially since there was no clue that the couple might have remarried ten years after the birth of their last child.

Lillian had bequeathed Tony $10,000 (of which he received $4,000), and she willed her doctor $40,000. She also left money to her two caretakers. She'd amassed about $280,000, which utterly surprised Mr. Ungaro, since she was employed merely as a clerk. But he added that, after Marion died, the copyright of Cummings's work went to Lillian, to the chagrin of Cummings's daughter (Nancy Thayer). Much of this had been depleted, however, by medical care for her and her brother, Benjamin, so the amounts received by those in the will were "less than specified." Tony was amused by the fact that, when Lillian's doctor eventually moved to Chicago, "she was angry at him for leaving her." When I noted that Lillian hadn't left anything to her distant relatives, he concluded that this was probably due to their estrangement.

Mr. Ungaro struck me as a completely trustworthy, thoughtful, and down-to-earth fellow. During our conversation, I could hear his wife occasionally speaking in the background, adding whatever she could to help trigger his memory. Although he was aware of the famous poet and his work ("E. E. Cummings wrote with those little letters, you know?"), he remained more interested in Lillian and in carefully preserving her memory. I respected his decision to honor the privacy of Lillian's parents but, at the same time, to be as helpful as possible while doing so.

In the months ahead, each of Mr. Ungaro's leads checked out. I was able to obtain various birth, marriage, and death certificates that verified his claims, and I eventually managed to extend the genealogy of both Anna Shortell and Benjamin Morehouse back a generation. I also located Anna and Benjamin's death certificates, which list the names of each of their parents, thus confirming Tony's pedigree data. City directories from Hartford and South Bend reveal precise locations where they lived, and they also chronicle Benjamin's various professions. Census results from Indiana, New York, and Connecticut helped to fill in other gaps. By the fall of 2014, I was able to reconstruct much of the background of Marion, Lillian, and their antecedents. These are some of the main events:

• According to the 1910 and 1930 census, Marion Morehouse was born in Indiana in 1903. The 1910 census, taken in Hartford, reveals that her mother, "Annie Morehouse," was married and was the head of the family. Note the absence of a husband in this listing, who would normally be considered as the head. Strangely enough, under a column for the "Number of Years of Present Marriage," the enumerator has left the space blank, although it's filled in for each of the other married couples on the page. Perhaps this indicates a separation just two years after the birth of Benjamin Jr.

• In the 1930 census, taken when Marion was twenty-seven, she was living on her own, renting a room at 5 Prospect Place, in the Bronx. Although the original building is no longer there, it must have been a high-rise, as there were 334 other "households" at this address. The enumerator notes Marion's "Occupation" as "Actress," her "Industry" as the "Theatre" (spelled the European way). Under "Class of Worker," she's considered a "Wage or salary worker." We also learn that she lived without a radio.

• Apparently, Marion didn't start fibbing about her age to the census takers until 1940, when she informed an enumerator that she was born in 1918, making her *twenty-two* instead of *thirty-seven* years old. (Oddly enough, 1918 is the same year that her parents remarried.) One wonders if E. E. Cummings was standing within earshot and Marion was merely propagating a myth that even her lifelong companion had remained unaware of. Upon learning this, Christopher Sawyer-Lauçanno remarked that, all along, he had the impression that Marion kept many things a secret from Cummings. "My sense," he said, "is that he didn't know much of any of this." (Of course, one must also allow for the possibly of a simple error on the part of the enumerator, which was common.) Although Marion's surname is misspelled ("Moorehouse"), it's undoubtedly her, for it correctly lists her address as 4 Patchin Place, the small mews where she and Estlin Cummings maintained separate apartments for many years. (Cummings first moved into 4 Patchin Place on September 8, 1924.) And consistent with the 1910 and 1930 census results, it records her birthplace as "Indiana." Under "Marital Status," it says that Marion was single. Her occupation is "Model," her industry is "Artist Model." Under "Highest Grade Completed," we read: "High school, 4th year." This is contradicted by the 1930 census, which indicates, under "Attended School," "No." But the 1910 census, taken when she was seven years old, shows that Marion was then enrolled in elementary school.

• One of the family secrets that may have led to the creation of those "walls of mystery" that Kennedy says "surrounded the facts of Marion's early life"* was that she was apparently born out of wedlock. In March 2015, I discovered that Benjamin Isaac Morehouse was previously married to Etta C. Harger (née Van Dalson), on December 22, 1889. About fourteen months later, Etta, also known as "Nettie," gave birth to a son named Otto Morehouse, in February 1891.* And on February 26, 1902, "Nettie" and Benjamin were divorced.

In 1903 Marion was born, and the following year Benjamin married Marion's mother, Anna Shortell, on June 30, 1904. The ceremony was held in the neighboring state of Michigan, in Niles: about eleven miles north of South Bend, Indiana. The marriage registry in Niles also includes the names of the bride and groom's parents; and it shows that, while Benjamin was residing in South Bend, Anna was then living in Hartford. Under "Profession," we learn that Benjamin Morehouse was a "Showman."*

Another intriguing detail: the "Person Performing [the] Marriage" bears the same surname as Benjamin's mother: Justice of the Peace W. I. *Babcock*. Further research revealed that his full name was Washington Irving Babcock, a fifty-one-year-old resident of Niles. One of the witnesses to the ceremony, Ruth (Hitchcock) Babcock, was Washington Irving's wife. They were each born in New York State in the 1830s and later emigrated to Niles, where Justice Babcock also worked as a lumber dealer. How (or if) he is related to Benjamin's mother, Elizabeth Jane Babcock, remains unclear. But if he is related, it might explain why Niles was chosen for the marriage ceremony.

• When I subsequently rechecked the information on the 1910 census for Benjamin and Anna, I noticed that, under "Marital Status," the notation "M1" appears beside Anna's name; while Benjamin's status is "M2." I then realized that the digits referred to their *number of marriages*, thus showing Benjamin to be married twice. Yet, Benjamin's enumerator has written "7" under "Number of Years of Present Marriage," even though the census was conducted about two-and-a-half months short of their sixth wedding anniversary.

• Earlier in his life, Benjamin lived and worked mostly in South Bend, but he appears in Hartford during the years 1911 and 1912 and from 1945 to 1954.* Besides working as a vaudeville actor and a scenery setter for the theater, Benjamin was employed as a carpenter and worked in various other working-class positions: wood finisher, paper hanger, painter for the Studebaker Corporation (manufacturer of the Studebaker automobile; the company was based in South Bend and was founded by two local blacksmiths), stage hand, night porter, watchman, janitor (during the Great Depression), maintenance man. (This despite Marion's tendency to pose as an aristocrat.)* The 1930 census shows that Benjamin received no schooling and that his parents (John Morehouse and Elizabeth Jane Babcock) were each born and raised in Indiana. Civil War records note that a "John Morehouse" was "enlisted in the Indiana 11th Light Artillery Battery on 17 December 1861 and mustered out on 7 January 1865," although it's unclear whether this was the same person. John married Elizabeth Jane in June 1865, and he fathered seven children, of which Benjamin was the third.

• Marion Morehouse's mother, Anna Shortell, was born in Hartford, as was Anna's father, William. William's parents, John Shortell and Mary Berry, were from Ireland. William's wife was named Anna Halpin, and she hailed from London. Her father, William Halpin, was also born in England; and his wife, Elizabeth Dryden, was from Ireland. Hence, the Anglo-Irish cast of Marion and Lillian's appearance.

• Marion's parents married each other a second time on December 20, 1918, in the Church of St. Francis de Sales, on East 96th Street in the Bronx. Although there's a record of Benjamin's divorce from his previous marriage, there's no record in the South Bend county clerk's office of a divorce between Benjamin and Anna Shortell, so it's possible that their 1918 marriage was simply performed as a religious ceremony.

Since Anna and Benjamin both vanish from Indiana and Connecticut directories around this time, there remains a strong possibility that the family relocated to New York. I could find no trace of Benjamin in Indiana or Connecticut directories from 1913 to 1924; while Anna disappears from these listings between 1915 and 1927. A 1927 Hartford directory notes that a Benjamin and Anna Morehouse were "removed" from the directory after a relocation to New York City, but it's uncertain as to whether this is the same

Morehouse couple. But they eventually returned to Indiana, and, according to a 1928 South Bend city directory, were living at 128 North Lafayette Street.

Marion could have attended school at St. Francis de Sales (in 1918 she was fifteen years old; Lillian twelve; and Benjamin Junior eight), since at that time the church hosted a school. Although Kennedy has conjectured that Marion and Lillian came to New York on their own in the Twenties in order to break into the theater, it may have been a family relocation that first brought them to Manhattan.

• Marion performed on the Broadway stage as early as 1923, at the age of twenty; Lillian in musical revues in 1925, when she was nineteen. Thanks to the online Playbill Vault and the Internet Broadway Database, we know that Marion acted in at least five Broadway plays between October 1923 and January 1931, which ran for a total of 412 performances. [hyperlink] (Kennedy says Marion "was able to get jobs as a showgirl in one or another of the musical revues such as the *Ziegfeld Follies* or to find bit parts here or there in plays," but the only play he mentions by name is "Gilbert Seldes's adaptation of *Lysistrata* in 1930": Marion's fifth Broadway production, which ran from June 5, 1930 to January 1931.)* The records also show that Lillian performed in two musical revues, Earl Carroll's 1924 and 1925 *Vanities* (a competitor of Ziegfeld), and a musical comedy, *Lucky*, with a total of 403 shows between September 1924 and May 1927.* [hyperlink] (*Lucky* was featured at the New Amsterdam Theatre, which also hosted the *Ziegfeld Follies*.) But since the archives contain only Broadway shows, there may have been other, Off-Broadway productions that featured the Morehouse sisters: a possibility that's bolstered by Tony Ungaro's comment that

Lillian and Marion "appeared together on the stage" (see below).

The earliest Steichen photo of Marion that I've seen so far dates from 1924 (see below): the same year that Marion was discovered by *Vogue* during a model search organized for Jean Patou. Since Steichen frequented the theater and the burlesque, it's possible the famous photographer also saw Marion perform in one of her early dramatic plays. For example, on December 26, 1923, Marion appeared in *This Fine-Pretty World* at the Neighborhood Playhouse, at 466 Grand Street. After thirty-three shows, it closed in January 1924. And later that year she performed in a play called "The Saint," which opened on October 11, 1924, at the Greenwich Village Theatre on Seventh Avenue South, near Christopher Street, in Cummings's neck of the woods. After seventeen performances, it closed that same month. Steichen also might have encountered Marion at the *Ziegfeld Follies* or in some other musical revue.* Kennedy says that Marion's tall, lanky figure made it difficult for her to find theatrical parts, but it was perfect for the role of a "showgirl." His 1978 interview with Marion's friend Aline Macmahon seems to have been the source of this information: "Because Marion was very tall," he writes, "she had a hard time finding roles to play on the stage, although her height and beauty were very suitable for work she secured as a showgirl in the *Ziegfeld Follies*. Lillian, an attractive blonde, was also a showgirl for Ziegfeld."* When I mentioned the *Ziegfeld Follies* to Tony Ungaro, however, he said he could recall no evidence of their employment with Ziegfeld in the papers he'd inherited but added that his memory was fuzzy when it came to the names of particular shows. Although the Playbill Vault has a complete archive of opening-night performers for the *Ziegfeld Follies* from 1907 to 1957, neither Marion nor Lillian appear there. Still, there's a possibility they were hired as replacements later on, after opening night.

Although Marion claims to have met Cummings following her performance in a play on June 23, 1932, she never revealed the title of this production to Kennedy: a highly suspicious omission. If they met after a *Ziegfeld Follies*-type of revue (Cummings was known to use dance hall-related material in his poetry), perhaps Marion considered such a venue to be lacking the glamour of the more "artful" theater. In keeping with her flamboyant persona, she may have felt the need to embellish upon this legendary encounter with one of America's most well known poets. However, all this remains speculative.

• Benjamin Isaac Morehouse's death certificate lists one of the causes of his demise as "rheumatoid arthritis": a malady that can be passed along genetically. Therefore, Marion, who suffered terribly from this debilitating illness, may have inherited it from her father.

*   *   *

Something that cannot be captured by mere vital statistics is the effect that Marion had upon the heart and soul of the poet. When we finally conducted our interview on February 2, 2015, I asked Christopher to describe her relationship with Cummings and to elaborate on how they supported each other emotionally and artistically.

"That story," he replied, "begins with two other relationships before that. The first woman he falls in love with is Elaine, who was married to his friend Scofield Thayer.

Scofield, as we know now, and as I'm sure Cummings knew at the time, was, if not 'bi,' gay."

"And very much in the closet for a while."

"Yes. An esthete, but not particularly interested in his wife sexually. Cummings falls head over heels in love with Elaine, with Scofield's wife. And Elaine herself is upper-crust. She's not the easiest person in the world to get along with; nor was, I think, Estlin himself. But basically, they have an affair, and she gets pregnant with Cummings's child. Thayer, being Cummings's best friend, knows what's going on, but he adopts the child – or rather, he allows it to be born as if it's his daughter. Eventually, Elaine and Thayer are divorced. Elaine marries Cummings, and it does not last very long. There are just too many differences between them. The daughter doesn't realize at the time that she's his child: that Cummings is her real father. They part ways; Elaine goes off to Ireland, and Cummings is bereft. I mean, he's absolutely bereft that Elaine has fallen in love with someone else and left him after he was hoping that this was going to be the love of his life.

"For all of Cummings's 'sexual identity' as a poet – because he certainly has one because of all the erotic poems, and being one of the first to write poems that were un-abashedly not just about love, but about sex – people think he must have had a million women. Well, he didn't. He had only *three* principal women. And they were each enor-mously important to him. He was a very tender, very sen-timental, and, in that way, very 'son of his father' old-fashioned man. Then he hooks up with Anne Barton, who is a flapper and totally unfaithful from the moment they get together, and this kills Cummings as well.

"He loves women as women, and I'll try to clarify what I mean by this. He enjoyed being in women's company. Probably among his closest friends was Hildegarde Watson, who was married to his friend James Watson. I don't believe there was ever a sexual attraction on either's part, but he absolutely adored being in her company. He *adored* women. He enjoyed who they were. He enjoyed the way they smelled [Laughs]. He enjoyed the way they looked, the way they walked. And so, in a pretty tough period for Cummings – financially, he's not doing well; he never did well, and his mother generally supported him most of his life – but here he is, a 'two-time loser' if you will, and suddenly here comes this angel out of the fog, Marion Morehouse. She is young. She is, unlike Elaine or Anne, really interested in being with Cummings."

"And not a gold digger, like Anne."

"Not a gold digger like Anne was, certainly. And so, she is gorgeous, and she makes it pretty clear, pretty early on, that what she wants to do is take care of this great man. And, *wow!* [Laughs] He's finally found the love of his life.

"Who knows what takes place in those kinds of circumstances? But clearly, there was a tremendous attraction. I didn't write this, because I didn't have enough evidence, but, from the little that I could glean, he was attracted to her initially because she was so gorgeous. It was certainly a major physical attraction. I think it took a while for him to let his guard down so that he could see her in a larger way. He kept her at a distance, initially; he wasn't quite sure of what to do.

"And so, what we have is hundreds of pages of writing about Elaine, maybe a hundred or so pages about Anne, but we have only about twenty pages about Marion. Why? Because he doesn't have to exorcise the demons. What he's doing with writing about Elaine and about Anne is trying to exorcise those demons. Because he wrote everything down; he was compulsive about trying to think on paper. You could see the guy pacing about the room, smoking endless cigarettes, then writing something down to help him try to analyze things. Once he meets Marion, this goes away. He writes about other things, but he's not obsessing about his relationship any longer. And that, in a way, tells you how perfectly matched they were.

"What happened as they spent more time together ... I would say she became much more of a 'gatekeeper' for Cummings. Allen Ginsberg told me a story: He'd gone to Cummings's house and knocked on the door, and no one answered. And he'd written him a letter and sent him a copy of "Howl." He really wanted Cummings's approval; it was enormously important to him for some reason. He finally gets to Patchin Place again, on another occasion, and he knocks on the door, and Marion comes down the stairs, takes one look, and says: *"You.* Go *away.* And *never* come back." He tries to explain who he is, and she just ... She was the *gatekeeper.* And that was very much a part of her function in later years. And with Cummings's blessing, because he became more of a curmudgeon as he got older. And by 'older,' I mean fifty-five. The man didn't live all that long. And she became 'the one you had to get through.'

"I believe her political views really began to affect Cummings's. She was very much a right-winger. At that time, Lindberg was on the radio, and various other right-wing isolationist, "Keep Out of World War Two" folks. And she would get Cummings to listen to these broadcasts, because these were the ones who were 'telling the truth.' She absolutely hated Roosevelt. Hard to know why; she was hardly an aristocrat! She hardly had any money, and she certainly had no reason to be a Republican, but then ... Oh, well!

"So, she's a model. She's in *Vogue*. And she's an *artist's* model: Steichen. At about the time she meets Cummings, it's likely she was also trying to achieve more in the theater. But suddenly she moves from being a sort of career woman – because she was certainly building a career – to being Cummings's protector and supporter."*

And I think no one has ever said it better than that.

*　　*　　*

After accumulating these various facts and anecdotes, on March 21, a day before his eighty-second birthday, I contacted Tony Ungaro for a follow-up interview. I asked him to go over the story once more, and I began by asking what year he'd first encountered Lillian.

"In 1960," he said, "I went to work for Heublein, Inc., and she was working in Central Files, as a file clerk." He offered her a ride home "within that year, and it was just occasionally. She was living with her brother."

"Do you know anything about the relationship between Lillian and Marion? Were they close?"

"Well, they appeared together on the stage." At this my ears perked up. This was new information, and it might explain the nature of one particular image in Tony's collection in which the sisters are each heavily made up and wearing what appear to be theatrical costumes. "I don't think there was any problem between them, frankly. Marion went her way, and Lillian went hers. And when Marion passed away … Well, Marion's husband had passed away first: E. E. Cummings. And of course, Marion inherited everything. When Marion passed away, she left, to Lillian, the income from his work. She continued to receive that. I think after Marion passed away, E. E. Cummings's daughter …"

"The last time we spoke, you said you heard that the daughter was a bit angry about that."

"Somewhere along the line, I'd heard that. I don't know how true it was. But I can believe she would have been a little disappointed, to say the least."

"The sisters performed together on the stage? I don't think anyone else is aware of that. Did you have some kind of documentation in the boxes that they were in a play together?"

"Yes."

"There's also speculation that they were employed as showgirls for the *Ziegfeld Follies*."

"That I don't recall. I had a whole bunch of papers, and playbills, and things like that, which I sent to the family. I don't recall the names of the shows. Lillian was quite attractive. In fact, she resembled, in my opinion, the actress Lillian Gish."

After summarizing Kennedy's search for embarrassing "family secrets," I asked Tony a few pointed questions about the inner dynamics of the Morehouse clan. "I'm wondering if you know anything about Lillian's relationship with her parents."

"I don't think there were any problems between the parents and Marion; I didn't see any evidence of that. I saw no evidence of family problems, frankly."

"And what about Lillian and the parents? Any estrangement there?"

"Not that I'm aware of, or saw at all. And let me tell you, I had a *ton* ... the lawyer sent me three boxes of material that he had left. And I didn't see any evidence of that, frankly."

"Do you know anything about what led to the parents' initial separation?"

"I know the mother was in a hospital in New York, and the father was trying to ... You know, holding down the apartment in Hartford. And those were some very difficult times." Although I was referring to the possibility of an estrangement between 1908 and 1918, I soon realized that Tony was actually referring to a later period, "in the Thirties," he said, during the Great Depression.

"Difficult financially?"

"Financially, right. And I don't know what specific years all this occurred, but there was that. It was difficult days. There was some correspondence between the parents. The father was in Hartford. And the mother was in some hospital in New York. I think it was a charity ward; I'm not sure. All this would have been in the letters, which I don't have anymore." (One wonders if this could have been St. Vincent's Hospital, which always catered to the poor and which was conveniently located near Patchin Place, at Greenwich and Seventh Avenue.)

At this point, we returned to the subject of Lillian. "When she worked at Heublein, I had to go right by her street. So when she was stuck for a ride, she asked if I'd drop her off.

I said 'Certainly, it's right on my way.' After she left Heublein, I sent Christmas cards and things like that. Her brother was still alive, and living with her. I think he worked part time, in a movie theater right up the street.* Other than these occasional communications, I never really saw her. Then I got a letter from the probate court, saying I have 'an interest,' and *blah-blah-blah*. And I said, 'What the hell interest could I possibly have?' [Laughs] You know, this woman didn't really have much; she worked as a clerk ... so far as I knew. She was living in this two- or three-family house. Then I called the lawyer, and he told me she'd remembered me in her will, along with this doctor, and two women who had helped her with her brother in later years. And she remembered everybody in her will. So I called the doctor, and he said, "Yeah, it was kind of strange, because when I told her I was moving out of state, she said, 'Why'd you take me out of the picture for, if you knew you were going to move?' [Laughs] And I said, 'That sounds like Lillian.'

"After all was said and done, I think there was about four thousand dollars left to be distributed. I was initially left ten grand. And I said to the lawyer: 'I don't need the money. I want to make sure she has a proper stone and all that.' He said, 'That was all taken care of.' She's buried with her parents at Mount Saint Benedict Hospital, in Bloomfield. That's where my parents are, and grandparents, and the whole family.

"I had 1040s, tax forms, in that pile of papers, and I could see where Lillian was getting the royalties from E. E. Cummings's work. Twenty thousand dollars, or something like that, a year. And that's how she managed to build up her inheritance if you will. But a lot of it went out for care-takers for her and her brother. She didn't die wealthy."

Tony spoke with a palpable affection for Lillian and with a lingering fascination with her past. "I'll bet you regret not having spent more time with her while she was alive," I said, "and getting to know her better."

"Well, yeah, in view of her history, which I had no knowledge of when I knew her at Heublein. When I started going through those boxes, I was floored. It was amazing. Full of photographic albums, pictures that went back easily into the 1800s. Which I wasn't going to throw away, and I had no use for. And I was ... 'What the hell am I going to do with all this?' My conscience wouldn't let me destroy it, other than the very personal letters between Marion's mother and father. So I tracked down relatives in Indiana, and I sent all that material to them. And what they did with it, I have no idea. But there were all kind of playbills from the shows, pictures of her in costume, and ... *oh!*"

"Pictures of Lillian and Marion in costume?"

"Yeah, on the stage. I think Marion was also in some movie. A small part with Lionel Barrymore. Whether she got credit for it or not on screen ... But there was some-thing; she was in Hollywood. And there were some letters she wrote that were not too kind to some people." [Laughs]

"Not too kind to people in the film?"

"No, in the movie industry. Written to a friend or family; I can't recall which. It's been a number of years now, you know? And there was something in there, I believe it was a film with Lionel Barrymore, back in the Twenties." So far as I know, this is the first compelling evidence that Marion had appeared in a Hollywood film. (Charles Norman, a friend of Cummings and Marion and the author of the authorized biography, *E. E. Cummings*, says that Marion was in two films that were shot in Long Island. But since Marion was the probable source of this information, this must be taken with a grain of salt.*) "She was obviously a talented woman. Too bad you didn't contact me fifteen years ago. I would have had a lot more information, and I would have made it available to you. What a book you could have written … You would have had a great time!"

After wishing Tony a Happy Birthday, he passed along the name and address of one of Marion's relatives in Indiana. "Maybe she can help you."

Thus, the search for the elusive model, muse, and starlet continues.

*   *   *

Although this brief genealogical foray into Marion's distant past represents only a minor footnote to the work completed by Richard Kennedy and Christopher Sawyer-Lauçanno, perhaps it will help future biographers to uncover more of the colorful history of the Marion Morehouse family.

• The Morehouse family recorded in the 1910 U. S. Federal Census, in Hartford, Connecticut.

• Anna (Shortell) Morehouse (left) and daughter Marion (right). If Marion was fifty years old here, the photo would be circa 1953, making her mother about seventy-three. This is the only known image of Marion with her mother, and, like most of the photos that follow, it has never before been made publicly available.

• The only known image of Marion's father, Benjamin Isaac Morehouse.

• An early photo of Lillian and her brother, Benjamin W. Morehouse.

• A young Marion Morehouse, her hair gathered in an elegant up-sweep, wearing a black wool jacket trimmed in mink over a bias-cut red silk dress, with draped wrap neckline and accessorized with leather gloves and a jeweled bracelet. I have not yet identified the photographer, although the style appears to be that of Steichen's. Steichen usually shot in black and white, but he began to experiment with color in the mid-1930s, utilizing more of an informal, "snapshot" composition. Since color photographs first appeared in 1935, Marion would have been at least thirty-two years old.

• Lillian Morehouse. (One of three photos that Tony Ungaro uploaded to "Find-a-Grave.)

• Lillian Morehouse, in later years.

• Marion's brother, Benjamin W. Morehouse.

• Marion's mother, Anna Shortell, wife of Benjamin Isaac Morehouse.

• Left to right: Benjamin Morehouse, Jr; Anna (Shortell) Morehouse; Lillian Morehouse. (One of three photos that Tony Ungaro uploaded to "Find-a-Grave.)

Mr. Matthews, a novelist ("Hange Stout, Awake!"), teaches at Ohio University in Athens.

E E Cummings
1939

• The poet Edward Estlin Cummings, the lifelong partner of Marion Morehouse, in front of a barn at Joy Farm, his New Hampshire retreat. The photo was taken by Marion Morehouse. (Note the inscription: "E. E. Cummings 1939," on top left.)

• Lillian Morehouse, her hair in a styled bob, modeling a satin dress with a cascading bow tied at the lower chest, with a matching cape over her shoulders. The gown has a train flowing to the floor. Note inscription: "Lillian," on bottom right. (One of three photos that Tony Ungaro uploaded to "Find-a-Grave.)

• Marion (left) and Lillian (right): The only known photo of the sisters together, and perhaps the earliest extant image of Marion Morehouse. According to Tony Ungaro, Lillian and Marion performed together on stage. This image appears to have been professionally composed, and it may have been taken while they were working together.

Partial Chronology of Marion Morehouse's Theatrical Work

Lysistrata
Opening date: June 5, 1930. Closing date: January 1931.
Total Performances: 252.
Marion Morehouse: Second Corinthian Woman.
Produced by Philadelphia Theatre Association. Adapted by Gilbert Seldes. Choreographed by Doris Humphrey and Charles Weidman. Staged by Norman Bel Geddes. Music by Leo Ornstein and Reinhold Gliere.
44th Street Theatre, 216 W. 44th St., New York, NY.
Seats: 1465. Built: 1912. Closed: 1945. Demolished: 1945.

Mr. Moneypenny
Opening Date: October 17, 1928. Closing Date: December 1928.
Total Performances: 61.
Marion Morehouse: Iris; The Dead Woman.
Comedy, written by Channing Pollock. Directed by Richard Boleslavsky.
Liberty Theatre, 234 W. 42nd St., New York, NY.
Seats: 1055. Built: 1904. Closed: 1933.

The Saint
Drama, written by Stark Young.
Opening Date: October 11, 1924. Closing Date: October 1924.
Total Performances: 17.
Marion Morehouse: Daughters.
Greenwich Village Theatre (later named the "Irish Theatre" in 1929), 7th Avenue South, near Christopher Street, New York, NY.
Seats: 425. Built: 1917.

This Fine-Pretty World
Drama written by Percy MacKaye.

Opening Date: December 26, 1923. Closing Date: January 1924.
Total Performances: 33.
Marion Morehouse: Delphy Boggs.
Neighborhood Playhouse, 466 Grand St., New York, NY.
Built: 1915. Demolished: 1927.

The Player Queen
Farce, written by William Butler Yeats.
Opening Date: October 16, 1923. Closing Date: November 1923.
Total Performances: 49.
Marion Morehouse: Second Countryman.
Neighborhood Playhouse, 466 Grand St., New York, NY.

Partial Chronology of Lillian Morehouse's Theatrical Work

Lucky
Musical, comedy, Broadway.
Opening date: March 22, 1927. Closing date: May 21, 1927.
Total Performances: 71.
Lillian Morehouse: Ensemble performer.
Book by Otto Harbach. Music by Jerome Kern. Musical Director: Gus Salzer. Music orchestrated by Robert Russell Bennett. Lyrics by Otto Harbac. Staged by Hassard Short. Choreographed by David Bennett. Ballets arranged by Albertina Rasch.
New Amsterdam Theatre, 214 West 42nd St., New York, NY.
Seats: 1747. Built: 1903.

Earl Carroll's Vanities of 1925
Musical, revue, Broadway.
Opening date: July 6, 1925. Closing date: December 27, 1925.
Total Performances: 199.
Lillian Morehouse: Ensemble performer.
Produced by Earl Carroll. Music by Clarence Gaskill. Book by William A. Grew, et al. Music interpreted by Ross Gorman. Musical Director: Donald Voorhees. Staged by William A. Grew.
Earl Carroll Theatre, 753 Seventh Ave. (West 50th St.), New York, NY.
Seats: 1025. Built: 1922. Closed: 1939. Demolished: 1990.

Earl Carroll's Vanities of 1924
Musical, revue, Broadway.
Opening date: September 10, 1924. Closing date: January 3, 1925.
Total Performances: 133.
Lillian Morehouse: Ensemble performer.
Music Box Theatre (September 10, 1924 – November 1924), 239 W. 45th St., New York, NY.
Seats: 1009. Built: 1921.

Earl Carroll Theatre (November 10, 1924 – January 3, 1925)

(Thanks to the Internet Broadway Database, the Playbill Vault, and the Internet Movie Database for the information contained in these chronologies.)

Footnotes

* Tobia Bezzola, "Lights Going All Over the Place," from William A. Ewing and Todd Brandow, *Edward Steichen: In High Fashion, The Condé Nast Years, 1923-1937* (W. W. Norton and Company, 2008), p. 192. Published for the international exhibition of the same name that was organized by the Foundation for the Exhibition of Photography, Minneapolis, and the Musée de l'Elysée, Lausanne. The collection was exhibited in eight different museums between 2007 and 2009, and it featured four photos of Marion Morehouse.

* Harold Koda, *The Model as Muse: Embodying Fashion* (New York: Metropolitan Museum of Art, 2009), pp. 19-21. Published in conjunction with an eponymously titled exhibit at the Metropolitan Museum of Art (May 6-August 9, 2000).

* A more accurate description would be: "not a *famous* model," but the point is well taken. Robin Muir, "Vogue's Earliest Celebrity Models," *FirstFT* magazine, September 24, 2010, ft.com.

* The earliest Steichen photo of Marion that Richard Kennedy seems to have been aware of is the one that appeared in *Vogue* on October 15, 1925 ("Model Marion Morehouse wearing a dress by Lelong and Jewelry by Black, Starr and Frost"). The portrait is reproduced in Richard Kennedy's *E. E. Cummings Revisited* (New York: Twayne Publishers, 1994), on page 112. In the words of Sawyer-Lauçanno, the photos from this period "reveal an absolutely stunning young woman, with large brown eyes, long dark hair, perfect full lips, and a Roman nose. By the early 1930s, her career as a fashion model was well established

and she was in high demand." *E. E. Cummings, A Biography*
(Naperville, IL: Sourcebooks, 2004), p. 363. In *Dreams in the Mirror*, Kennedy calls her "one of the great beauties of her time," noting her "long elliptical face," "high cheek bones," "swanlike neck," "delicately curved breasts." Echoing Steichen, Kennedy notes: "Her training in the theater helped her to become a renowned fashion model, for she had the knack of adapting herself to the character of the clothes that were chosen for her." Kennedy, *Dreams in the Mirror. A Biography of E. E. Cummings* (New York: Liveright Publishing Corporation, 1980), p. 337.

* Although a marriage of seven years would have made Marion's birth legitimate, Benjamin and Anna were actually married for about six years at this time.

* Kennedy, "The Elusive Marion Morehouse," *Spring. The Journal of the E. E. Cummings Society* (Flushing, NY: E. E. Cummings Society, 1996), Number 5, p. 9.

* Otto Leo Morehouse was employed as a chauffeur and taxi driver during the Great Depression (while his father was a janitor) and later as a clerk. He died three months before Marion, in February 1969.

* A county clerk from South Bend informed me that crossing over the state line in order to marry after a divorce was a common practice; otherwise, one might be forced to wait up to two years to marry again within the state. Anna's surname appears here as "Shortelle." Lillian Morehouse's birth certificate says that Benjamin worked as "shoeman" (sic). Most likely, the person gathering the information mistook the (spoken) word "showman" for "shoe man."

* Since the information contained in city directories is gathered during the year prior to their publication, a listing in a "1904" directory actually reflects a person's residence and employment status in 1903.

* "In her social views, she posed as a 'monarchist' and an 'aristocrat' and often offered her opinions with *hauteur*. Like many people lacking in educational background, she enjoyed looking

down on others – working-class people or people outside their social circles – in order to elevate herself." Kennedy, "The Elusive Marion Morehouse," p. 12.

* Kennedy, *Dreams*, p. 337. According to the Playbill Archive, the play "Lysistrata" starred Hortense Alden (from the New York Theater Guild), who made her Broadway debut as a teenager and who performed in fifteen Broadway productions between 1919 and 1939. She would later appear in a 1964 episode of the TV serial, *The Doctors and the Nurses* (1962-1965). In 1941, Hortense married James T. Farrell, author of the *Studs Lonigan* trilogy. For more on the production of *Lysistrata*, see my "Partial Chronology of Marion Morehouse's Theatrical Work."

* Although neither Morehouse sister appears in the online *Ziegfeld Follies* archive, Lillian's name is listed in two of Earl Carroll's *Vanities* productions, which were *Ziegfeld Follies*-like musical revues. Carroll constructed his own Broadway venue, The Earl Carroll Theatre, which in 1925 featured Eugene O'Neill's premier of "Desire Under the Elms." Carroll's theater on Seventh Avenue was purchased by Ziegfeld in 1932 and renamed the Casino Theatre. It later hosted the Woolworth's Department store. It was demolished in 1990.

Steichen's widow, Joanna Steichen, briefly mentions Marion and Cummings in her book, *Steichen's Legacy*: "Once, Steichen suggested making a series of nude photographs. Morehouse agreed and posed wearing only long black gloves and stockings. Later, Steichen heard that she had married. To save her any possibility of future embarrassment, he destroyed the negatives of the nude sitting. Then he learned that she had married the avantgarde bohemian poet e. e. cummings, who, Steichen believed, would have relished the pictures." *Steichen's Legacy* (New York: Knopf, 2000), p. 106. Thanks to Christopher Sawyer-Lauçanno for alerting me to the fact that Steichen and Cummings were friends.

* *Edward Steichen: In High Fashion, The Condé Nast Years, 1923-1937* contains many portraits of dancers, actors, and ac-

tresses from the early Twenties, including one captioned "Actress Mary Eaton from the Follies, 1923": the same year that Steichen arrived in the United States. Plate 33 features one of the earliest photos of Marion taken by Steichen and is captioned "Model Marion Morehouse wearing an evening gown by Chanel, 1924." This gelatin silver print first appeared in the February 15, 1925 edition of *Vogue*.

According to author Nancy Hall-Duncan, Marion "was first seen in Steichen's photograph of November 1, 1924 for American *Vogue*. Nancy Hall-Duncan, *The History of Fashion Photography* (New York: Alpine Book Company, 1979), p. 54. Considered a classic in the field, this catalog was published in conjunction with the History of Fashion Photography exhibit produced by the author for the International Museum of Photography at the George Eastman House in Rochester, New York. The exhibit also traveled to several other museums in the United States.

* Kennedy, "The Elusive Marion Morehouse," p. 9.

* This was the same conclusion reached by Cummings's friend Charles Norman, who says, "When she married Cummings, she put her career behind her." Charles Norman, *E. E. Cummings: A Biography* (New York: E. P. Dutton & Co., 1967), p. 10. Norman was personally acquainted with Cummings from 1925 until his death in 1962.

* According to Benjamin Jr's death certificate, before he retired he was employed at the Webster Theater in Hartford. City directories list his occupation as "assistant manager."

* "She appeared in two films, and I have heard that whenever she arrived on location, in a Long Island studio, spectators and technicians ceased watching the stars to watch her." Charles Norman, *E. E. Cummings*, p. 10.

Interviews

Albert Hofmann: An Appreciation.
A Brief Exchange with the Discoverer of LSD*

Through its profound influence upon art, culture, and history, Dr. Hofmann's "problem child," LSD, has affected us all, in one way or another. Yet, rather than sensationalize it – as many others chose to – Hofmann always addressed the subject with reverence and responsibility. He spoke of LSD as if it were a living entity: a spirit that demanded propriety and respect. To the end, he considered it a "sacred medicine": not something to be toyed with or abused. Thus, it was with a sense of relief that he described how lysergic acid was finally being administered in an institutional scientific setting in Switzerland.

Although Hofmann's time was limited (he was receiving guests) and his English was rusty, we managed to share this delightful, if brief, exchange.

Rob Couteau: Do you believe that, in the future, LSD will be used in psychotherapy again?

Dr. Albert Hofmann: It is now officially used – in the medical practice – by dying or very ill persons as a narcotic. By a dying person, by a very ill person, it is used officially now, as an *anti-schmerz mittel* [painkiller].

RC: It's used in Switzerland?

AH: Yes. It's legal. It has started a half-year ago. We got, from the health authority, this permission to use it officially. By a dying person or by a very ill person.

RC: That's wonderful.

AH: It is wonderful.

RC: You must be very happy about that.

AH: Yes, that I can see that happen.

RC: Did they ask you for help to establish this treatment? Did they ask for your ideas? Did they consult with you?

AH: No. The properties and the possibilities of LSD are known. I have not to explain.

RC: I recently read your book, *LSD: My Problem Child*. I thought it was a beautifully written account.

AH: I am very happy that LSD is now officially a medicine, a medicinal product. It is no more needed to use it in the black market. This is very important for me, that I can see this happen. LSD, really, now it becomes what it is. And I wanted that. Especially for this application: for people with very heavy …

RC: [In French:] *Douleur*?

AH: *Douleur*, yes.

RC: In pain? People in pain?

AH: People in pain, in very heavy pain, especially. And now, dying people. This research is now officially working in Switzerland.

RC: With people who are dying, and people in pain, do you think it helps them to contact the spiritual aspect of life before they die?

AH: We don't know.

RC: Do you think that LSD is a spiritual medicine?

AH: Yes. Yes, of course!

RC: So, with some people, it could be an important experience before death, yes?

AH: Yes.

RC: How is your health, doctor? How are you feeling physically?

AH: Oh, I must say, I'm very, very happy. I am 102

years old.

RC: I know! [Laughs.]

AH: [Laughs.] Yes. And I have no pain. And so, I am thankful to my destiny.

RC: It's incredible that your friend, the German author, also lived to be 102.

AH: Who?

RC: Your friend Ernst Junger.

AH: Yes, yes ...

RC: You both lived to be so old! [Laughs.] It's very interesting, yes?

AH: [Laughs.] Yes.

RC: Thanks so much for speaking with me today.

AH: I don't know you, but I am happy that it has a meaning for you to speak with me.

RC: You must be very happy that LSD is now officially used in Switzerland.

AH: Yes, that's very important for me. That I can know that LSD has a place, begins to have a place, which it merits.

RC: Do you think that, for the artist, LSD can provide an important experience for creativity? For art?

AH: Maybe. Yes.

RC: It can?

AH: It has been! Many, many works have been done on the influence of LSD.

RC: Doctor, thank you so much for your time.

AH: Good-bye. Thank you.

Just two weeks after our conversation on 13 April 2008, Dr. Hofmann suffered a fatal heart attack. I was honored to have conversed with him and felt as if I were in the pres-

ence of an Old World Gentleman: One effusing kindness, awareness, discretion.

Reflections on Dr. Albert Hofmann's memoir, *LSD: My Problem Child*

I'm often drawn to authors that truly attempt something new. In literature, it's the stylists who captivate me: those who stretch the language in a manner that's so innovative and complex that, no matter how often we return to such work, it always holds more, both in what it says (content) and in how it's said (style). The novels of Hubert Selby are an example of this, as are the works of Thomas Bernhard, Gabriel Garcia Marquez, Henry Miller, Céline, and Walt Whitman.

Although Albert Hofmann wasn't a literary stylist, the story of his life is far more amazing than that of most novels. Therefore, it's the content of his memoir – the innovative adventure he embarks upon and its far-reaching social consequences – that renders it unique.

While his writing wasn't avant-garde, it was wonderfully understated and articulate. He was also well read, both in the classics and in contemporary works. For instance, in *LSD: My Problem Child*, Hofmann briefly mentions an exchange of letters with Henry Miller. His friendship with the German author Ernst Junger is also of note. Junger was a World War One pilot, and he later befriended Hofmann, who introduced him to LSD. In the course of one trip, Junger hallucinated miniature airplanes circling round his head. As a result of this experience, he wrote *The Glass Bees* (1957): a forerunner of magic realism with elements of science fiction. The novel chronicles an inventor who creates miniature wonders, such as robotic insects. (Indeed, we are now living in the era of the glass bees, as the CIA has recently used artificial insects – fake dragonflies – to monitor war protesters.)

Regarding Hofmann's understated manner, here's an example. Recounting his various attempts to synthesize the elusive properties of LSD, he remarks: "LSD spoke to me. He came to me and said, 'You must find me.' He told me, 'Don't give me to the pharmacologist; he won't find anything.'" And: "Under LSD ... I entered into realities which were as real and even more real than the one of everyday.... [I] became aware of the wonder of creation, the magnificence of nature and of the plant and animal kingdom. I became very sensitive to what will happen to all this and all of us." I admire the subtle way he turns that last phrase.

I also admire the grounded, human quality of this man. The tale I recall most vividly from *Problem Child* is one in which a distraught hippie girl shows up unexpectedly at Hofmann's door. As was the case with many of those divine "lost children," she viewed him as a sort of guru. But instead of wearing a toga, burning incense, and trying to seduce her – as Timothy Leary might have done – he helps to land her a job singing at a Zurich restaurant. In short, he attempts to link her back to the everyday world.

One must remember that Hofmann was thirty-seven years old when he accidentally dosed himself with LSD. His ego was strong and healthy and he had firmly established himself in the mundane world. Undoubtedly, he understood the importance of keeping at least one foot anchored upon the earth. Contrast this awareness and sense of responsibility toward others to someone like Leary, who advocated giving

LSD to children (and often did).* Perhaps Hofmann kept his phone number listed all his life because he keenly felt this responsibility, especially toward those who had stumbled while tripping along the magical LSD path.

When Leary visited Hofmann in Switzerland, Hofmann politely questioned his irresponsible approach to such matters. Leary's bizarre response was that American teenagers were more mature than European teenagers. In his typically reserved fashion, Hofmann remarked that he never understood what Leary "really intended" and concluded that he was simply "naive."* He wondered why Leary and his followers were traveling all the way to India for mystical experience when they could simply admire the flowers in their own gardens.*

Problem Child also explores the relationship between hallucinogens and the Eleusinian mystery cults of the past. For centuries, leading figures of society were initiated into these experiences, and there exists strong evidence that an LSD-like substance was involved in this ritual.

Research on the relationship between hallucinogenic experience and cultural evolution continues, although it remains inadequately explored in our educational institutions. Hofmann's later writing delves into this area.

---

* Both this interview and essay were published in the *Rain Taxi Review of Books*, summer 2008.

* "The psyche of very young persons should ... be considered as unstable, in the sense of not yet having matured. In any case, the shock of such a powerful stream of new and strange perceptions and feelings, such as is engendered by LSD, endangers the sensitive, still-developing psycho-organism. Even the medicinal use of LSD in youths under eighteen years of age, in the scope of psychoanalytic or psychotherapeutic treatment, is discouraged in

professional circles, correctly so in my opinion. Juveniles for the most part still lack a secure, solid relationship to reality. Such a relationship is needed before the dramatic experience of new dimensions of reality can be meaningfully integrated into the world view. Instead of leading to a broadening and deepening of reality consciousness, such an experience in adolescents will lead to insecurity and a feeling of being lost." Albert Hofmann; Jonathan Ott, trans., *LSD: My Problem Child* (New York: McGraw-Hill), p. 70.

* "I never could make out what he [Leary] really intended. I had the feeling he was naive. He was so enthusiastic about LSD that he wanted to give it to everyone, even to very young people. I told him: 'No, give it only to people who are prepared for it, who have strong, stable psychic structures. Don't give it to young people.' He said that American teenagers are so experienced that they are like grown-ups in Europe." From "Interview: Albert Hofmann," *Omni* magazine, July 1981, p. 70.

* "I've never been able to understand these people. What I got out of LSD, I carry about inside me. I have to stay in my own daily life. To see the flowers in my own garden is to see all the mystical wonder of existence, of creation. You don't have to go to India to see it." Ibid., p. 72.

The Charmed Life:
A Conversation with Michael Korda*

A former editor-in-chief at Simon & Schuster, Michael Korda was one of the most influential people in the recent history of publishing. He's also the author of the memoirs Charmed Lives, Another Life, *and* Horse People; *the biographies* Ike *and* Ulysses S. Grant; *as well as several best-selling novels. A powerful public speaker and gifted raconteur, he attributes his storytelling ability to the creative influence of his father Vincent and his famous uncles Zoltán and Sir Alexander Korda, "who were brilliant at that," but adds, "I've never met anyone who was Hungarian who wasn't." After speaking at the State University at New Paltz, NY, about the future of books and book publishing, he kindly agreed to this interview, which took place on 22 April 2010.*

Rob Couteau: One of the things that struck me about *Charmed Lives* was that, throughout the book, you speak of your shyness, and you say you were "frequently at a loss for words … in social situations," and you found the accents of the English very intimidating. How did you go from this rather introverted figure to being such an articulate, powerful public speaker?

Michael Korda: It would be almost impossible for me to know how I do that. Probably the answer is that somewhere very deep in my genetic pattern is my mother, who was a very gifted actress, and that that emerges from time to time. I also think there's a huge difference between speaking to an audience and speaking to individuals. I can certainly suffer from nerves from time to time when speaking to individuals. But faced with an audience, I'm able to separate them from individuals, if you see what I mean. And I was certainly never trained for it; it just comes out on its own. I didn't know until I started, when I wrote my first book, *Male Chauvinism*, then did an unexpected and large amount of publicity for that book, that I had a gift for it. I would have thought that I probably didn't. But there it was. I attribute that entirely to my mother. My mother was a terrific actress, and I must have inherited that as a part of my gene pool. Along with the teeth.

RC: I can think of many actors who are quite nervous without a script.

MK: I used to be able to speak quite easily without a script. And had no difficulty extemporizing when I stood up. That's not true anymore. I find that it's difficult for me to do unless I have a script in hand. With a script in hand, I find it comes naturally. But I have to know what I'm going to say now. Before, many years ago, I was able to just get up and speak, and it would work, but I wouldn't dare to try that now.

RC: It reminds me of a story I heard recently about Robert De Niro. He was speaking at the Tribeca Film Festival, and a friend of mine was one of the judges there, and he was shocked at how nervous De Niro was, introducing the whole thing. So, that's probably something many actors go through, I would imagine.

MK: Oh, yes. Almost every actor I know has a degree of stage fright. And I think that's healthy. Because it makes you perform better.

RC: To bring one's adrenaline up, and so on?

MK: Exactly.

RC: Just before he buys you a motorcycle, your Uncle Alex Korda says: "Years ago, I remember that Lawrence of

Arabia was coming to see me to talk about a movie of *Seven Pillars of Wisdom*, and he was killed on the way in a motorcycle accident. I still own the rights." Did this anecdote plant a seed in your mind for your later desire to write about Lawrence?

MK: I've always been interested in Lawrence. That item, by the way, is not entirely correct. Alex met Lawrence and bought the rights not to *Seven Pillars of Wisdom* but to *Revolt in the Desert*, which is the condensation of them. And did so on the promise that he would never make the movie in Lawrence's lifetime. This was extremely important to Lawrence. And Lawrence comments about it very nicely in his letters, about how Alex had removed from him this fear that somebody would make the movie during his lifetime. And that as long as Alex owned it, nobody else would be able to do it.

He was not killed on his way to see Alex. I may have supposed that when I wrote *Charmed Lives*, but on further examination it isn't so. But they did meet, and liked each other enormously, and Alex made him this promise.

It certainly played a part. My Uncle Zoltán would have directed the movie, which was to star Leslie Howard as Lawrence, and the screenplay was written by Miles Malleson, who later became that famous character actor. And Winston Churchill was working as screenwriter for my Uncle Alex in the '30s, since he was then in political, not exactly exile, but he was removed from any kind of political power, and also in desperate need of money because of his lifestyle. So I knew a great deal about this, and it certainly steered me in the direction of Lawrence. And there are numerous resemblances, quite accidental, between myself and Lawrence. In the sense, for example, that I joined the Royal

Air Force; in the sense that I've always owned motorcycles, until quite recently, when I'm really too old to be riding around on one anymore; and that I've been in the Middle East and liked it and, of course, spent time there.

So Lawrence is certainly somebody who was put in my mind a very long time ago, no doubt by the connection between Lawrence and my Uncle Alex. And the fact that Alex would have made that film before the war if he could have, after Lawrence's death. But he couldn't get the financing for it, because the British government very much wanted the film not to be made in the 1930s, for very obvious reasons. They didn't want to offend the Turks. There was constantly an Arab resentment toward the portrayal of the Arab revolt as being something for which Lawrence was in any degree responsible. That's one of those things that are just built in, but in the 1930s it was a serious concern on the part of the British government. They were asked to prevent it from happening. And Alex, who had a very acute political sense, simply shelved the film and put it to one side and made *Four Feathers* instead. Which my Uncle Zoltán directed and my father art directed.

And then, after the war, it was even harder to make a movie about Lawrence immediately. First of all, it was enormously expensive and difficult to do, and secondly things were even more exacerbated because of Israel. So he put it to one side completely. Then, as with so many other things that he owned, he sold it for a considerable profit to Sam Spiegel, who eventually got the backing to make his film.

It's interesting to speculate on what it would have been like as a film, but we'll never know. Leslie Howard would have been very good actually, as Lawrence. So, I don't doubt it would have been an interesting movie.

RC: You've just finished the book on Lawrence?

MK: I finished writing it. I'm now involved in the details: permissions, artwork, fact checking, and copy editing. But it is written, yes.

RC: How long were you working on it?

MK: About three years.

RC: The other day, you said that it was the most difficult book you've worked on, in part because he was such an unsympathetic character.

MK: No, I never said he was unsympathetic. I said "difficult to work on" because he's like an oyster. There are lots of things going on in Lawrence's life, but he had a great capacity for hiding what he thought and what he was really doing. Sometimes, even from himself. So, with Lawrence, you have to probe constantly beneath the surface and try and figure out what it is that's really going on there. Which is not the case for example with Eisenhower or Ulysses S. Grant.

RC: What drew you to doing this book on him? Was it the similarities you felt you shared with him?

MK: No, I don't think so. Lawrence is just a wonderful story. And one that interests me a lot and that I know quite a bit about. So, when I'd done the *Battle of Britain* book, it was fairly natural, in looking for a new subject, to think about Lawrence.

There was a suggestion that I should do a book about the marriage of Winston Churchill and Clementine Churchill, and that interested me. But there's so much about Churchill, and even about their marriage, that I had a degree of doubt about it, which nobody else seemed to share. And then, all of a sudden, when somebody mentioned Lawrence, I said, "Of course that's what I should do." [Laughs] And I think it's worked out. I think Lawrence was in need of a contemporary clearing away of some of the cobwebs that had gathered around him. And that's a valuable thing to do.

RC: How would you rate *Seven Pillars of Wisdom*?

MK: The *Seven Pillars of Wisdom* is one of those strange books. It's not an easy book to read, in part because Lawrence tried so hard to make it a great work of literature. You can kind of feel, throughout the book, Lawrence doing what amounts to weightlifting in the mind to create a great work of literature. I think it can be argued that he succeeded. But it's one of those books that are not by any stretch of the imagination an easy read. There are great scenes in it that are absolutely spectacular. But it's a little in the category of reading James Joyce's *Ulysses*. Which is that, you know, it is admittedly a great work of literature, there are great scenes in it, you can recognize it as a masterpiece and a classic, but it's not an easy read. And I certainly feel that about *Seven Pillars of Wisdom*. *Revolt in the Desert*, which is the condensation of it, is in fact much more readable. But for all that, *Seven Pillars of Wisdom* is a more interesting book. Certainly, the fact that it's still in print after all these years, and in two versions, and continues to sell, is some indication of the fact that Lawrence succeeded.

RC: Was it his greatest literary work? When I say literary, that could include letters, nonfiction, whatever. Was it his greatest piece of writing?

MK: Lawrence's best writing, and most interesting writing, was as a letter writer. He was a prodigious letter writer.

RC: I had a feeling you were going to say that.

MK: And his letters are amazing. And quite extraordinary. And represent one of the great bodies of letters of any English figure at any time.

RC: Would it be fair to say, then, that *Seven Pillars* is a bit strained in its style, whereas the letters …

MK: I think it tries too hard to become a great work, and you can feel that constantly in reading the book, but there are whole scenes that are among some of the most striking in English writing. And certainly, it's one of the great non-fiction books about war that I've ever read. Or that anyone's ever read.

RC: In your work, do you focus more on the historical aspect of his life or the literary, or both?

MK: Everything. You can't separate the one from the other.

RC: Getting back for a moment to *Charmed Lives*. You call your Uncle Alex "a man who at heart disliked intimacy, and could never share the innermost part of his life with anyone, except his brothers." You also say "there was a ruthless streak in his nature" and that "when ego or self-interest were involved Alex could be harsh, authoritarian and vengeful." "He did not take kindly to disagreement, and disliked being thwarted or contradicted." Much of this could serve as a classic, textbook definition of narcissism. If you were to agree with that, how much of this was a destructive narcissism and how much what psychologists would term a healthy or character-building narcissism? Did he have a real empathy for others or only a need to assert dominance over them by forcing his "assistance" on them?

MK: I think the book makes it obvious that Alex had enormous charm and that I was very fond of him. That he was a narcissist is probably true enough. There's a streak of narcissism in anybody, I suppose, as successful as Alex was. But I don't think I could analyze it beyond what I've done in the book.

RC: By the way, I thought the ending of *Charmed Lives* was really touching.

MK: I like the ending of the book; I think it *is* very touching. It really was the best way to end it. I have no regrets about having ended it that way.

RC: Especially since your father was normally so reticent. I believe that was the last meeting you had with him.

MK: Yes ...

RC: And then, it's so poetic, he says, "It's not been such a bad life, my boy, has it? We had some good times, no?"

MK: It's wonderful. That was exactly what ... he did say that. So, it rounds itself off very well.

RC: In terms of the three brothers, you devote the most time to describing Alex. Then, secondly, your father. And the middle brother, Zoltán, the least of all. This creates a kind of mystery around Zoltán.

MK: He lived in California whereas we lived in London. I saw much less of Zoli than I saw of Alex. And obviously, much less of Zoli than I saw of my father. I simply know less about his life; so, I don't think there's anything deliberate about that. If I knew more about Zoli, I would have put more in.

RC: He possessed a sort of amalgam of traits of the older brother and the younger brother. On the one hand, Zoli had much of the artistic integrity that your father refused to give up, yet, on the other hand, he was able to successfully work within the movie-industry system. This is an interesting part of his character.

MK: A lot of people felt that Zoli was by far the most talented of the three, although an equal number have felt that my father was the most talented. For what it's worth, I'm inclined to say that all three were very talented in their own special ways, but their particular abilities were different. My father had a much broader range of talent in some ways than the other two. Obviously, Alex had an ability as a producer and as a businessman, as a showman, on top of being a movie producer and a movie director. He was a very special figure. Zoli I simply know less about. He was a brilliant movie director and, you know, what else filled his life, apart from collecting gold coins, I don't really know.

RC: You said your father was a gifted raconteur.

MK: Yes, very. In his own strange English; yes, he was.

RC: Was he the most gifted storyteller of the three brothers?

MK: No, all three were wonderful storytellers. I'm not sure that isn't just a Hungarian characteristic. But they were all wonderful at that.

RC: One of the most amusing portraits in *Another Life* is the one you paint of President Nixon. You describe his odd behavior as a tragic inability to communicate on an interpersonal level. But I was wondering if you felt there was a deeper pathology there.

MK: He was a very strange personality; there's no question about that. I don't claim to have known him any better than I described in the book. So, there's a limit to my ability to parse him. But even Henry Kissinger would always agree that the president was a very odd personality.

On the other hand, he's in that curious range of people who set out to become something totally unlikely, which is the president of the United States. He prepares himself for that role in his own way, and then succeeds in doing it. And also succeeds in being an extraordinary and revolutionary president for a Republican. For all Nixon's faults – and I would be the last to deny that there were many – his grasp of foreign policy and his strategy for getting what he wanted out of foreign policy was altogether extraordinary. Henry Kissinger, whom I also have edited for many years, is the first to agree that even though Nixon's genius in choosing Henry Kissinger – not an obvious first choice at all for somebody like Nixon – to be his foreign policy advisor and then secretary of state is a curious but very powerful stroke of genius, none of Henry Kissinger's achievements in foreign policy could have been made without the president first accepting or agreeing to them. And, in many cases, without the president first coming to that knowledge.

The opening of the China policy is not something Henry Kissinger brought to Richard Nixon on a plate and said, "Why don't we do this?" It's something that Nixon, in that lonely and sometimes embittered but very determined isolation of his, thought out. Now, that's a very unusual thing for a West-Coast Republican, when every other Republican was in favor of Chiang Kai-shek and Taiwan and against any agreement with the Communist Chinese. For Nixon to sit there in the dark and come up with the brilliant notion of recognizing China and using China as a third party in negotiating with the Soviet Union so that, in effect, the United States would become the dominating power by being able to manipulate the two Communist powers against each other … This is something that Nixon thought up. Once Nixon had introduced it, then, certainly, Henry was probably the only person in the world with the patience, the charm, and the ability to make this happen in the way that Nixon wanted it to happen. But it should never be forgotten that this was Nixon's policy, not Kissinger's.

RC: Why do you consider Ulysses S. Grant's memoir to be the *Moby Dick* of American nonfiction?

MK: Well, it just *is*. [Laughs]

RC: I know you believe that; I'm just wondering if you could elaborate on it.

MK: There are two great American classics. In fiction, it's *Moby Dick*. In nonfiction, it's Grant's memoirs. You could make an argument for *Huckleberry Finn* instead of *Moby Dick*. And that argument has been made by several people. And it may be true. But if you look at nonfiction, I don't think there's another book in the American literary universe that is as powerful and as much of a classic as Grant's memoirs.

RC: I'd like to quote an excerpt from the memoir and have you react to it. This is from chapter eight, volume one: "Every Sunday there was a bullfight for the amusement of those who could pay their fifty cents. I attended one of them – not wishing to leave the country without having witnessed the national sport. The sight to me was sickening. I could not see how human beings could enjoy the sufferings of beasts, and often of men, as they seemed to on these occasions." Then he goes on to characterize the matadors as "murderers"!

MK: Where are you quoting from?

RC: It's from Grant's memoir. I thought it was fascinating, because we'd probably be hard-pressed to find such a sympathetic general in the United States military today saying something like that.

MK: Although Grant was a West Pointer, remember that

he resigned from the army as a captain because of his drinking problem and only came back in the Civil War because of special circumstances. You can't think of him as a normal general. And Grant's fondness for animals and his dislike of the sight of blood is a very deep characteristic of Grant. It's not just that he didn't like bullfighting; he didn't like to be anywhere on the battlefield near where the wounded were being taken care of and operated on. That's why he was out in the rain at the end of the first day of Shiloh. It was the only place where he could have sheltered from the rain.* They were operating, in the manner of the day, by cutting off limbs. And Grant had a very low tolerance for that. Which, by the way, does him credit. He was not afraid of effusion of blood, as he would have put it. He was a very tough general and understood exactly how best to win on the battlefield. And he was certainly not afraid of casualties. But he was the last person in the world to have enjoyed cruelty for its own sake. Or to have condoned it. That's a genuine aspect of Grant to be taken into consideration.

RC: My father's from roughly the same generation as you are; he was born in 1929, and he's fascinated with the whole World War Two period. So I bought him a copy of your Ike biography, and I asked what he would have liked to ask you, regarding the book. He said, "I'd like to know his opinion as to why the right constantly refer to Ronald Reagan as their paragon of past greatness but never refer to Ike in that mode."

MK: Ike was never a natural Republican. You know, probing Ike's deeper opinions is something I am reluctant to do, because I can't "channel" him, as it were. But he never had a natural taste for the Republican right wing.

After all – talk about bullfights – he had to fight Robert Taft almost to the death to get the Republican nomination. The Republican right wing was always much more sympathetic to and determined to have as a presidential candidate Robert Taft than Ike.

When Ike ran for the presidency in '52, the Republican Party and those who supported Taft were against NATO; wanted to get American troops out of Europe; talked about preventative war against the Soviet Union; or wanted the United States either to resume the war in Korea or felt that the war in Korea should never have been ended, except for the victory. None of these were things that Ike believed at all. Ike was an internationalist; his strength was that he got along well, in general, with the British and the French and even with the Russians. He enjoyed Stalin's company when he was in Moscow. He is virtually the creator of NATO. The last thing he would have wanted was to draw American troops out of Europe.

In social terms, it's difficult to know what Ike was interested in or what he was for, if only because Ike was too clever to be pinned down by it. He was certainly, in modern terms, slow to move on civil rights, although very firm when he finally did move. But then, for a mid-Westerner of Ike's generation, that's just par for the course. JFK was not in any way fiercely committed toward civil rights.

RC: Until push came to shove, Kennedy wanted to avoid it as long as possible.

MK: He wanted them to stop demonstrating. And so did Bobby Kennedy.

RC: Actually, Truman was far ahead of his time in this regard.

MK: Very far. Although whether he was far ahead of his

time in terms of his personal feeling about blacks is a separate matter altogether. Once again, he was born in the nineteenth century, in Missouri.

RC: We have to judge these things in their context, obviously.

MK: Yes. But Ike was an atypical Republican. And by the way, no sooner had Ike left the presidency than the Republican Party moved a huge step rightwards. Where it has remained ever since. And rejected Nelson Rockefeller, and ...

RC: It's certainly moved *several* steps to the right in the last five to ten years! I mean, it's quite unimaginable where things have ended up.

MK: Exactly. Yeah, that would have infuriated Ike, actually.

RC: Perhaps one of the reasons he hasn't been characterized as a paragon of the right is that when he brought Federal troops to enforce integration in that Arkansas high school, a lot of the right wing – with their State's Rights concerns – must have been furious about it, and this probably still resonates.

MK: Yes, probably so. It is going back in time, but I think it took a good deal of pushing to get Ike to where he wanted to do it. But once he did it, he did it in a very forthright and strong way. And instead of using marshals and FBI agents, he used the 101st Airborne. There you have to give Ike credit. He figured a segregationist mob might not be stopped by FBI agents, but they sure would be stopped by the 101st Airborne! [Laughs] He didn't have any doubts about that.

RC: Perhaps we can briefly touch on some of the ideas you spoke about the other day, on the future of publishing and the form of the book. You were saying the form itself is not so important; it's the *book* that's important. And we have to compare the book in its present form not just to an electronic book, like the Kindle, but we have to apply our imagination to it much further, in that it might become something that's *beyond* anything we could imagine today.

MK: Well, I think that that's true. You know, you're looking at the Model-T Ford and trying to look ahead to what road transportation will be like in 2010. I mean, ultimately, it'll still have four wheels, and some form of propulsion, and a steering wheel. But beyond that, you're trying to imagine something that is *beyond* imagination, if you see what I mean.

Now, there are two important differences. One is that the speed of progress is now so rapid, and transition is so quick, that the next step in reading-technology will come very rapidly, rather than very slowly. There's not going to be a long lag between its inception and its development and any changes that take place. Already, the iPad is a huge step ahead of the Kindle. Although whether it's a useful step ahead for readers remains to be seen. I don't have a comment about that, and I'm not equipped to; I don't have an iPad. But clearly, it's a big step ahead.

On the other hand, also clearly, it's a rather large, cumbersome device, which needs to be replaced by something altogether different. But that is going to happen with such incredible rapidity that we really can't forecast what it will look like.

Ultimately, my guess is that all the world's literature and knowledge will be contained in something the size of a refrigerator. And you'll be able to pick it up with your computer, or with a handheld or pocket computer of some kind, with some system of payment, with no problem at all. I can't see how, exactly, that will take place. But my guess is that, in ten years time, it will be in place, and nobody will have a problem with it. It's just amazing the degree to which things are changing rapidly.

RC: There are many who say, "Well, I would miss the *feel* of the book." But if you unleash your imagination, it's easy to imagine that, at some point in the future, a book could be what appears to be a single piece of paper, which is not actually a piece of paper, and the text is appearing on that pseudo paper, which looks just like text on a normal piece of paper. And you could hold it and feel it, but every time you want to get to the next page you touch something, and there's the next page. It could even be something like that, to appeal to the tactile sense. It doesn't have to be just a visual innovation; it could also be something that involves more than one sense.

MK: Yeah, no doubt. But you know, I don't have a clue. The person to talk to about that is Steve Jobs. [Laughs] Unless he dies first, he'll probably be the one who will invent it. But it'll be something quite different.

In any case, I don't think that that's something that one should be afraid of. People react the same way about a whole variety of things, ranging from smoking cigarettes to using typewriters or fountain pens. But nevertheless the technology simply leaps ahead, and people simply adapt to it.

RC: About ten years ago, you mentioned this in your memoir. In *Another Life*, you spoke about the sudden appearance of computers and word processors, and how a lot of people at Simon and Schuster were terrified that this would be like movies being replaced by videocassettes, and everyone was going to go out of business.

MK: Yes, exactly. And some people *will* go out of business. [Laughs]

RC: But other things, other businesses, will be created.

MK: Right. If you had said to somebody ten years ago, what do you think the music business will look like, nobody would have guessed that people would be downloading individual songs into their computers and that the record stores would have gone. A very similar thing is going to happen to reading. It's not going to take place in a huge, explosive way. The book will continue to be a major factor, certainly for as long as I live, and maybe for as long as you live. But eventually it's going, in the form of something else.

RC: What about the future of publishing?

MK: It will have to be reinvented with that in mind. Already, it's evident that the major publishers are looking to find a partner in Steve Jobs. So that Apple will become, in effect, a kind of publishing house. How that will work remains to be seen. There isn't anyone in the book publishing business who can tell you, because nobody knows at this point in time. But that's what everybody is clearly attempting to move toward.

RC: What about the role of small press publishers?

MK: They can only be improved by this, because they will have access to a media that's open to everybody. How they'll make money, I don't know. But then, how do they make money now? I mean, that's enough of a mystery right there.

RC: So, that part might not change very much.

MK: That part will be better. They may come out ahead. I mean, I'm not sure I wouldn't rather be a small publisher than, say, Random House.

RC: Right now?

MK: Not right now, but five years from now.

RC: And why is that?

MK: Because how are you going to keep a large organization like Random House – with a lot of editors and a headquarters in New York – functioning if books are going to be sold from scratch for between ten and fifteen dollars, by downloading them into some device that hasn't yet been invented? And will not the publisher then, in effect, become Apple or whoever makes the device?

But a small press could be placed in New Paltz and issue a book on the Internet, and it could either be read on the device or printed off the device without any particular problem. All of that is surely coming in the future. And given that, the small press should do better, if anything.

I mean, there'll be no difficulty in finding a way of doing small books. It's whether the big publishers will, in fact, have a place at all that remains to be seen.

---

* This interview was conducted on 22 April 2010 and originally appeared in *Rain Taxi Review of Books* (online) in August 2010.
* The battle of Shiloh (1862) was extraordinarily bloody, shocking the public in both the North and the South. There were about 20,000 total causalities, mostly in one day, and more fell in the battle than the entire number of dead and wounded in the Revolution, the War of 1812, and the Mexican War combined. During the conflict, Grant converted his field headquarters into a hospital, and he spent the night under a tree in a driving rainstorm. Greater horrors were yet to come in the wholesale slaughters of Antietam, Gettysburg, Vicksburg, etc.

Remembering the Deluge:
An Interview with Jeffrey Jackson, Author of *Paris Under Water* and *Making Jazz French**

Jeffrey Jackson is associate professor of history and director of environmental studies at Rhodes College. After spending over a decade researching in the Paris archives, in 2007 he was named a "Top Young Historian" by the History News Network, and he received an international fellowship that enabled him to continue his archival work in Paris. His first book, Making Jazz French: Music and Modern Life in Interwar France, *considered the best work on the subject, explores the complex reactions to jazz in France and its ultimate integration into the national tradition. This was followed by the widely acclaimed* Paris Under Water, *a history of the nearly forgotten deluge of 1910 that almost destroyed the City of Light.*

As a child, Jackson attended an elementary school that required French lessons, beginning in the first grade. It was the combination of this early training and the influence his globe-trotting grandparents – who brought back exotic tales of Europe – that led to his interest in French culture.

Rob Couteau: You've received quite an enthusiastic response to your new book!

Jeffrey Jackson: I was very pleased and pleasantly surprised at how much play this has gotten. Unfortunately, you could say that natural disasters are always kind of exciting in a strange way. [Laughs] There's always that drama built in. And people are always interested in Paris.

One of the things that's been nice about this project is that it's allowed me to tell something about the history of the city that people didn't really know. Many have read about the history of Paris, and it is a well-known history; much has been written about it. But because this was something that hadn't been written about very much, it opened up a new light, or a new window, to a familiar story.

RC: The same could be said of your first book, about jazz in Paris. It touched on many little-known facts regarding that history.

JJ: That's true. It was my dissertation originally, and, of course, it was revised for the book. When I began working on it in graduate school, I started looking around to see what else existed about jazz in France. And really, very little had. I was kind of surprised. So, it was another one of those things where I was able to open up a new perspective on something. People had known a lot about Josephine Baker, or particular, specific musicians, or certain aspects of the jazz story. But there hadn't been a lot that had pulled it all together, into one narrative. So, that's what I was trying to do.

RC: I feel as if there are two principal heroes in your account of the flood. One is Louis Lépine, who served as the prefect of police. The other is the average citizen of Paris, with his system of *débroullard* or, as it's commonly known, *système d*. It was wonderful to finally read an account of *système d* in an English-language book. I lived in Paris for twelve years, and I constantly heard references to *système d*. In your book, the prime example of *système d* would be the wooden walkways or *passerelles* that were constructed throughout the city to allow people to get around. I believe you said this was copied from the Venetians.

JJ: Yes, the Venetians have been doing that for quite a long time, because they always have that high water every year. It probably is a combination of people knowing that Venice had done that, but also that kind of extemporaneous reaction of: "What are we going to do? We need to get around the neighborhood, and we've got some planks, and let's put them together." That's why I talk about it as a prime example of *système d*.

It's funny you say that it's nice to finally read a description of that in English. Because I knew what *système d* was, and talked to people about it, and had heard of it, but when I went looking, just to put a footnote or to cite something about *système d*, I couldn't find anything in print. It's one of those things that people know about but don't feel the need to write about.

RC: The Larousse defines *système d* as: to sort out, to disentangle, to manage. But when I lived in Paris in the 1990s, I heard it used in a sense similar to what we would call *finagle*. That is, to achieve by devious, crooked, or crafty means. The first time I heard of it was when one of my French English-language students showed me her method of secretly turning back the dial on her electric meter, in order to lower her utility bill! You don't really touch upon that in your book, but the more common usage often indicates something a little underhanded.

JJ: Yeah, I can see that. [Laughs] Obviously, I was trying to emphasize the positive spin on that. But I can certainly see how it would cut both ways, depending on the circumstances. Getting yourself out of a scrape could be turning back your electric meter, just as much as putting up a wooden walkway. It depends on what you're trying to get out of.

But getting back to back to your initial statement, I think you're right: I try to talk about both sides of that story. I focus on leadership and on people who are in charge. And Louis Lépine is of course the one who really pops out. Because the police oversaw so much of the city, even beyond what we think of as just crime and punishment sort of stuff: all the management of the urban space. And I talk about President Fallières, and the prefect of the Seine, Justin de Selves, as other leader figures who were important in providing that kind of top-down, official response.

But I think you're right: at the same time, it's something that goes hand-in-hand with the bottom up. You know, with the people in the street, working together, to save themselves and to save the city and their neighbors. You can't really have one without the other. You could've had the police doing all they could do, but that still wouldn't be enough. It never is, really. And you could have people responding locally, but without someone working to coordinate it all, you'd just have sporadic, scattered efforts. So, you see both of those groups of people working together. That's part of what helps to make the city survive at this point.

RC: Louis Lépine served in that role from 1899 until his retirement in 1913. What special qualities did he bring to his position that helped him to become an effective leader during the flood?

JJ: He definitely saw himself as a man of law and order. He wanted to be someone who could tame the city. And that has both positive and negative connotations. For him, that meant good public health, regulated traffic in the street, public safety: all the good things. But it also meant *his* vision of what order was. In the book, I refer to him raiding bookshops and taking out what he thought were inappropriate books or photographs. You know, a bit of a censorship aspect. But I think in a disaster situation like the flood, that desire for orderliness was something he brought to the table that really did help in this time of need, because it was something people needed at that moment.

He called himself "the prefect of the streets": someone who wanted to be out in the street, wanted to be visible. I'm sure part of that was a way of him saying, "I'm in charge." But I think it also allowed him to say, "I feel some sense of connection to, or commonality with, the man on the street." He could sympathize with that suffering in a moment like the flood.

There are numerous accounts of him leading the charge. It's hard to tell how accurate some of these depictions are: leading the firefighters and others into the vinegar factory that had exploded. And coordinating that effort. Or coordinating the evacuation of the Boucicaut Hospital. He's supposedly there, overseeing the whole thing. And it's hard to know exactly, but it doesn't seem too out of character that, at the very least, he would have been there. Whether he was really the one barking out orders, or whether he was overseeing, it's hard to know; but he was definitely there, and bringing that sense of orderliness to the situation.

RC: People often forget that there's a long history of censorship in France. In our literary community, we often regard Paris as an open city. But even the Marquis de Sade was thrown into the Conciergerie.

JJ: Right.

RC: What's your estimate of the number of homeless in Paris during this crisis? About 200,000?

JJ: I think so; I don't have it right in front me of me. I know there were at least 50,000 people who were put into hospitals. Something like 20,000 households, depending on how you count people versus households. You know, it's always hard to come up with an exact number.

RC: Many of those were recent arrivals from outside the city, right?

JJ: Some of them would have been. Many would have been from the immediate suburban towns, just outside Paris, which were very much a part of the city's life. Of course, I focus mostly on Paris itself. But I do try to talk about a few of the towns that adjoin it: Alfortville, Charenton, Gennevilliers, and others. Because they were very much part of the city and its life. And so, many of those who had recently arrived would have been living in these suburban villages, working in factories or in occupations that were tied to what was going on in Paris.

RC: Perhaps the unsung hero of your account is Eugène Belgrand, Baron Haussmann's chief of water services, who originally proposed raising the height of the quay walls to prevent flooding. But the engineers refused to do so, because of aesthetic reasons. Perhaps you could speak about Haussmann, Belgrand, their role in designing modern Paris and, in particular, their creation of the Hydrometric Service.

JJ: They're very much part of the story. Of course, they pre-date the flood. But you can't talk about Paris at this moment without at least having them standing there, in the background.

One of the things I tried to emphasize was that, when Haussmann and Belgrand worked to renovate the city in the 1850s and 1860s and to really modernize it, part of what they do is, not only do they make it beautiful, they make it modern. They widen the streets; they re-do the sewers and all these things that make Paris cleaner, newer, brighter. But what that also does is, it reinforces the idea, which was very much a nineteenth-century idea, that we can control our environment. We can shape the city to our human needs. That we really are in charge of nature and our surroundings. That was one of Haussmann's operating principles, this belief in technology and engineering.

You see it as well in the Hydrometric Service. Part of what Belgrand was trying to do was to study the river. To understand how it worked so that he could figure out how to engineer it better: to engineer the sewers and the water system to prevent flooding. Or to manage the water for the better use of the people living there. Haussmann and Belgrand shared this nineteenth-century belief in the power of technology.

On the one hand, it served them well; it served the city very well. But in 1910 it didn't quite match up to what they had hoped. That's one of the great ironies of the story that was particularly interesting and that really fascinated me: to see this unending belief in science and technology have this moment of crisis where people were like, "Does it really work the way we've always been taught?" Especially when I quote the British journalist Gerald and his descriptions of Paris: Will Paris die? Is this the death of Paris? Is this the end? This whole "end of the world" scenario. It was such a shock to read those kinds of words, where somebody was actually musing openly about whether this might, in fact, be the end of civilization in this place.

RC: You write: "The growing mountains of garbage, collapsed sidewalks, clogged sewers, and dislodged paving stones transported the city backward in time to the era before Haussmann's renovations." It's incredible to imagine that Paris, which we conceive of as a kind of eternal city – one that even survived quite intact after two World Wars – might be so vulnerable to a natural disaster. Especially one in which the water came largely from beneath the ground, and through the city's infrastructure, rather than over the embankments of the Seine. The image you paint of concierges pulling the drain plugs in the basements of buildings, only to incur worse flooding, is quite striking.

JJ: I thought that was really interesting, when I found out about that. It's another example of people putting their faith in the engineering of the sewer system and then it actually backfiring. Again, that irony at work.

I think you're right. The idea that Paris could be this vulnerable is really something that drew me to the project. It's probably another reason why a lot of people found the book to be striking and why it's gotten a number of reviews. Because we don't think about that. San Francisco, New Orleans, places that are in high-risk zones: we think about those kinds of cities. Or Venice, which is slowly sinking. But as you say, we have this image of Paris as an eternal city, even though, of course, it's evolved over the years. It's never been eternal; it's always been changing. But we have this idea of it as somehow being eternal. And for it to be vulnerable, and to see it in this moment of vulnerability – both through the descriptions and through the amazing photographs, where you see the streets ripped up, and you see the water everywhere – I think it is shocking, because it's so unexpected. It certainly was that way, too, for people at the time. That was another reason why this was such a powerful moment. Especially with the city having been rebuilt, and having the sewers expanded and modernized, they really didn't expect this to happen.

RC: You say: "the flood challenged many of the era's most basic assumptions about the inevitable force of progress. Railroads, telegraphs, steam engines, electricity, sewers, and hundreds more inventions had promised a better life.... In one week, the flood made that promise seem false, and their faith in an ever-brighter future seem so fragile." The French in general have long been known to resist change. I wonder if this exacerbated their fear of the new.

JJ: Well, it's interesting; I think it cuts both ways. For all the French interest in the past and resisting change, there have also been moments when they have not only embraced it but have also been at the forefront of it. Some of that engineering stuff is part of that. That's why I start with the image, in the first chapter, of the 1900 World's Fair. Because that was one of those moments. The whole purpose of these world's fairs or expositions was to celebrate the new; the modern; the newest, latest, coolest invention. And to think about how that might make your life better.

This could be one of those moments that's both a forward-looking and a backward-looking moment. Some said, Look at what technology has brought. It's destroyed our city. These sewers, that were supposed to keep us safe, have in fact made things worse. The subway, all these things, this new stuff, has made our life worse. And, yes, maybe we should go back. But others said, the city's been destroyed, but we can rebuild it. We have the power to renew and continue it even further. In the book I say that, for many people, this was not the end of Haussmann's dream of modernizing the city. It just provided them with another opportunity to move that project forward.

And so, I guess it depends on who was looking at the scene, who was talking about their response to the event. For some, I think you're right; it would be a kind of confirmation of how we've deviated too far from the old ways. But for others, it was just a blip on the radar screen of this inevitable progress.

That's why, when they form a commission to study the flood, and they write this enormous tome, this huge book that has all this – their study of what happened and what went wrong – even with all the discussion of what went wrong, much of the book is about how we will fix it for the next time. It's very much an engineering document about, or blueprint for, rebuilding the city and getting back to where we were: getting back on track.

RC: It's funny you mentioned the world's fair. I just finished reading Jill Jonnes's *Eiffel's Tower*. And the story of the Eiffel Tower is a typical example of what you're talking about. In France, there's often a general collective resistance to change; yet, on the other hand, change often comes from a single individual who is resisted at the beginning but who finally must be embraced. Because there's also in France a respect for culture. And if one respects culture, one must embrace change, because change only comes via that route.

And Eiffel was an example of this. His tower was fiercely resisted until it was a little more than halfway built, and then, suddenly, people began to appreciate the aesthetic. She says in the book that, at the beginning, when just the foundation was constructed, many regarded it as ugly. But by the time it was finished, there were postcards and souvenirs all over Paris.

JJ: I'm going to read that at some point soon; I just haven't had a chance to. But it sounds like an interesting book.

RC: You have this incredible thing, Eiffel's tower. And then, Buffalo Bill and Annie Oakley are there, as part of the 1889 World's Fair. [Laughs] It's such a bizarre, almost surrealist thing. And it dovetails with your story. The Third Republic really needed something to prop themselves up, and the world's fair was an exhibition of progress and the belief in engineering. Thomas Edison had a display there, and there was a pavilion for industrial machines and electrical engineering. So, I think this is also part of your story.

JJ: Yeah, that's true. The way I've always thought of the Eiffel Tower is that it looks very much like – and I don't think I'm making this up, I've read this somewhere else – the sort of thing that one would see on a bridge support or something. Like it itself could be a piece of engineering. It sits alone; it has its own aesthetic beauty. But the shape of it, the form of it, could be a kind of functional piece, if put into some other context. Yet, it's sort of extracted from that and made into a monumental sculpture on its own. As a way of saying, "Progress can be beautiful."

RC: Yes, it's a monument to modern industry, cast in a beautiful, art nouveau, turn-of-the-century style. Eiffel was well known, before the tower, as an engineer of bridges. He would have been remembered as a significant figure for what he'd accomplished before the tower: spanning enormous distances with railway bridges, and things like that.

JJ: Yes. And you're right of course; there's the politics of that moment, too. That it's also about the Republic. And the Third Republic linking itself: We are progress. We are a new, modern political regime for a new, modern era in French history, and in world history.

RC: Another interesting thing about the 1889 World's Fair was that it was the hundredth anniversary of the storming of the Bastille. Many European countries refused to participate, because they regarded it as a celebration of the beheading of the king and the end of the monarchy. So, this was the subtext to the whole thing.

JJ: Yeah, the politics are interesting, that's for sure. And I was trying to draw on the same kind of stuff when I was talking about the 1900 World's Fair.

Of course, in 1900, you've got the fact that it's the turn of the century, too. It's that round number, you know: *1900*. It's the idea that we're finishing the nineteenth century, moving into the twentieth century, and what does that mean? I remember, a few years ago, when it was 2000, there was that sense of the zeroes turning over, and what does that mean? It's a moment to look forward.

RC: It's a psychologically significant and symbolic notion, the "turn of the century."

JJ: Yeah, right, exactly. Then, ten years later, you have this kind of ... I tried to talk about it as a "return to the primitive" in many ways. Like that quote you were citing a minute ago; it's almost like a reversion to a pre-Haussmann period. It's a going backwards. That's another thing that's so shocking for people.

RC: One of my students in Paris was a government consultant who participated in the revolt of May 1968. When I asked what the essential difference was between pre-'68 and post-'68 France, he said before '68, the world "change" always had a negative connotation. "After '68," he said, "*peut-être ... peut-être ... peut-être*, it could be positive."

JJ: [Laughs] That's interesting!

RC: And the '68 revolt is another example of this collective holding onto the past and the strong resistance to change, but, when it does come, it's been repressed for so long that it explodes.

JJ: Right.

RC: In your book, you remark upon the motto of Paris: "She is tossed about by the waves, but she does not sink." This is also the symbol for the ancient city of Lutetia: the boat tossed on the stormy sea. You're probably familiar with the large mosaic of this image in the courtyard of the Hôtel de Ville.

JJ: Yes, absolutely.

RC: In light of your work, I thought it might be interesting to note that the meaning of the word *Lutetia* isn't known with certainty, but many historians interpret it to be a Celtic word for *mud*. In his book, *Paris: The Secret History*, Andrew Hussey writes:

> The Roman name for the settlement in fact derives from its original Celtic one. The Celts had the habit of naming their settlements after their physical qualities. The islands, whose stinking and greasy banks made the site an unlikely halting-post, were for this reason originally named *Louk-tier* or *Louk Teih* – the place of the mud, marshes and swamp. Another half-accepted etymology is *Loutouchezi*, said to be a Gaulish Celtic term meaning 'among the waters.'… The name *Louk Teih*, the most widely accepted approximation of the Celtic was simply absorbed by them into Latin as 'Lutetia' … Other translations of *Louk Teih* have it as a pre-Celtic word, meaning variously 'the isle of crows,' 'the isle of rats,' 'shelter from the water.'*

I thought that was interesting in terms of the long history of Parisian floods, and that the original name for Paris –

Lutetia – means *mud*.

JJ: Yes. I tried to evoke a bit of that in the first chapter. I didn't really do extensive research into the many floods that have occurred in Paris. I did a little, to build a context, but I think that could be a whole other book: writing about the history of Parisian floods.

It's also very much about the city's relationship to the river. Now, people don't think about that as much. You walk by the Seine, and it's beautiful, and it's picturesque. You may have a little picnic by the river, or spend some time walking by, but you want to see all the other things in the city. But historically, as with most cities that are built on rivers, it's built on a river for a reason. It's because that's where so much of the early work, and life, is centered. You know, the water is life. So, that's definitely the case for Paris, too. That motto and that symbol of the ship tells something of a much longer story about how the city has relied on the river for so long: for commerce, for trade, for industry. And for the life of the city itself.

Another one of those ironies is that when the river floods, it brings so much destruction and devastation. It's that double-edged sword of the river. That's a mixed metaphor [Laughs] but, you know, the idea that the river brings life, but the river is also a threat, too, at times.

In that brief section at the beginning of the book, where I talk about some of the other floods, you can get a sense of some of the moments in the city's history when the river did wreak havoc. Of course, the city was so different in those earlier moments. There was no electricity; there were no gas lines. All the modern infrastructure wasn't there in 1658, when the other worst flood, the one that was higher than the 1910 flood, occurred. So, it had a very different effect. But at least you get a feel for the fact that there's always been this kind of lurking: the river is always there, in the background, possibly creating some kind of havoc.

RC: It's not just a pretty touristic thing. It's a natural force that we must respect.

JJ: Right, exactly. And that's easily forgotten, because of the desire and the ability to tame it. You know: to channel it, to create a canal that goes round the city, to add locks and other kinds of devices, and to raise the walls and so forth.

RC: Do you have any idea when the quay walls were built? If you look at Île Saint-Louis and Île de la Cité, you see that they're standing on top of these beautifully sculpted stone walls. When were those walls first constructed?

JJ: In that early section, I mentioned that some go back to the sixteenth century. I'd have to look it up; I don't have it right in front me. But I think some of the earliest walls were built in the time of François the First, which would have been in the early sixteenth century.

RC: That must have been quite an undertaking. Did they divert the river to accomplish that?

JJ: I don't think so. Some of the earliest walls were built just to make it easier to cross the river. Especially when the king wanted to cross, he didn't want to get muddy, so you build a wall to support bridges, and it just makes it easier to cross. I think that, over time, the walls just evolved; they were built bit by bit, over the centuries.

RC: At the time of the Celts and the first Roman conquest, the Seine was twice the width that it is today. This must have greatly influenced how a flood would play itself out then, as opposed to now.

JJ: Yes, I think that's true. I talk a little about the ancient arm of the Seine that had dried up many centuries before 1910. When flooding would occur, you would see that ancient arm that dried up be reactivated.

If you look at the map I have at the beginning of the book that shows the flooded zone, you see how it reaches up on the Right Bank. Part of that was because it was following the subway line around Concorde and up to the Opera. But part of that was also because it roughly follows where this dried up arm of the Seine was. It seems to want to naturally fill in that space.

RC: Is this the same thing that you were discussing in the book: that there was a passage reactivated that turned the area around the Opéra Garnier into a lake? I believe it was an underground system that was activated.

JJ: There was the Bièvre River; is that what you're thinking of? That was a tributary that ran for many miles, and it cut across the Left Bank. It's still there; it's just been driven underground. They've covered it over.

The Bièvre had been very important for industrial purposes in the nineteenth century and even before. It was another water source in the area. Many factories found their way there and used the water. But it became polluted, because so many factories were using it for dyes and all kinds of chemical things. It was so polluted that they drove it underground and covered it over. There's a movement afoot now to reopen it, to uncover it.

RC: I believe you discussed this in the book.

JJ: I mention it at the very end. I don't know much more about it, other than that. I found out about it on the Internet, actually. There's a website devoted to a group that wants to uncover the Bièvre. It would be interesting to see what would happen if they did that.

RC: The other notable figure in your account is the almost animate statue of Zouave: a uniformed colonial soldier who stands with a solemn expression along with the other statues on the Pont de l'Alma.*

When I lived in Paris there were many times that I passed Zouave, often accompanied by a Parisian who might point to the high-water mark of 1910 near Zouave's neck, but other than that I never heard anyone discuss the flood in any detail. You say: "the story of the 1910 flood is largely forgotten." "It is oddly absent from the written history of the city. Somehow Parisians have erased much of this moment from their past." Why did this happen? Was it because World War One occurred just a few years later and it eclipsed this big event?

JJ: It's a question I've struggled with in many ways, and thought a lot about, in working on this project. People often ask, "Why haven't I heard of this before?" There are probably a number of reasons. Part of it is timing. With the war that comes only four years later, when people look back to that moment at the turn of the century, 1910 becomes part of the prewar era.

When we think back, when we create a kind of historical periodization, we talk about that as the run up to the war. All the things that are happening are related to what we know now, looking backward, will be the outbreak of war. So, when people think about the big cataclysm of that moment, it's not flood, but it's war.

And then, if you think about the anniversary dates of the flood, the fifth anniversary would have been in the middle of the war. The tenth anniversary, of 1920, would be just after the war. People are rebuilding; they've got other things on their mind. In 1930, it's the beginning of the Depression. In 1940, there's another war. So, even if you're thinking about commemorating the flood, there are other events that are pushing this down and out of people's active memory.

Another reason is the fact that the city is rebuilt so thoroughly. It's hard to know exactly how long it took, but I'd say that, within a year or so, the city was back to normal. A few things took a while to re-do; but within several months, or up to a year, things were back to normal. So, there weren't those visible markers that you could look at: a pile of debris, or some destroyed building. All those things were gone. Without any physical reminder, it easily passed into memory.

Also, it's the kind of thing that people want to forget. In some ways, it's not something that's …

RC: It's not a happy memory.

JJ: It's not a happy memory, yeah. It goes back to what we were saying before, about how it challenges people's assumptions about their ability to control their environment and their destiny.

It's easier to remember wars, and things like that, than it is natural disasters. Obviously, there are very important natural disasters that do get remembered, even of that same era, such as the San Francisco earthquake of 1906. And there are other disasters that, for various reasons, have also been remembered. But with this one, there are many factors that helped to push it to the side.

This was something that was surprising to me when I started doing this research. Certainly, I had a few people who knew about it, and who would talk about it as a kind of memory, and would say, "Oh, my grandmother told me a story about that when she was young," or something like that. So, it's not totally forgotten. But when I looked in histories of the city – even in some of those large, multivolumed histories – it might show up in a paragraph maybe, or a footnote, but in many cases not at all.

RC: In the official French history, there's often a tendency to downplay the negative things. Even the Second World War is referred to as an "Occupation"! So, that's possibly part of it, too.

JJ: Yeah, it certainly could be.

RC: At least since the Enlightenment, the French have often exhibited a paternalistic attitude toward nature. You write that, although some regarded the flood as a "natural result of environmental degradation" such as "deforestation upstream from Paris," most considered it "a freak event that people had failed to manage but could control the next time around." You add: "In France, people talk about saving nature through technology rather than giving up on the kind of urban industrial society that harms nature in the first place." Is this attitude likely to change at any time in the near future?

JJ: I doubt it. Actually, that's something that's not unique to France. It's typical of Western society generally. That we believe we can mitigate environmental degradation through additional technological means. Rather than saying, "Well, gee, the technology that we're using is messing things up, so maybe we should stop using that technology."

RC: But isn't it worse in France because there's always been, since the Enlightenment, this attitude that nature is just another colony that we have to teach civilization to in some way?

JJ: I think that's definitely true. And I cite that book, *The Light Green Society*, by Michael Bess, who was one of my mentors when I was an undergraduate.

RC: You say there's "ambivalence toward considering environmental questions" there.

JJ: It's sort of like: we can be green, but without giving up a modernistic kind of vision. In some ways, the best example is France's reliance on nuclear energy. Nuclear energy is of course much greener in the sense that it doesn't produce greenhouse gas; it doesn't produce carbon emissions. But what do you do with the waste? [Laughs] You know, that's very much a double-edged kind of thing.

RC: When I was living there in the Nineties, many of my English-language students said there were higher rates of leukemia and other cancers around these plants, but it's completely suppressed in the media. The French mass media is very government controlled, so most people don't get that information. But perhaps now they're getting it, through the Internet.

JJ: Right. But it's not too surprising that they wouldn't want to talk about those kinds of things. I mean, I'm sure that would be the case in this country, too. But it might have an easier time of getting out, through media or other ways.

RC: I think there's more awareness here that this is going on. But until the Internet came to France, for most people there was only one source of information. In the literary community in America, there's a kind of "positive prejudice" about France being an open society. But it's a little more complicated than that.

JJ: Yeah, much more complicated, for sure. [Laughs]

RC: At the time of the flood, Métro tunnels were still being constructed, and this further aggravated the situation, allowing water to rise up from below and to enter parts of the city that were quite a distance away from the Seine. You conclude: "Unlimited faith in urban engineering can sometimes create a false sense of security about our ability to withstand natural disasters." As you know, Paris as well as the rest of France is riddled with catacombs. This must have contributed to the swelling up of water from beneath the city streets, yes?

JJ: Yes, definitely. There were natural caverns and caves as well as human-made ones, too. It's the combination of those things. You know, Paris is like a Swiss cheese. There are caves and catacombs, then you add tunnels and sewers and all these things. You've got old, Roman-era wells and crypts that have been built over. You've got porous soil, but there had been so much water that it was saturated. So, it's got to go somewhere. And so, it seeks out caverns and caves, and then people's basements.

There's no way of knowing what the volume of water in the ground would have been. But when you think about it, that's a huge amount of water. I mean, if it could fill up all those natural caverns, and all the human-made ones, too, that's an awful lot of water. Then, for it to push up and come into the streets: the volume is overwhelming.

RC: Just to read in your book that the water in the Seine alone was about to overflow the embankment near the Louvre! It's an incredible amount of water.

JJ: Yes. It's even hard to visualize mentally. I've seen the photographs, but when I stand on the banks there, and think of how much water that would be …

RC: And it's continually being drained, into the Atlantic, yet it still keeps coming.

JJ: Right. And moving up to twenty-five miles an hour. That's an amazingly fast current.

RC: Racial tensions in Paris, particularly between the Algerians and the French, have continued to mount, especially over the last twenty years. You suggest that, today, France's identity "must expand to include people of color whose origins are in other parts of the world. Until it does, should the Paris region undergo a similar kind of catastrophe as in 1910, the same level of social unity might simply not exist." In this regard, what do you think would happen if Paris were suddenly flooded tomorrow?

JJ: Of course, I can only speculate. But the thought I had as I was writing this, and as I was thinking about that issue and about the way Paris has changed so much since 1910 – and the demographics, the politics, and especially the politics of race and the suburbs – the fear would be that people in those suburban towns, who are from other parts of the world, and not as fully incorporated into many people's understanding of the identity of France and the identify of Paris itself, that they might be left to fend for themselves.

One of the things that struck me so deeply in writing about how the city survived was the fact that people were able to pull together. They saw their own individual self-interests as bound up with the common survival of everyone. To me, that only makes sense if you understand yourself, and your neighbor, and everyone around you as part of a common community that you want to save. That you identify yourself as a Parisian, and this other guy over here as a Parisian, and we're working together to save ourselves as Parisians and as residents of this place. That's why I wonder whether this same sense of connection – of the social bonds – would extend to those suburban communities. Would that sense of common cause extend to those people today? I don't know. Maybe it would. Maybe the government would step in; who knows? That's why I say it's only speculation.

If you think of the way the social ties were so strong in 1910, including across class lines, it's rather remarkable. Clearly, there were many divisions in Paris. There were many ways in which Parisians were divided against one another: class, neighborhood, religion, politics. There were many ways that people could easily have fractured and pulled apart. Instead, they pulled together. Could this happen today, in the same way? Hard to know. I hope we never have to find out, but that's what was in the back of my mind. There's so much tension there; there are so many ways in which the people who live in those suburban, *banlieue* areas feel detached from Paris. And feel so excluded from much of French society, and of Parisian society, that I just wondered what might happen along those lines.

RC: You made that point very well in the book, as well as tying it to other disasters around the world. You write: "What the flood provided was a moment in which Parisians, who were normally divided by class and politics, could act out a different kind of relationship. The solidarity they created out of necessity during the flood would again prove useful during World War One." You go on to talk about how "the flood also served as a kind of dress rehearsal for the war. It gave Red Cross administrators additional experience in coordinating relief efforts." That was a very interesting insight. Probably, no one's made that connection before.

JJ: Thanks. It's something that occurred to me as I was thinking about the way people acted during the flood. As I mentioned in the book, I was looking at photographs of

Paris during the war, and I noticed how similar they are to photos during the flood. I was thinking: What are those connections, and what are those links? And the way in which the flood experience could easily have been a moment that allowed people to do it all again, just a few years later. To do all the things they had done: to find ways to work together, communally; to find ways to save their city.

RC: I understand that your wife, Ellen Daugherty, who's an art historian, helped you to realize that the photos of the flood, which were plentiful, were in fact primary documents and should be utilized as such.

JJ: She deserves a great deal of credit. As an historian, I've always known that photos make great documents, and I try to teach my students about that. But for some reason, early on, when I was working on this – and initially that's all I had, before I really got into the archival stuff – I couldn't figure out *how* to use them. I knew I could use them, but I wasn't sure how. And so, because she's trained to look at visual sources, and to read them and think critically about them, she was the one who said, "Look at what they're telling you. Look at what's going on in those pictures. What's the story that's emerging from them?" She helped me to clarify, and pushed me along those lines, and gave me insights that helped me to think about how to best use those sources. Once I was able to have the documentation and things from the archive, they really blended well together and just went hand in hand. Talking about the photographs, and looking at the photographs, really enriched the story I was trying to tell.

RC: Of all the images, which was the most evocative?

JJ: The image that's always stood out is the one of the old woman on the raft. I don't know why, but, for some reason, that's the one that's always stood out for me. Initially, I was going to propose that as the cover photo until a friend of mine said, "You've got to have a picture of the Eiffel Tower on the cover, because that's Paris. Everyone identifies that as Paris." And I was like, "You know, you're right!"

Anyway, it's an older woman on a raft, sort of hunkered down. And I guess there's another one. There's a great one of people on the *passerelles* …

RC: With the little girl?

JJ: No. I love that one, too. In fact, I bought that in a flea market in Paris.

RC: It has an impressionistic quality.

JJ: It does. I think it's because they're in motion, so it's a little blurry. But there's one – I don't think it's in the book; it's on the website – of three people crossing a walkway. One of them is looking at the camera, and they're all dressed up. There are two women, and they're wearing big hats, and dresses, and it's very 1910.

RC: Yes. The contrast between the upper-class accoutrements and the mud and the water; is that it?

JJ: Right, exactly. Those two images have always stuck out for me. They're very human: very much about the human experience. It's fascinating to see pictures of destroyed buildings or streets. It's interesting to see destruction on the urban landscape. But for me, it was more interesting to think about this as a human story and to study pictures that show people. Usually they're not pictures of people suffering. Usually they're of people being rescued, or crossing a walkway, or sweeping. Or doing something: rebuilding.

RC: Utilizing *système d*.

JJ: Yes. But still, even though the old woman on the raft is being rescued, you know she's afraid, and she's dealing with the emotions that go along with that.

RC: It's a serious moment.

JJ: Exactly. So, those photos have always been the ones that have jumped out.

RC: For me, the most dramatic moment in your account was certainly the near-disaster at the Louvre, when the Seine would have gone over the embankment if the workmen hadn't been piling up all those bags of cement, and sand, and so forth. You quote a British journalist who said: "'A few hours later, and the river would have won. All the basements of the Louvre would have been flooded.'" In fact, "water had already breached the basement of the Louvre." But fortunately, "the barricade held fast." It's amazing that this is not more widely known in France today. It's a really significant moment in French history: that the treasures of the Louvre could have been destroyed!

JJ: And if they had been, people *would* remember! [Laughs] It's another one of those things where it's like a "near miss," you know? People forget those near misses. Even though these are the things you should remember, because you never know what's going to happen the next time around. But if the Louvre had been flooded, if the Mona Lisa had been destroyed, everyone would know about the flood of 1910.

RC: I recently listened to a BBC interview with the *administrateur générale* of the Louvre, in which he said that not only are they expecting another flood, but, when it comes, they'll have just seventy-two hours to remove over 100,000 works of art from the basement of the museum. In a culture that doesn't treasure spontaneity and rapid decision-making, such a quick move sounds like wishful thinking.

JJ: Again, I hope we'll never have to find out what happens. There is a flood plan in place. The police have a flood plan, and that plan, at least in part, is based on the experience of 1910. It's a touchstone for thinking about what they would do today.

I don't know if you've seen it, but there's a movie called *Paris 2011: La grande inundation*. There's also an English version that, for some reason, is called "Paris 2010." I don't know why they added a year for the French version or took off a year for the English version. It's considered a *docufiction*: a fictional documentary about the city, which has just lived through a flood. They made this mock documentary about how we just lived through a flood and what happened. They use the police flood-emergency plan as the basis for the film. It's kind of an imaginative, "what would happen if this happened again."

And it's interesting, because this film has all the drama; it has all the "everything floods and everything goes wrong." But the way they depict what happens at this moment of crisis is that everything works smoothly. You know, the museums pack up their artworks. They actually show it in the film: the Musée d'Orsay, people are in there, packing away. [Laughs] And they go through this whole thing, and, of course, it's a happy ending. Everybody survives, and everything's fine.

I've always interpreted this film, which was produced by the same people who made *March of the Penguins*, as a kind of way to say to people: Don't worry; everything will be OK. We have a plan; we have an administrative structure in place. You know, the French love administrative structures. We have experts. We have all these things in place, and everyone knows what to do. But I mean, that's the film version of it. [Laughs] The actual, real-life version? That could be another story.

RC: When I taught English in Paris, many of my students would say, "You know, Robert, we really are *individualistic*." But in fact, my experience was that there was a real respect for authority, which they're often unconscious of. There's a respect for authority, a desire to blend in and not to stick out, and a general faith in this logical, rational, Cartesian approach, which doesn't account for acts of God. [Laughs] But since the Enlightenment, God doesn't exist; so, that's the problem, you know.

JJ: Yeah, I think you're right. There is a weird paradox in French culture, very much, of this kind of individualism but, at the same time, yeah, what you said, that respect for authority. Also, that there's a standard procedure for how things need to be done.

RC: There needs to be more questioning of authority there.

JJ: There are moments like '68, where authority clearly was questioned. But I think that deference to experts, in particular, is very much still there.

RC: Again, *système d, débroullard*: it's wonderful that it exists. But often it's sparked by a crisis; it's not a natural tendency there to respect spontaneity. They turn to it only when they can't turn to anything else.

JJ: Yeah. And of course, *système d*, that's one of those myths. I don't mean myth in the sense that it's false. But myth in the sense that it's a story they tell to make sense out of the world. Of course, we all have this ability; it's our natural, French-born ability to get out of a crisis or whatever. I know it's a bizarre comparison, but, in the American context, the only thing I can think of is that thing about "Yankee ingenuity." That's a myth we tell ourselves, too: that story about how we're a resourceful people. There's truth to that; there's truth to *système d*, too. But at the same time, it's a way that we craft our identity. Whether it's Yankee ingenuity, or *système d*, or whatever, every culture has a similar sort of thing.

RC: It's shocking that it took them until 1969 to finally do something to prevent another flood. I'm referring to the construction of the Grands Lacs de Seine. Perhaps you could briefly describe what that system is.

JJ: I haven't read extensively about it, and I'm not an engineer, but my understanding is that, basically, it's a series of reservoirs upstream: three or four of these lakes. The idea is that, if a large volume of water came down the Seine, they would open up the locks and allow the excess water to flow into these reservoirs, and fill them up as basins that would take the pressure off the rising Seine itself. To alleviate the rising level of water.

They've used it several times. It has proven to work, up to a point. The big question is: would it work if it were a 1910-level flood? It's worked for smaller floods. But it's impossible to know if it would work for a flood of the same magnitude. Again, I hope it's one of those things we never have to find out. But that's my understanding of how it's supposed to work. It's a pretty simple idea and, so far, effective for what they've needed at this point.

RC: In your bibliography, I noticed that Denoël published a biography by Jean-Marc Berlière, *Le Préfet Lépine*, and you mentioned Lépine's memoir. Is there much else written about him? Is he a well-known figure in French history?

JJ: I don't get the sense that he's particularly well known. There are a couple of biographies. And then his autobiography, or his memoirs.

RC: Is the memoir an engaging read?

JJ: In some ways it is. I mean, obviously, he's writing it toward the end of his life, and he wants to shape his own story. Of course, he emphasizes the positive things. But it's sort of interesting on its own. That's where he talks about himself – there, especially – as the *préfet* of the street, wanting to be in the street. And he wants to be known by people around town because that's where his sense of authority comes from.

As I mention, there's a "place Louis Lépine," right across from police headquarters in Paris. And there's this "Concours Lépine." Apparently, he sponsored a show of new inventions, which still goes on in Paris today. So, I suppose if he's remembered today for anything, it's probably more for that. It's a yearly competition for new inventions.*

He's a fascinating figure. Someone asked if I'd ever thought of writing a book about Louis Lépine. That's probably not in the future: not in the works for me. But someone should write something in English, or translate these things that have been written in French, because he's an interesting figure, for sure. And at a particularly interesting moment in French history.

RC: You briefly mention Geneviève, the patron saint of Paris, "long revered for having rallied Paris against an invasion of Attila the Hun in 451." In 1206, when "nearly half the city flooded," she "came to the city's aid in spirit." "Following the mass chanted at Notre-Dame with her relics present, the waters miraculously began to recede." Were any masses said for her in 1910, or did any of the devout turn to her then?

JJ: I don't know of any masses; I didn't see any reference to that. There were plenty of masses said, but I don't know of any said specifically to her. But it wouldn't surprise me if she were invoked widely, because she was thought about not only as the city's patron saint but, specifically, as the saint one turns to during a time of flood. So I would imagine that, among the devout, she would have been evoked.

RC: How old were you when you first visited Paris?

JJ: It was during graduate school, so I would have been in my mid- to late twenties.

RC: You started studying French in the first grade. Was this unusual for your generation?

RC: Probably so. The school I went to was a private school, and it was just the language that they taught. They didn't teach Spanish, which is more common, or anything else, but they taught French. So, I did that all the way through high school.

RC: Is this what first triggered your interest in French culture?

JJ: Probably a combination of that and my grandparents who, when I was a kid, started doing their world travels. They traveled everywhere, all over the world, mostly going on package tours, and they returned with stories, photographs, and souvenirs. They went to Paris and to Europe many times. So, it was a combination of hearing them talk about Europe and studying French in school. All this came together in my background and pointed me in the direction of being interested in European history, and French history in particular.

JJ: What was your emotional reaction upon first walking

through the streets of Paris?

JJ: It's funny because, the first time I went to Europe, I flew to London and, after a couple of days, I took the Eurostar, which was still relatively new at that point. So, when I arrived in Paris, I arrived in the train station at Gare du Nord. And that was beautiful and amazing, but I still hadn't seen the city at that point. Then I boarded the Métro, and I went to the place where I was going to meet the person from whom I was renting an apartment, up in the twentieth *arrondissement*. And so, that whole way, I traveled *underground*. I still hadn't seen the city.

I didn't really see Paris until I came out of the Metro. I looked around, and my response mentally and emotionally was: "Oh my gosh, it's Paris!" [Laughs] It looked like the postcards; it looked like the pictures. You know, it was almost too good to be true. Like, does it really look like all the movies and all the images? And this was in the twentieth *arrondissement*; this was not in central Paris. It wasn't near the Eiffel Tower or anything. It was out in a residential neighborhood. But it still looked like what I thought it would look like, in some way. There was a little café there, and all these things. So, it was a surprise of strange familiarity, in many ways.

RC: When my brother first visited me in Paris he said, "It's like a dream here." We were standing in front of the Centre Pompidou at that moment, and he was looking at the buildings in the distance. And then it came to mind, that quote from somewhere that goes: "It's one of the few places in the world where the reality exceeds the dream." It's an amazingly beautiful city.

JJ: Yeah, it is. That's a good way of putting it. It's a funny place, for so many reasons. It's funny because, whenever I go, there are so many beautiful things, and so delicious things to eat, and amazing things to see. Then I have moments where it's a big dirty city, and you walk around and get exhausted trudging through the streets – and almost get hit by a bus or something like that happens – and then I'm like: "Damn Paris!" [Laughs]

RC: There's a lot to curse about in Paris, that's for sure!

JJ: Yeah, I go back and forth. Then I sit in a café and have a pastry, and I'm like, "This is so wonderful; I'm so glad I'm here." [Laughs] It's a weird sort of back-and-forth thing.

RC: For me, the Seine is really the soul of Paris. It's the most beautiful and powerful thing in the city. To sit along the quay near Pont de la Tournelle, across from Notre-Dame ... it's such an amazing experience that goes beyond mere words.

JJ: Yeah, it really is. If there's an eternal part of Paris, that's it. As I was saying, the city itself is always changing. It's always being built, torn down, whatever. But the river has this kind of feel, because it's been there for centuries and centuries. That's where the eternal part of Paris is.

RC: I don't want to keep you, but I thought we could touch a little on your jazz book. A large part of your first work is devoted to the efforts of Hughes Panassié, a jazz aficionado who took it upon himself to publicize "le hot jazz" and to educate his fellow Frenchmen about the intricacies of this new musical form. He even formed Le Hot Club de France. I found this to be a typically French reaction: the need to bring art and artists into institutional frameworks and organizations. Artists are often part of a "collective" in France. Even members of the avant-garde feel compelled to form groups.

JJ: Yeah, that's interesting; I hadn't thought about it in quite that way. But I think you're right; there's something very French about that sort of response to form a club. Of course, there were similar kinds of jazz clubs in this country, too, and they were trying to connect up a bit. You know, I talked about the International Federation of Hot Clubs that they tried to get going. This trans-Atlantic association, which, so far as I could tell, never came to anything. They talked about it; there was some discussion in the magazine *Jazz-Hot*. Marshall Stearns, who's a big jazz critic in this country, who founded the Institute for Jazz Studies, was the American connection. They were supposed to create this international network of clubs; but, so far as I can tell, they only talked about it on paper. It never really became anything.

RC: Regarding the Hot Club, I thought it was typically French that he not only tried to create an institution to preserve and promulgate hot jazz, but, in addition, there was a pedagogical aspect to his work: trying to show people how to think about this particular form, and how to psychologically assimilate it, and so on.

JJ: That's definitely true. Some of this may have been because there were so many people who just didn't get it: didn't understand what this was supposed to be. I tried to talk about it in the first part of the book: the response to jazz. For some, it's brilliant and amazing and they love it. And it's dance music, and it's fun. And others are like: this is the end of the world [Laughs]. This weird sound is just the primitive jungles of Africa, or it's some weird thing from outer space, or we don't know what to make of it.

To some extent, that was the case in this country, too. Jazz was very controversial in the Twenties. A lot of people were like, this is devil music; this is black music. You know, all the weird associations that people brought to it. And they said, we don't know what this means.

But in the French context it was even more outlandish, because it was coming from another country; it was coming from outside of France. It was seen as something that was doubly foreign, because it was American, it was black, it was not from within. And so, there's really no frame of reference to understand what it's about. And Panassié and Delaunay and others in the Hot Club, and just in that whole scene, felt they had to do some teaching, early on, to say, "No, we can appreciate this too; we can perform this music too."

RC: And they were successful to some extent.

JJ: They were. As far as one can measure, the number of jazz fans is still relatively small until after World War Two. That's really when you see the big explosion. But you couldn't have gotten to that point without those guys in the Twenties and Thirties, like Panassié and Delaunay, who were building the groundwork, and making it OK to listen to and to play. So, in that sense, they were successful at their teaching.

RC: As I previously mentioned, often, there's a fear of anything spontaneous in France, and the dominant cultural consciousness is that of a logical, rational Cartesianism. Yet this the whole notion of jazz improvisation flies directly in the face of that. As you say, for many, it must have been viewed as something satanic. You talk about how the same adjectives that were used to attack jazz by its critics were also used to extol it. For example, the "brutal force" and the sounds, and the dancers who were "elevated," "hypnotized, driven mad." I found this quite interesting and ironic. It suggests there are two fundamentally opposed temperaments at work, each experiencing the same thing in a completely different manner.

JJ: Yes, that's right. It really does come down to which side you are coming at it from. Some of this is generational, perhaps. But are you a traditionalist who wants everything to remain the same? Or are you open to a new, avant-garde idea?

Those who were open – and there were plenty of people in Paris in the Twenties who were open to new, avant-garde kinds of things – were looking at this and saying, Wow, this is amazing stuff. And then, those who were looking at any kind of avant-garde thing, whether it was jazz, or some new art form, or new literary, or new other kind of musical form ... you know, people who were listening to Stravinsky and saying this is horrible and walking out; they were the same people who were walking out of jazz, or not going to jazz performances, because it was not traditional music. So, it depends which side of that divide you're on.

RC: It epitomizes two diametrically opposed tendencies. On the one hand, "Why do something differently if we've always done it this way before?" And on the other, an enduring need to be at the service of culture, which necessitates an openness to innovation and change.

JJ: I think that definitely makes sense. As I said, clearly, in the 1920s especially, there were many who were interested in something new and innovative. You're right, there's always this tension in France, and in Paris in particular. Paris wants to be the capital of art, innovation, culture. And so much of that is about the new, right? Coming up with something that's shocking, even. Dadaism, or something that is in your face. But then, at the same time, there's a deep-seated desire to link back with tradition and to see how this fits into a broader, deeper flow of tradition.

That may not necessarily be uniquely French. It's probably something that's broader. You find expressions of that in other cultures as well, including this country, too. But it's something you see very much: the duality there, the tension between those two things comes to the fore in a place like Paris.

Because there were so many who were doing, and who were interested in doing, shocking and avant-garde things in the Twenties. And so many who, at that same moment, were pushing back against that. So, there's a culture war happening in the Twenties in Paris. That's why jazz becomes a touchstone. It's one of the many things that shocks people, and if you want to be shocked you're drawn to it. And if you don't want to be shocked, you push back against it with all your might.

Some of this is about the postwar period. You're coming out of the trenches; you're coming out of the experience of war. And the culture has undergone this tremendous upheaval. For many people, they want nothing more than a return to sanity. There's this whole artistic movement, *le rappel à ordre*: the return to orderly things. [Laughs] And so, there are many, even in the artistic community, who say we need to get back to basics and forget all this craziness. But there are plenty of others who say, No, let's push forward. The old culture is dead. The war proves it. Now, let's try something new. We must reinvent ourselves in this moment.

RC: The ironic thing is: the great avant-garde artist is always working through tradition, and forging a new link to a long chain in tradition. But very few can actually see that, particularly when the new form is first manifesting.

JJ: Yes, I think that's true. There were people who were trying to understand jazz within that tradition. There were many who said, "Well, jazz has its own tradition. That is a tradition that is linked back to Africa." They saw it explicitly in racial terms, that this was an expression of "blackness," in musical form.

But there were others who were trying to say, "OK, but this is also *music*, and we can understand it in the context of the history of musical tradition. And so, maybe there are ways we can understand it, even though it's coming from outside. We can think about it and how it fits within the idea of musical tradition."

For instance, the notion of syncopation is not something that jazz invents. It's an older, traditional musical technique. There were composers and others who were trying to think about that. And to connect jazz – this avant-garde form – to a deeper tradition. Just as you were saying.

RC: After jazz gained wider acceptance in France, it became "a symbol for what it meant to be French in the interwar years." Maybe you could expand on that.

JJ: One of the things I was interested in was not so much writing about jazz per se but writing about the reception of jazz. To some extent, I was more interested in audiences than in performers. What I wanted to know was, what happened when people heard this music? What did they say; what did they do; what did they think about it?

That's where this plugs into the question of French tradition, identity, and culture. Jazz provides a language, or an opportunity for people to debate these questions about what it means to be French. Is it French to accept an artistic musical form that comes from another part of the world? And to bring it into our tradition and to have French musicians who perform it and play it as well as the people who created it? Or is it more French to see it as an outside thing and to push it away? In the response to jazz in the Twenties and Thirties, you see this debate going on. You know, what does it mean to be French? What is the definition of Frenchness? Is it openness to new things? Or is it a kind of conservative, traditional vision? And where does that debate go, with jazz as the thing that … You know, we're talking about jazz, but really we're taking about all these other issues.

RC: It's like a Rorschach test.

JJ: Yes.

RC: How would you define "hot jazz"? Is it synonymous with jazz improvisation?

JJ: Hot jazz refers to that kind of Twenties-era, sometimes referred to as Dixieland, jazz. It's the early jazz that's very much about improvisation and spontaneity. Often, it was a collective improvisation, early on.

RC: Where each takes a turn on his instrument?

JJ: That's part of it. Or just the sense that the group as a whole is improvising on the theme. It's out of this that come the "big name" people like Louis Armstrong, who become soloists doing this kind of improvisation. It's all the same thing; it's all related. The thing for Panassié, which was crucial, was the fact that you had to have that spontaneous improvisation.

RC: Otherwise, you were banned by Panassié! [Laughs]

JJ: Yeah, exactly. The way he puts it, he has this quote – I don't know why it always sticks in my brain – he says: "Where there is no swing, there can be no authentic jazz." And so, the music has to swing. For him, that means it must be rooted in this improvisational expression. Here, he was really talking about what he referred to as "real jazz," the music of the New Orleans players – Armstrong and others – versus that kind of orchestral jazz: the stuff of Paul Whiteman and Jack Hylton, who orchestrated and scored it, and there was no need or room for improvisation. So, for Panassié, it's not just "pretty" band music, but there's something live and in the moment. That's where the "hotness" comes from.

RC: What led to the creation of your book? Are you a jazz aficionado? Or was it coming out of what we were previously discussing: jazz as a sort of Rorschach test to define other aspects of French culture?

JJ: A little of both. I'm not an aficionado; I'm an enthusiastic amateur when it comes to jazz, because I'm not a musician or anything like that.

As I said, it was my dissertation originally. The way it came about was, I started with the time period. I wanted to do something on the interwar period. I'd always found that to be a fascinating era, and I wanted to do something on that. I remember saying to myself in graduate school: I know I've heard something about jazz and Paris, and maybe I could look into that and see what was there. It started as a seminar paper in one of my classes. I found that very little had been written. And the light bulb went on over my head and I said, "Well, since I'm interested in this time period, and not a lot's been written about it ..." And as someone who appreciated jazz, and who was interested and listened to jazz, I was attracted to it for that reason, too.

The other reason it made sense to pursue it was that I went to graduate school at the University of Rochester, and one part of the University of Rochester is the Eastman

School of Music. Eastman and Julliard are the two preeminent music schools in this country. I knew I would have access to an amazing music library, which I did, as well as the faculty at Eastman, who could give me their insights. I thought that, even though I'm not a musician, I'm surrounded by musicians, and I have access to those kinds of resources. So, it just made sense to work on that.

And I felt it really came together, too. I was very proud of that book

RC: I'm glad we had a chance to talk about the jazz book. Thanks so much for your time.

JJ: Thank you. It's a great honor and pleasure to talk to you.

---

* This interview was conducted on 20 June 2010. It was published in the *Rain Taxi Review of Books* (online), in December 2010.

* Andrew Hussey, *Paris: The Secret History* (New York: Bloomsbury, USA, 2006), pp. 7-8.

* The French Zouaves were infantry soldiers originally composed of Algerian recruits, and known for their colorful uniforms and showy drilling style.

* The Concours Lépine also makes a brief appearance in the annals of modern art. On 30 August 1935, the conceptual artist Marcel Duchamp rented a booth at the Concours Lépine to launch his "optical play toy," an invention later known as the *Rotoreliefs*.

An Interview with Robert Roper, author of
Now the Drum of War: Walt Whitman and His Brothers in the Civil War

In Now the Drum of War, *Robert Roper makes a unique contribution to the ever-growing body of Walt Whitman scholarship. His book features an in-depth exploration of Walt's relationship with his siblings, and it maintains a special focus on his brother George, who served in some of the bloodiest battles of the Civil War. Roper casts a completely new light on these family ties, and he questions some long-held beliefs regarding the influence of Walt's father and the characterization of his mother, Louisa, as being an unsophisticated illiterate. Drawing on the often visceral, earthy, and moving letters exchanged between Walt, George, and Louisa, Roper's lyrical narrative depicts both the Whitman saga and the extraordinary events of the time.*

Roper is the recipient of numerous awards for works of fiction and nonfiction. His Fatal Mountaineer, *a biography of the climber-philosopher Willi Unsoeld, won the 2002 Boardman Tasker Prize. He currently teaches at John Hopkins University.*

Rob Couteau: Are you on a cell? I'm not picking you up very well; you're breaking up on me.

Robert Roper: Maybe if I go outside the building … How about now?

RC: This is interesting, that you're outside. It's very Whitmanesque. [Laughs]

RR: The thing about Whitman is, he's so large, almost everything is Whitmanesque.

RC: Right. It's like a Sears and Roebuck of the soul.

RR: That's good; that's good!

RC: So, what led to your interest in Walt and in *Leaves of Grass*?

RR: It was a funny derivation. In college, I took an American literature seminar, and we read a lot of Whitman. And I really wasn't much taken with him. It could have been my age at the time, but I think a crucial element was that we read from the "deathbed" edition. He had bowdlerized his own poetry pretty severely at that point. I had the impression of a lot of clotted rhetoric, and an occasional terrific line. And maybe the professor wasn't that good either. But there was something about him that attracted me.

Then, about fifteen years later, someone sent me a postcard with a picture of Whitman from about 1854. This romantic, seductive, handsome guy. Completely at odds with that bearded old fellow with the wispy white hair. And it just arrested my attention. Then I learned he had been a nurse in the Civil War hospitals, and that intrigued me. I mentally made a note: read up on this someday.

Three or four years ago, I learned he had a younger brother who was in the war in a very active way. I liked the dichotomy of the nurturing homosexual poet and the ardent, fierce, warrior brother. I thought maybe there's a story there. That's when I started reading more intensely and looking at the letters.

So, the postcard was crucial. It had an image of him really looking out at *me*. He knew how to pose. In 1839, the daguerreotype was introduced in the U.S., and he had his first daguerreotype taken in 1839. He was kind of smart about that.

RC: When I was in my early twenties, I had that postcard tacked to my wall. It's an unusual photo, especially when compared to typical nineteenth-century portraits. Whitman's friend, Dr. Bucke, referred to it as the "Christ likeness."

RR: I wouldn't say it's Christlike; I'd say it's more the ardent young man. Like you might send that photo to your girlfriend or your boyfriend. You know, you're thinking about him in a certain way. But that was even rarer in nineteenth-century photography.

RC: The camera clearly liked him. You can see that in the picture, can't you?

RR: Yeah, I agree with you completely; he's a very handsome guy. But there's something else. He's like, *projecting*, into the camera. In most of the nineteenth-century portraiture, you had to sit really still. Often, if you see group photos, or family photos, the only thing that looks alive is the dog. [Laughs] Everyone else is frozen and trying to look proper. And, somehow, already, Walt wasn't doing that.

RC: There's something of the bearded sage as well as the youth setting out on his life's journey in that picture. There's a line in "Song of Myself" that could serve as a wonderful caption for it: "I am of old and young, of the foolish as much as the wise, / Regardless of others, ever regardful of others, / Maternal as well as paternal, a child as well as a man, / Stuffed with the stuff that is coarse, and stuffed with the stuff that is fine". It's an image of all these opposites that merge together in him.

RR: I still say it's the sexual element that dominates there.

RC: Oh, I see; you feel it's a *seductive* image.

RR: Yes. From a very early age, he was also acting the sage. George said that when Walt was a teenager, people in the neighborhood came in for sage council. Then, pretty early, he started going gray. He had no vanity about appearing youthful particularly.

RC: In your biography, you encourage us to rethink certain assumptions about the Whitman family. One is the so-called failure of Walt Whitman Senior. As you point out, although he wasn't a millionaire, he always provided the essentials for a family of nine children, and he passed a number of valuable skills on to his sons.

RR: I was reading a little more generally about the social history of the early nineteenth century: the terrible destitution that people fell into after the panic of 1837 and other times. This was a cruel economic period, when all these skilled artisans are, for some reason, unable to feed their families. They don't understand it, but they were falling through the cracks. An industrial economy was emerging, and the fact that you were skilled didn't mean anything. In fact, it disabled you; it made you less resourceful in going where labor was needed, back and forth. So, the stories of fathers who really were failures – I mean, I don't consider them as failures, but who couldn't put bread on the table – are just legion. And somehow, the Whitmans always had a roof over their heads. I thought it was interesting that Hannah, the favored sister, went to a fancy school. Probably, their fortunes waxed and waned, but basically the fact that nobody starved to death, and nobody succumbed to childhood tuberculosis, it's all right.

RC: It's certainly an accomplishment, especially during this rough time.

RR: Right. And as you said, because he was trying to be a spec builder and making a few mistakes, the sons were smart in that way; George and Walt picked up on it and were successful at that. So, that's kind of a success.

RC: Walt's father was "an acquaintance of Tom Paine" – which I find so fascinating – "and an ardent admirer of *The Age of Reason* and other iconoclastic, anticlerical works." He was "born on the very day of the storming of the Bastille" and "bequeathed to his sons and daughters a certain radical élan." Was this the key contribution he made to Walt's intellectual inheritance?

RR: I think so. That's the only thing we have evidence for. Walt spoke of his mother as a great storyteller and a great mimic: "Everything I have in the way of a talent comes through her." So, let's just assume that the father wasn't a literary influence or a model. I think he was an intellectual influence, but it doesn't seem like he was the kind of guy who sat around the fireside and told the kids fascinating stories. And there's that famous photo of him, and, so far as I know, it's the only photo of him ...

RC: It's always tricky to interpret a photo, but he looks *grouchy* in that picture.

RR: Yes, he does! [Laughs] He doesn't exude that gemütlich warmth. He looks troubled. And of course, he didn't live that long; it's close to the end of his life. He might have had a stroke or two already. But I think the Tom Paine-ish iconoclasm is something Walt treasured.

RC: Tom Paine was a rabble-rouser, and often a rabble-rouser has an innovative side. So, if we broaden the definition, we could say the father was a literary influence in the sense that Walt inherited a taste for rabblerousing and innovation. Especially the innovation in content and in form that we see in the first edition of *Leaves of Grass*.

RR: Yeah, I guess that makes sense to me. But to nail something down so that literary scholars could sign on to it, it's a little harder. The fact that the father was a close follower of a Quaker – a kind of renegade – preacher, and that he read Tom Paine: those are high waters of reading. He knew Tom Paine, but he also read *Rights of Man* and his other works. The father, who was considered a failure, and certainly no intellectual, and perhaps a baleful influence on Walt, a cranky old guy: he was reading Tom Paine's books. I don't know if you could say that about many working-class guys these days. You know, guys who are working hard construction jobs. So I think there's an intellectual inheritance there.

RC: How do we know he knew Tom Paine?

RR: That's a good question. I think there are a number of mentions of it. But I don't think any of the other siblings mentioned it.

RC: It would probably be less important to them than it would be to Walt.

RR: Yeah, possibly. Again, this is not something that holds up in court. I know people who write fiction and poetry are inventing all the time; certainly, people who make their life story the wellspring of their writing. But a tremendous amount of what Walt said about himself paid out. He was scrupulous. After two or three years of being in his company – in the sense of the research for this book – I came to really trust him. Again, that wouldn't hold up in court, where you want to have three or four sources.

RC: We can trust him except when it comes to his creation of a heterosexual persona, right?

RR: [Laughs] Yeah, I think we've got him there.

RC: You also point out that although Walt's father was a heavy drinker, so were many working-class men of that day, because alcohol was safer than the unsanitary water in many of the polluted Brooklyn wells.

RR: As recently as the early twentieth century, workmen in the U.S. and in France drank two or three bottles of wine a day, because the wine didn't make them sick the way bad water did.

RC: I lived in Paris for twelve years, and I can tell you that workmen in France still drink a lot! On one of my first visits to Paris, I got off the plane, and it was extremely early – six or seven in the morning – and I needed a coffee really badly. I couldn't speak a word of French. I walked into a brasserie, and there were all these working-class guys – what they call *ouvriers* – around me. And I just listened to one of them, and he said *"Un demi!"* So I said to the waiter, *"Un demi!"* thinking it was a demitasse. But a *demi* is a huge glass of beer! [Laughs] And that's how I started my day. I didn't want to be looked at strangely, so I just downed the thing.

RR: That's a good story!

RC: You've done a great job of portraying Walt's mother, Louisa, and of questioning the notion of her being a simple-minded illiterate. Instead, she served as a valuable sounding board for Walt. She was able to absorb and to intelligently respond to his letters, especially his Civil War letters.

RR: Right. She was probably doing the same thing for George, although her letters to George at the front didn't survive. Over and over again, I saw Walt – in his letters to his mother and to the rest of the family – was just cheerful when he felt he could possibly pull it off. But sometimes he'd write a letter just for her, and he was being overwhelmed; he was breaking down psychologically. Her responses were very moving. And her grammatical way: she spoke exactly to it. You know: "I understand, Walt, how you've become fascinated with this difficult work, seeing the boys die."

When I read the letters she wrote, and George wrote, and Walt wrote about, let's say, George's postwar-building career, she was right in on every aspect of it. She was smart about going into debt to finance construction, and she knew about gathering tools and buying the right kind of residential plots. She was just *smart*. And they came to trust her because, probably, the "old bat" was right.

RC: Will her letters to Walt ever be published in an unabridged version, and hopefully one that maintains her lack of punctuation and idiosyncratic grammar, as you did when reproducing them in your book?

RR: It would be a wonderful project. Sure, why not? George's letters made a very good volume; it came out in 1975, and Jerome Loving was the editor. But to me, her letters are more fascinating, as much as I enjoy George's, too.

RC: You show how George was closer to Walt than previous biographers have realized, and that his writing was not without its merits.

RR: They were quite brotherly. I don't know if you have brothers, but often people seem so heterogeneous in a family. Later, Walt made this comment that George was interested in pipes, not poems. And that was true. George read all of Walt's poetry, but he was an entrepreneur and a contractor.

I found his letters really unusual in the amount of focused intelligence he brought to the problem of trying to understand the confusing, overwhelming battles he had just been in. It made me look at a lot of other Civil War correspondence. You see other soldiers trying to describe the battles they were in, but George's descriptions are quite solid and detailed.

When I went to the battlegrounds, they really held up as maps. You know, George says: "We got pinned down under withering fire by a little rise in the ground by a terribly muddy creek, and I had my face in the mud for three hours" – and I can find that creek! His descriptions and his surmises about what went wrong with battles were often what the Civil War historians say. So, besides having whatever the skills are of a warrior who survives, he also had a mind for battle.

RC: You say he had a gift for literary detail, despite the fact that people like Gay Wilson Allen claim that he didn't. And that his letters "often strike a tone of rustic foolery."

RR: His descriptions are really apt and funny at times; he's definitely not without humor. Maybe you can start to infer his character from this. It seems like he was a by-the-book company commander but a human being, too. In the book, I describe how his soldiers gave him a sword and scabbard. It was an unusual honor for a guy of his rank.

RC: One of the most important issues you've raised is Walt's inability or unwillingness to allow the soldiers to speak in their own unique voice when they appear in his Civil War poems. You call him "a writer ... intimate with thousands of wounded men and their personal stories, who yet appears not really to be listening." Several lines from "Song of Myself" strangely anticipate this approach: "I do not ask the wounded person how he feels – I myself be-come the wounded person." "I act as the tongue of you, / Tied in your mouth, in mine it begins to be loosened." Even the opening line echoes this sentiment when he says: "what I assume you shall assume".

RR: Yeah. He's very much under the influence of Emer-son: the poet is a representative being, and he subsumes all of us, and can speak for us, because he has a gift we don't have. And Walt's may have coincided with his own high, justified estimation of his abilities. But he really took that and ran with it. He sort of thought: Well, that's the respon-sibility of the poet. He'd speak for these people who, in some sense, are dumb. Emerson says the impressions fall too weakly upon most of us. We feel things, but we're not quite stirred to memorable utterance, whereas the poet can do it for us.

You know, it sounds like I'm condemning him, and I don't intend to do that. I just noticed this being a salient as-pect of his war poetry. I think it's overwhelming; what are you supposed to do if you're talking to thousands of young boys? Are you supposed to give *all* of them a voice? Are you supposed to quote ten of them, or a hundred, or fifteen hundred? He's also a poet who wants to produce books. So, he tries to say the truth, trusting that, when it comes through him, it's going to work.

RC: In the 1860 "Song of Joy," he writes, "To see men fall and die and not complain!" He also says: "I will show that nothing can happen more beautiful than death." Throughout his work, death is often portrayed as an entirely positive thing. Is this the result of his mystical view of death? That it's of no consequence; therefore, one should meet it calmly, and we don't have to focus on its negative aspect?

RR: That's very plausible. He had this great truth he wanted to communicate – among many other truths – that death comes like a lover. It's greater and more beautiful than anyone has said yet. That might have been part of why he doesn't let the soldiers scream and be horrified, the way I imagine I would be in that sickbed and a lot of people would be. Perhaps because to be true to that would drown out this other thing that has its own truth, which he really wanted to communicate. That's partly it. Again, there's the need to produce a book: to subsume all of this.

It's tangentially related, but as I talk about in my book, he set out to write a regimental history of George and the 51st: this very hard fighting, famous regiment. And many regimental histories have been written. But finally, I think it was a little, I don't know, beneath him, or he felt he had more important books to write. But it's also, if you start talking about cases, if you try to get historically accurate and detailed about everything, you're going to lose yourself in that. And that just wasn't his vocation.

RC: Yet, he wasn't averse to at least privately admitting to the horror of war. He writes: "Mother, one's heart grows sick of war … when you see what it really is … I feel so horrified & disgusted – it seems to me like a great slaughter-house and the men mutually butchering each other."

RR: Yeah, that's pretty frank, isn't it? But of course, he'd probably distinguish war from death. Death is a deliverer. He saw these guys with unspeakable wounds, dying for ten, fifteen, twenty days, then death finally takes them. It's like a great blessing.

RC: His war experience was, in part, an exploration of what might be termed a death consciousness. He writes to Emerson: "A new world here I find … surely a medium world." You add: "By 'medium world' he meant a world of the spirit … and he intended to use the wounded soldiers to penetrate its mysteries."

RR: Yes, and David Reynolds makes good use of that in his Whitman biography. Walt is very much of his era, in so many ways: phrenology, and the obsession with séances and mediums. I don't know if it's because these are things he really believed, or if he had an eye on the market. Probably, a combination. You know, every poet speaks through the tropes of his era. The ideas that are obsessing us in 2010, you know …

RC: Whitman, especially, was doing that, and you can see it in the various editions of *Leaves*, how they change so dramatically, in certain ways.

RR: Well, I guess I don't really know about thematic changes …

RC: Perhaps not thematically, but in terms of how he starts off being a very provocative writer, and he ends up really trying to be accepted. That's a very big change. And this parallels the cultural changes that take place from the 1850s to the post-Civil War era. Reynolds says that, in America, the 1850s resembled the 1960s; it was a time of great cultural upheaval. So we see that in the first edition, but we don't see it as much in the deathbed edition.

RR: Yeah, good point; that's a great way to describe the first *Leaves of Grass*. It goes too far, and it's provocative. But I think we might have a hard time showing the Gilded Age, Grant's administration being a time of slowing down and embracing. The culture is healing itself in some ways.

But Twain and Whitman talk about what was happening in the 1870s and how disgusting it was, politically and economically: the money worship. And he tried to make himself more grandfatherly and anodyne, maybe because he was aging, and maybe because it was a good role and it was appropriate to play.

RC: Regarding the notion of a death consciousness, Reynolds brings up an interesting point. The cholera epidemic and the widespread incidence of tuberculosis in urban centers in the United States, where proper sanitary conditions were lacking, made death a palpable part of everyday life, especially in nineteenth-century Brooklyn.

RR: Yeah, there were probably corpses on the street all the time. Maybe that mid-century adoration of the corpse was an attempt to …

RC: Come to terms with it in some way, with this prevalence of death?

RR: Yeah. And my crude understanding of it is that, you know, you lose your child – this unspeakable sadness – then you keep the corpse around for a couple of weeks, trying, by staring at it, and thinking about it, to go over that threshold, into the spirit world, where the child, you hope, *is* now. That's sort of what I think they were doing.

RC: Let's talk about the importance of the first and third editions of *Leaves*. I've always felt that the first edition was by far the best, followed by the third, of 1860, which introduces some of Walt's last great poems. It seems you also feel this way. You write: "Of the poet of 1860, almost anything might have been expected. By no means conventional in thought, nor in the emotional colorations he introduced into poetry, the Whitman of 1860 was a wonder, an astonishment." The third edition included "a few longer, more ambiguous poems ... that gave evidence of a doubled, skeptical, half-despairing cast of thought. The great mystery of Walt's poetry is that this new turn, this potent beginning to a process of promising change, finally came to little."

RR: Yeah, I agree with that guy you quoted. [Laughs] I took a little heat from Ed Folsom, who's kind of the dean of Whitman scholarship. A very estimable man, and a remarkable scholar. He reviewed my book in the *Walt Whitman Quarterly Review*. He wrote a pretty long review, and he found a few things to praise; that was generous of him. But he's kind of angry about my statement that, really, with the war, Whitman's great poetry was over. Except for "When Lilacs Last in the Door-Yard Bloom'd." I mean, I looked at the poetry that was written after 1865; I just didn't find any great poems. In the 1860, they're knocking you down everywhere you go. I think nobody will ever know exactly. And certainly people will disagree with that: with your estimation or my estimation. But I think the labor in the hospitals took something out of him. It was an exhausting life labor. Then he started to get sick. Too soon, he started having strokes, and it took other energies out of him. You know, it's amazing how intact he was and how, after a long recuperation at George's house, he really pulled himself together. And I was cheered to see him carrying on with good-looking young men, right up to the end. [Laughs] His letters are wonderful and witty, and he's clearly a formidable guy, but the great poetry was over.

RC: Discussing this same period of 1860, Roy Morris writes: "In their bitterness and cynicism, 'The Eighteenth Presidency!' and 'Respondez!' are light-years removed from the utopian expansionism of *Leaves of Grass*....

Whitman himself … had undergone a similar transformation. Gone was the gladsome, celebratory poet of the open road; he had been replaced by a detached, world-weary onlooker."

Unlike the bulk of *Leaves*, which reeks of utopianism, "Respondez" reads like a dystopia. Here are some of the more disturbing lines:

"Let there be apathy under the stars!" "Every one who can tyrannize, let him tyrannize to his satisfaction!" "Let every man doubt every woman! And let every woman trick every man!" And this is strangely prophetic of the Internet and of a whole generation sitting beside a monitor: "Let the reflections of the things of the world be studied in mirrors! Let the things themselves continue unstudied!"

RR: That is remarkably predictive, but he's probably also talking about Plato's cave. Yes, I think he had his moods. And he never stopped the labor of trying to find new avenues of poetry: the new veins he was going to write great poetry out of.

It's like, just today, I've been writing an article about John Updike, for some intro. Trying in a few hundred words to talk about his whole career You know, Updike, who wrote about sexual shenanigans in the suburbs. And then, later on, in some of his lesser novels, he's writing dystopias, he's writing sci-fi, he's sort of doing Philip Roth lite: talking about the failures of his body, and writing long, long passages of kind of funny but self-indulgent sexual stuff. Well, you know, he's a writer who has a career he wants to keep alive. I think all writers do. And Whitman probably wrote out of the great, overwhelming emotions of given moments in his life. Things that were driving him and obsessing him. And so, he feels great disgust and distress. I mean, the Gilded Age was …

RC: But would you agree with Morris that he was depressed during this period because *Leaves* didn't receive the acclaim he thought it should have, and he was drifting aimlessly, so this was reflected in his mood?

RR: Morris wrote a book I really like, *The Better Angel*, but I think it's really wrong about many things. He doesn't quite understand that the Walt of 1860 had just written the greatest book of poetry of that era: the 1860 *Leaves of Grass*. He was probably bitter as hell it had sold only 300 copies. [Laughs] And he was in a foul mood because the country was tearing itself apart. But I don't know that he was depressed and then went into the war because of that.

RC: So you're saying *that's* what these types of poems are really reflecting.

RR: Well, I don't know. I mean, I hate to be vague. But with someone like Whitman, there's probably a lot feeding that.

RC: You know, you're absolutely right. Who is to say what is behind a particular painting or poem? I often read art-history books, because I'm also a painter. And I don't know if you've ever read an art history book, but they're among the most ridiculous examples of an author trying to explain why someone did something on a canvas. It's quite humorous at times!

RR: Yeah, yeah! I mean, this is the problem I have with David Reynolds, who's a very interesting scholar. But he thinks that if he adduces all the cultural currents of a moment, then, QED, we have *Leaves of Grass*. But you know, there were millions of other people who were around phrenology and daguerreotypes and opera who didn't write anything!

RC: I agree with you. This is typical of a hyperrational, academic approach to the mystery of art, isn't it?

RR: Yeah. I don't want to sound snarky about him, because I've read his stuff with great interest, but yeah. I think it's good to do that kind of research and then say: "But I stand in front of a mystery when I try to explain 'I Sing the Body Electric.'"

RC: One of the reasons I enjoy your work is because it doesn't have that dry, always-trying-to-be-balanced point of view of an academic.

RR: I have the advantage or disadvantage of being just a commercial writer. To a large extent, I live on my books. I'm teaching these days at Hopkins, but I'm not a tenured professor, so ...

RC: So you want people to *read* and *enjoy* your work! [Laughs]

RR: Yeah. And these are the books that I respond to, which rest on a great deal of research but where the writer makes strong judgments, and tries to decide. Yeah, what you say reminds me of Joseph Blotner's Faulkner biography. I love Faulkner, so I rushed to that book. But it was one of those books that just pile it on. It's got everything in there, but, you know ...

RC: Perhaps the contrast between "Respondez" and the rest of *Leaves* provides a key to understanding Whitman's attitude toward the soldiers. Because if *Leaves* is a utopian document, then it can only allow a utopian notion of death and of suffering. Walt claims to absorb both good and evil, but, really, evil is ameliorated in his overall vision of

Leaves. His portrayal of the soldiers is utopian but not holistic.

RR: I would agree with that. My only problem is that, when I read *Leaves*, I find an awful lot of dark stuff in there. This is years before he saw a battle, but he talks about clots of blood falling on the floor, and people getting their brains blown out. There are images that are very raw and not, you know, "Happy bedside poet." He was a poet who had good news for mankind without it being Christian at all.

RC: He almost puts himself in the role of a Savior or Redeemer, doesn't he?

RR: Yeah, pretty frankly, right. His friend O'Connor wrote a book basically saying this guy is the Christ. And Walt very calmly nodded, "Uh huh." [Laughs] "Sure, if they want to write that, great!"

RC: Would you agree that after a short spate of this kind of bitter, dark verse, what followed was a less provocative poetry: one that he hoped would appeal to larger numbers and, in the process, make him a celebrity rather than a hermetic poet who celebrated himself only to a handful who could possibly understand?

RR: Yeah, although when he was a hermetic poet, he was always hoping to win over the *entire nation*. He had the biggest hopes. You know, what does he say, that the poet embraces his people, and they all embrace him? I don't think he ever thought he was writing for a small audience.

RC: "The proof of a poet shall be sternly deferred, till his country absorbs him as affectionately as he has absorbed it."

RR: Right. Maybe I'm overemphasizing the sexual element, but I thought most of his editing down of himself later on was just, you know, some of the things he said were a little too risqué. And he's trying to make himself look like Longfellow: one of those guys who could be served at the Harvard Club. And again, he was conducting a career. You know, Walt at age sixty-five, it's time to become a gray eminence.

RC: So you would agree with Reynolds's point that Walt was growing impatient with that deferment and finally decided to do something about it, even if it meant being more palatable and less provocative?

RR: I would agree except, again, is he just being careerist, or is he actually feeling something different each day when he gets up? Do you know what I mean? His fires are somewhat banked, and I think he knew better than I know, or you know, or anybody knew that his great imaginative poetry was not happening. He was still writing, and he wrote good stuff, great prose, in his later years, but he must have known that the things that had happened in his great calling weren't happening. So, I hesitate to say it was just some clever cutting of his jib in a certain way: tacking this way rather than that way. He was always smart, and trying to be smart commercially. That was always an element in his shaping of himself. But I don't want to say he was "just a hack."

RC: Although the changes he made to "Song of Myself" in the deathbed edition are for the most part unsuccessful, I think it's important to remember that this isn't a completely black-and-white, absolute thing, and that, here and there, we can find improvements over the original edition.

RR: Yeah, I think so. I can't remember any good examples now. But probably Gary Schmidgall,* or somebody like that ... I've seen people show where he really clarifies things. But the preponderance of the change is disheartening. And I'm so happy we still have the original: that he didn't buy up all the 1855's, and 1860's, and burn them.

Since he seems so prophetic, I don't put it past him to have thought: Well, all those texts are out there. Now, I'm writing this deathbed edition, and maybe that will be part of my story. Somebody will put it together: as I aged, I made these changes. I mean, it sounds pretty fanciful, but he's certainly a half step ahead of me as far as the largeness of his imagination of himself, and his soul, and what he might have meant.

RC: Although the deathbed edition is replete with a lot of filler, not very interesting lists of things, and much bloated verse, some of these tendencies are evident in the first edition, which also features prosaic lists and so on. The difference is that the treasures first appear there; it's sprinkled with absolute gems, of a kind we've never seen before in poetry.

RR: Yeah, although remember, the 1855 is pretty slim. The only impression I had of wordiness was from the preface. You know, "bloated lists," he's got a few of those, although sometimes he pulls off these tremendous lists with great aplomb. But I don't think somebody coming to the first edition of *Leaves of Grass* would mainly have said: this is bloated and full of filler. I don't think the critics said that.

RC: Around the time of his father's death, Whitman "became the poet of original ideas, expressed in *Leaves* in an idiom never heard before in the history of the world." Perhaps you could talk about the nature of this originality and innovation.

RR: That's the big mystery of his poetry: where did this intimate tone come from? I mean, there were good poets. Emerson was writing good poetry. And Longfellow. You know, they scanned; the diction was sophisticated. But it wasn't like your friend grabbing you by your shirtfront and saying, "This terrible thing happened to me last night. I saw this drunk get run over in the street." That's the kind of intimacy Walt evokes. He doesn't have it in every line of *Leaves*, but, gosh, he's really got it there. And it's original in poetry. Maybe there's some classical poetry that has it. I mean, Shakespeare doesn't have it. Shakespeare has other fantastic things, but that originality, I don't know. And, in all the scholarship about who he was trying to sound like, and who he was reading carefully – you know, they say he was reading Whittier! [Laughs]

RC: Although the point has been made that, in the nineteenth century, certain Eastern sacred texts were translated into English, and this may have been one of the primary sources of literary influence on *Leaves*.

RR: But what are those texts, and do they have this kind of intimacy?

RC: Specifically, Hindu texts, in which there's a discussion of the Self, and the Self with a capital 'S,' not the personal self. And of how this higher Self comes through the personal self.* After all, this is "Song of Myself." When Whitman talks about himself, it's an archetypal self; it's not just the small ego. It's what, in the East, they would call the Bigger Self. But on the other hand, those texts are certainly not written in an American idiom: of a guy from Brooklyn talking to you on a street corner and, as you say, grabbing you by the shirt – and even trying to kiss you! [Laughs] You know, there's a section in the 1860 version where he ends it by trying to kiss the reader, which is just unimaginable for that time!

RR: [Laughs] Yeah. I mean, the tone of intimacy is independent of the subject, the subject matter being the Self. So, where the hell does that come from? I just don't know. I find it somewhat persuasive that he was bowled over by opera: by these voices singing words, intelligible words, that were causing him to have near-orgasmic feelings in the theater. You know, an intimacy that went right into his soul.

And not everyone's going to be responding that way. Already, there's something in him that's capable of being inspired that way. He tried to make a poetry, a verbal art, that could maybe have the same effect. Could go right into the heart, into the whole being of someone else. And having the ability to do that is one thing, but having the idea: that's really original. That's the start.

I was talking to a guy I just met who's from Romania. His name is Voytec. For some reason, we talked about poetry. And he said, "Oh – Whitman! Whitman! Me and my friends, we all read Whitman!" You know, he's read everywhere. Because he was the start of this poetry that could really talk to people.

RC: One often hears about his influence on American poets, but it was really a worldwide influence.

RR: Yeah. So many people read him and – wow – it changed their lives. It was so *hopeful*, to hear him speak frankly about his sexual life. But that whole tone: it's a modern tone. I never heard it before him.

RC: It's completely unique. Here's an example of this worldwide influence. In a letter to his sister from 1888, Vincent van Gogh writes of Walt: "He sees in the future, and even in the present, a world of healthy, carnal love, strong and frank – of friendship – of work – under the great starlit vault of heaven a something which after all one can only call God – and eternity in its place above this world. At first it makes you smile, it is all so candid and pure; but it sets you thinking for the same reason."

RR: Gosh, what an incredibly astute characterization! And that he got so much of Walt in a few phrases. I particularly like where he says, "At first it makes you smile, it is all so candid and pure." Whitman's forthright approach to all the big questions seems naive, at first, and braves a kind of ridicule. But who else can put it all together the way he does? Van Gogh hits the mark.

RC: When I interviewed Hubert Selby, he brought up a wonderful point about growing up in Brooklyn. He said there's a music of language in the street that you just don't have in other places. You know, this marvelous melodic way of speaking: the argot, the slang, the mixture of immigrants and so on. I wonder if this had something to do with Whitman's unique use of a vernacular tone.

RR: Yeah, he's real frank about that. He loved the density of New York and Brooklyn – the variety of folks – and he rejoiced in slang. That's a part of why he hung out with cart drivers and stage drivers – the equivalent of bus drivers – who had this argot. Yeah, he loved that. Was it more intense in Brooklyn and New York than anywhere else? Well, probably, because it was so densely populated.

I read *Last Exit to Brooklyn* when I was a college student. It just knocked me and all of my friends over. Wow.

RC: It's such an important book. It was banned in England until 1968, and there was a huge censorship trial, the equivalent of what we had here, a few years before, with *Tropic of Cancer*. Are you also a Henry Miller enthusiast?

RR: Well, I've read Miller, and I love him.

RC: At various points in his writing, he speaks about the influence of Whitman on his life and work.

RR: Sure. He's a Whitmanesque guy.

RC: Like Miller, Whitman is also a great *flaneur*: just strolling along, absorbing the atmosphere around him. So much of *Leaves* is about this almost mystical ability he has to absorb, to take things into himself. As I said before, the Sears and Roebuck of the soul: to take every element in, and transfigure it in some way, and hand it back to you. Perhaps there's a phrenological term for it.

RR: I'm not fully up on my phrenology, but I know Walt was very proud of his phrenological report. They felt his bumps and said, "You're a genius. What are you, a poet?" And suddenly, we find phrenological terms in his poetry.

Yeah, I think Miller was very much like him. The other very different sort of guy who was profoundly affected by him, of sort of the same era, is D. H. Lawrence. He had to struggle with Whitman. And he wrote a very affectionate, slightly mocking, but loving essay, in *Studies in Classic American Literature*, about Whitman. Walt was very important to him.

RC: You quote him in your book; he called Whitman the "great postmortem poet."

RR: Right. For trying to go over into death – and bring back the news.

RC: In one of those fascinating coincidences of history, shortly before Walt finds his wounded brother George, he pays a visit to the Lacy House mansion, where Clara Barton is serving as a nurse for the wounded. You felt they had certain things in common.

RR: Yeah, that vocation to nurse: their serious version of it. They both got the job done. I've been to the Lacy House; it's not that big a place. I'm sure he was jostling against her.

RC: "Both were in their early forties, both decidedly unorthodox – disinclined to hand out Bible tracts to dying men, unlike other hospital visitors – and both had a proud faith in their own physical health, believing that they could 'out-robust' the threats to themselves, and were too fit to catch infections." Do you think Walt died from whatever infections he caught in the Civil War hospitals?

RR: I don't think you can prove that. Well, maybe somebody could dig up his corpse and conduct sophisticated DNA testing. But look, this was the nineteenth century, and he lived to be seventy-two or seventy-three. He lived and lived and lived, and then, suddenly, the body was giving out. That was a long life.

He was incredibly strong and resistant. Most residents of Brooklyn of his class were TB-positive. Whether it flared up and killed them, or whether it stayed in suppression most of their lives, it probably killed them in the end. It was almost universal. And he did have a brother, Andrew, who died of it.

RC: Walt writes of President Lincoln: "We have got so that we always exchange bows, and very cordial ones." Has anything emerged since your book was published that reveals more about the Lincoln-Whitman connection?

RR: A book was written about it by Daniel Mark Epstein. He explores it and discusses the meaning of it. But I think Walt gave a pretty accurate account. He said, "I didn't want to impose myself on him."

What I found interesting was that Lincoln read the first edition and loved it. He had a copy of it in his digs that he shared with his really good buddy, Joshua Speed, in Illinois. They lived together like bachelors, and many people think there was more than just bachelorhood between them. But Lincoln loved that book. And it was considered a very racy, dirty book.

RC: And Lincoln recommended it to others, as well.

RR: Right, he did.

RC: I enjoyed the way you brought the Whitman saga to its somewhat tragic conclusion. By "moving to the country, George fulfilled an old dream of the family's ... Once the Whitman's had been Long Island gentry ... now, wealthy with the earnings of a modern economy, George returned to the land." But George's wife died without leaving any children behind, although Walt's brother Jeff was survived by his daughter, Jessie Louisa. Perhaps you could talk about Jessie's final years.

RR: She was very long lived and died in the 1950s. She was apparently charming and lovable. And so, when she became an elderly lady, there were people who wanted to take care of her. She had a kind of magnetism that was unusual. I thought it was very unusual that this nurse of hers – playing a variation on the Walt Whitman nursing theme – just took to this old lady.

When she and her family moved to New Mexico in their station wagon, they took the old lady with them. She was probably ninety years old at that point. So, there was something of Walt's charm, or maybe Mrs. Whitman's charm, or the family charm, in this daughter of Jeff's.

In the 1940s, an independent researcher went to Long Island's North Fork, to Greenport, looking for Whitman relatives. She found two daughters of his sister Mary Elizabeth, who had lived out there. They were really big, robust women with spookily clear blue-gray eyes that people said Walt and George both had. They were very handsome large women.

RC: So, it's possible there are Whitman descendants walking among us.

RR: Yes. And that researcher wrote some wonderful stuff about Whitman haunts on Long Island: where he taught and so on. It was very like her to have stumbled on these Whitman women.

RC: Which of his biographers do you most admire, and what do you think of Horace Traubel's memoir of Walt?

RR: I haven't read all of Traubel, but it's a wonderful source. Far and away the best book I've read is Paul Zweig's book. Zweig was an American poet who died in the 1980s, who published a book about Walt's youth, and how this poet came out of being kind of a junk journalist and poorly educated. It's a wonderful book. It's called *Walt Whitman: The Making of the Poet*. That's my favorite. But there's a lot of great stuff about Whitman. As I said, I enjoyed Roy Morris's book although, in the end, I disagreed with him about a lot of stuff.

RC: On the subject of Walt's mother helping to shape *Leaves*, I thought this was a very fitting psychological assessment. He said the "reality, the simplicity, the transparency" of his mother's life were "responsible for the main things in the letters, as in *Leaves of Grass* itself." Those three adjectives – *reality, simplicity, transparency* – describe something essential about the style and modernity of the first edition.

RR: Yeah, and the fact that he slowed down to say it so precisely, what he got from her. Right there, that's a strong testimony to her importance to him. You know, all sons have a "nice mother," a "good mother"; after the mother passes on, her memory is precious to them. But they don't spell it out so carefully. As we were saying, she was a great mimic and a great storyteller, with a natural sense of drama. And he got that from her.

I found her character fascinating. Walt uses "mother" as a general term; but often he seems to be talking about his own mother as this calm, benign, good, solid, enduring presence in the home. But what I saw in the letters is that she was also a snake, and sharp. She got a case on her daughter-in-law. She had this adoring daughter-in-law who could never please her. And she said vile, vicious things about people. In her letters to Walt, she really expressed herself. She was nothing like that pious angel in the home.

I mean, if you and I were the guests, and Walt was bringing us home one day in 1853, we might have that impression of Mrs. Whitman. She'd be wearing a clean, Quakerish outfit, and she'd be a lovely woman who'd serve us up a nice dinner, and she might say a couple of witty things. She was very kindly. But she had her moods. She definitely had a sharp side.

As far as making her an interesting person, that was significant to me. I read those letters of hers, and I had the impression of a complex, rich personality. A very interesting woman.

---

* This interview was conducted on 12 October 2010. It originally appeared in a slightly altered, abridged form in *Emerging*

Civil War in October 2011.

* See Gary Schmidgall, *Walt Whitman: Selected Poems 1855-1892* (New York: Saint Martin's Press, 2000).

* Emerson referred to *Leaves of Grass* as "a blend of the *Bhagavad Gita* and the *New York Herald*."

The Mystery of the Man: Justin Kaplan
Talks About America's Greatest Poet*

Awarded a Pulitzer Prize and a National Book Award for Mr. Clemens and Mark Twain, *Justin Kaplan is the author of* Lincoln Steffens, A Biography *and* Walt Whitman, A Life, *which won an American Book Award. He's also the editor of several editions of* Bartlett's Familiar Quotations. *Kaplan lives with his wife, author Anne Bernays, in Cambridge and Truro, Massachusetts. In 2002 they co-authored a "double memoir,"* Back Then: Two Lives in 1950s New York. *His latest work is* When the Astors Owned New York: Blue Bloods and Grand Hotels in a Gilded Age *(2006).*

Rob Couteau: Joe, what led to your fascination with Walt Whitman?

Justin Kaplan: That's a big question. It was the mystery of the man, partly. That is, the sudden efflorescence of *Leaves of Grass* after what appeared to be a very unpromising first thirty years. There's something vaguely sacramental about that. And he resists all attempts to get people to explain what he's done. You just have to take it as a given.

I really feel there's a vaguely religious aspect to biography. Especially with creative people, you're dealing with sort of a mystery. And you can describe the circumstances before and after some great innovation, but you can't explain or describe the moment or the time that it happens, or the way it happens.

RC: I'm glad to hear you say that; I agree with you so much about that. And I have some other questions about this mysterious aspect of it. Do you recall the first time you read "Song of Myself" and the effect it had on you?

JK: Yes, I recall it very vividly. I was a student at the Horace Mann School for Boys, in New York. And we had as a text – the sort of high school edition – of Louis Untermeyer's *Modern American and British Poetry*. That was the first time I had ever really read ... I mean, I knew much of the familiar Whitman stuff: "O Captain! My Captain!" But this was a real revelation. That is, that beautiful lyric about being on the grass. And I never got over that feeling of "Wow. This is like nothing else." I still feel that.

RC: You paint a wonderful portrait of Louis Untermeyer in your memoir *Back Then*.

JK: Ah, good. He was a great man. He got pissed on a great deal because he was written off as a popularizer. But he did more than anybody else to really introduce modern British and American poetry. Even though he publicized himself along with his poetry.

RC: I remember, in one of the editions of that book, he had his picture on the cover, along with the other "great poets" of all times. [Laughs]

JK: I wouldn't put it past him. [Laughs] But he deserved it. I mean, there were a lot of second-rate poets in his collection.

RC: That's a wonderful story in the sense that you ended up working with him, years later. It's quite amazing, isn't it?

JK: It was fortuitous.

RC: This is another very big question. Why is "Song of Myself" such an important poem?

JK: Well, let's say there are two aspects. One is historical. How original and innovative this poem was, especially if you read it in the context of the kind of poetry that was being written and loved in 1855. Tennyson, for example, who writes in an English that is literally English, whereas Whitman's English is strictly … it's very much like *Huckleberry Finn*. It's the same sort of crossing over into the colloquial, and being able to handle the colloquial with great ease. That is, you don't hear any grinding of gears. This is his natural idiom.

The trouble is, as Whitman got older and older, he tended not only to imitate himself but also to pick up some of the bad habits of Victorian poetry. He should have stayed at the age of thirty-six.

RC: Walt read his father's copies of Frances Wright's *A Few Days in Athens* and Constantin de Volney's *The Ruins*, and you say that *Leaves* "borrowed the insurgent and questioning spirit of these mentors along with literal quotations from their writings." Were these the key contributions Walter Whitman Senior made to Walt's intellectual inheritance?

JK: I never thought of it that way. I suppose it was a contribution, but I couldn't go beyond that.

RC: And I understand the father also knew Tom Paine and read Tom Paine.

JK: These claims really have to be looked at rather critically, because this is Walt writing in retrospect. And little things get magnified, and little encounters turn into anecdotes. It's inevitable. So, I don't know how much actual weight you can put to these stories.

RC: I guess it's impossible to say. One of his father's favorite aphorisms was: "Keep good heart, *the worst is to come*."

JK: That's a cheery way to grow up, isn't it? [Laughs]

By the way, that reminds me of the advice of a publisher to someone whose first book is about to come out, and he's complaining about the lack of excitement. He says, "This is the calm before the storm; *before* the calm, *before* the storm, the calm remains." Well, anyhow, that's a very downhearted piece of wisdom.

RC: We know very little about the father, but what temperamental traits do you think he may have passed on to Walt?

JK: I don't see the two of them as being at all close. It's the mother, in this instance, that was the vital link. The father is relevant as far as business and daily living is concerned. In fact, he very rarely refers to his father specifically, as I remember.

RC: When we look at Walt as a journalist, he was a very opinionated man; he was a thinker, and he had strong ideas and opinions, and I've often wondered if there was some imprinting from the father in that regard.

JK: I'm sure there must have been. Because if the father had definite opinions, Walt, as a beginning journalist, also had extremely definite opinions, some of which are kind of untoothsome. Some of those attitudes, judged by current standards, would be rather unpleasant.

RC: When Walt was ten years old, he heard the preaching of a radical Quaker named Elias Hicks. You write, "His 'passionate unstudied oratory,' neither argumentative nor intellectual, turned into a naturally cadenced prose that at times seemed to strive to achieve the condition of poetry." That description bears a strange resemblance to *Leaves of Grass*. Perhaps you could discuss how the phenomenon of oratory influenced "Song of Myself."

JK: If you look at the voice in "Song of Myself," it is

somewhat addressing a group of people. It's not private poetry. He's maybe writing about private experience, but the
stance, the communicating stance, is very public, and very
open, and therefore very oratorical. In fact, there are places
in the "Song of Myself" where he practically says: "Now,
listen here." He's forcing the audience to pay attention.
And remember, at that time, oratory was much more highly
valued than it is now. We tend to be suspicious of oratory,
whereas then it was the making of a politician, for one
thing.

RC: You say, "Hicks's presence persisted in Whitman's
passion for oratory" and "in his wooing of ecstasy and in
his fundamental creed, that 'the fountain of all naked theol-
ogy, all religion, all worship, all the truth to which you are
possibly eligible' was the single self and its inherent rela-
tions." Is it possible that Walt's very Eastern-sounding notion of a transcendental self can be traced back, in part, to
Elias Hicks?

JK: I'm sure you're correct in that. Because Hicks becomes the absolute model of, let's say, a transcendent person, especially in his oratory. He's comparable in some
ways to Father Mapple in *Moby Dick*. Remember the great,
great sermon before the ship leaves? Mapple is sort of a
fierce Elias Hicks.

RC: You write that many of Walt's "Chants Democratic"
were "all too nakedly in the manner of the orator." Would
you agree that the first edition of *Leaves* was by far the
best?

JK: Absolutely. One of the horrible accidents that has be-
fallen Whitman is that, when you say *Leaves of Grass*,
people immediately think of this big, fat, 1892 edition,
which has a lot of garbage in it. And the 1855 poem, or po-

ems, eleven of them, are sort of buried in this enormous book. Yeah, I certainly think there's no comparison between the 1855 version and the big so-called *Leaves of Grass* volume. It's a pity, really.

RC: It's also a pity that he spent all that time constantly reworking it when he could have been creating something fresh.

JK: Well, can you predict that?

RC: No, you can't. [Laughs]

JK: [Laughs] You postulate that, but you can't ...

RC: Well, this is another thing that you can't really logically answer, but, if you could speculate, what led to Walt's relative decline as a poet after 1860? Was it the extreme physical toll the war took upon him?

JK: It's a number of things. It's the toll of the war; it's failing health; it's strokes; it's feebleness and so on. Also, quite aside from these disabilities, you can't really project creativity. You might say he used up a great deal of it, and there's a fair amount left over for the late poems, for the late poetry, but this is not a poetry factory.

RC: Interpreting a single photo is a tricky business, but when you examine Harrison's "Christ-likeness" of Walt, what qualities do you imagine it captures most strongly?

JK: The intensity of the gaze. The very strange expression in the eyes. He's looking at you, and he seems to be looking beyond you. Maybe I'm reading too much into that picture, but it's a very Christlike image!

RC: And it's an unusual image for that time, when everyone else is posing in a rigid, deadly way. He reaches out at you in that picture, doesn't he?

JK: Well, that's true of that picture, and it's certainly true of the frontispiece of the 1855 *Leaves of Grass* where he's obviously an outside person, a worker. He's not a library person or a literary person.

RC: "One of the roughs," as he liked to say.

JK: Yes, exactly.

RC: You write, "No other poet of his century wrote about the body with such explicitness and joy, anatomizing it at rest and cataloguing its parts, celebrating it as an instrument of love." It might be interesting to compare this to the rather sexless, although equally profound, writing of Mark Twain. If Walt was clearly fascinated by sex, death, and rebirth, how would you characterize the literary keynotes of Twain?

JK: Mark Twain was very reticent about sex and the physical, except when he was with his cronies. I'm not sure I understand the drift of the question, though.

RC: I thought it would be interesting to compare Whitman's over-the-top celebration of the body and of sexuality to Twain. When you read Whitman, the sacredness and sexuality of the body are so intertwined, and there's also a great focus on death. And on psychological, emotional, or spiritual rebirth.

JK: Yes.

RC: I think these are the keynotes. So, if you compare these two writers, what are the keynotes of Mark Twain?

JK: The keynote would be a sort of inspired skepticism about just about everything. Almost a religion of being skeptical. Of certainly not taking anything at face value. Certainly never accepting anything that's pretentious or imitative. It's a very compact value system, I think.

RC: And a wonderful use of satire and irony.

JK: To cut through all the ambient bullshit, yes.

RC: [Laughs] That's a great answer! I recently interviewed Robert Roper, who authored a book about Walt and his brothers during the war. When I asked him to discuss the nature of Whitman's originality, he said: "That's the big mystery of his poetry; where did that intimate tone come from? There were good poets" during this period, "but it wasn't like your friend grabbing you by your shirt and saying, 'This terrible thing happened to me last night. I saw this drunk get run over in the street.' That's the kind of intimacy Walt evokes." Would you agree with Roper, and can you think of examples of classical or antique poetry that feature such an intimate tone?

JK: The only source I can think of as being comparable is Christian mystics. But poets in general … [Pauses] All right, Keats's "Nightingale" ode, which makes the transition from the poet standing there to a beatific and almost mystical vision of reality. And then it fades, as the nightingale goes away.* But I think Whitman is almost unique in this hyperreligious, mystical style. Where did it come from, as I suggested before, nobody knows. [Laughs] It's a sacred mystery; it really is.

RC: That's one of the things I enjoyed about your book. Yours was the first Whitman biography I ever read; I was about twenty-three at the time, and it had a great influence on me. One of the things I loved about it was that you really address the spirituality, and mysticism, and mystery of Whitman. And not everyone does.

JK: I don't see how you could write about Whitman without doing that.

RC: Well, for example, with David Reynolds's book, it's almost like a vast attempt to trace every cause and effect in society to a result in the poetry.

JK: It's a very workmanlike, very thorough approach to

Whitman, but it's not transcendent in any sense.

RC: You quote Henry Adams, who "asked himself 'whether he knew of any American artist who had ever insisted on the power of sex, as every classic has always done; but he could think only of Walt Whitman.... All the rest had used sex for sentiment, never force.'"

JK: That's a great quotation from Adams.

RC: It illustrates that it isn't just the portrayal of sex that makes Whitman unique, it's the poetic discussion of it as an inherent *power* and life *force*: even one through which spirituality is experienced and expressed.

JK: Yes.

RC: This lends him a kinship with certain writers of antiquity. I'm thinking of Sappho or Catullus.

JK: Yes.

RC: Or of Petronius' *Satyricon*. Would you agree that he seems to share a greater affinity with them than he does with writers of his own time?

JK: I don't see quite the relationship with Petronius; tell me how you see it.

RC: When I read the *Satyricon*, it's as if those two boys are captives, not of a particular relationship, but of a kind of cosmic power of lust and sex ...

JK: Yes.

RC: And sensuality. But again, the main point being it's not just the portrayal of sex that makes Whitman unique.

JK: No, it's not just sex; it informs the poetry.

RC: That he attempts to address the archetypal power of sexuality as it's expressed through the life force is something that's very impressive in *Leaves*. For example, his poem "A Woman Waits for Me." It's not just about a particular woman, but it's through this woman that the future of the whole nation is somehow assured.

JK: Yes, he's talking about the future generations, isn't he?

RC: Yes, it's almost as if having sex becomes a patriotic act!

JK: Yes. [Laughs] It's a very powerful poem.

RC: Writing about Walt's life circa 1850, you say: "Whitman turned to the gospel of the self redeemed through art." This notion of a "gospel of self" reminded me of something Joseph Campbell once said about how the modern artist – and *not* the religious institution – is the one who bears the new spiritual content. From your point of view, does *Leaves* primarily contain a spiritual message?

JK: Yes. Very definitely. Not in any doctrinal way. [Laughs] But a *spirit*. And you can't pin spirit down.

RC: About halfway through your work, you conclude that, ultimately, "It is useless to look outside Whitman himself for the matrix or occasion for *Leaves of Grass*." I like this very much because it honors the mystery of art and of the creator. Sometimes, there's a tendency in biography to try to pin down every cause-and-effect relationship between an artist's environment and his work, and, as every artist knows, this is not only impossible but it's also misguided. I particularly appreciate your approach because, while it explored every possible artistic influence and connection, one also senses that you revere the mysterious, inexplicable spirit of artistic creation.

JK: Yes. You can write about it, as I tried to do it, without getting misty eyed. It's a matter of, lets say, balance.

RC: You say: "Supreme American inheritor of Romanticism, Whitman too believed the poet was the agency of a transcendent power and created 'rapt verse' in an 'ecstasy of statement,' 'a trance, yet with all the senses alert.'" Although his manuscripts show he labored over his verse and continually edited and revised, is it your sense that the essential inspiration for much of his early verse came to him in a kind of trance state?

JK: Yeah, I'd certainly like to think so. It depends on how literally you're going to take that part of it. How autobiographical is your reading of *Leaves of Grass* going to be? And when he talks about that afternoon on the grass, you can't help believing this is referring to a particular experience, which he generalizes from. But you can't go too far with that, because poetry is not autobiography.

RC: It's coming from somewhere else, as well.

JK: For the biographer and critic, it really comes down to a matter of *respect* for the so-called creative process. You can't pin it down; you can't literalize it; you've got to live with it.

There are pre-"Song of Myself" fragments that I found very moving and really indicative. In one of them – it's a two or three-line quote – he uses the image of the sleeper. That is: "I'm now awake; have I been asleep all my life?" It's a way of describing illumination. And I found that very crucial, because you have the feeling that, yes, the same ecstatic mood that pervades "Song of Myself" is partly, if not rehearsed, at least recorded.

RC: You say *Leaves* "was to celebrate the conquest of loneliness through the language of common modern speech." About a year ago, I heard Barney Rosset* lecture …

JK: Yes, I see he's one of your heroes. He's a great man.

RC: I didn't know much about Rosset until I saw a documentary that was recently made about him, *Obscene*. I was so moved by the fact that he sold off millions-of-dollars worth of beachfront property to pay for the court trials of *Tropic of Cancer*.

JK: He was a very generous man.

RC: When he lectured, he said there was a direct line of literary descent extending from Whitman to Henry Miller to the Beats. In your Whitman biography, you spoke of how *Leaves* was to "celebrate the conquest of loneliness through the language of common modern speech" ...

JK: [Laughs] I thought that was a neat sentence; I was very proud of it.

RC: It is a great sentence! And it brought to mind Rosset's remark, and also that Ginsberg often said the Beats attempted to address this sense of separation and ameliorate it through poetry.

JK: You mean, suggesting a conscious program?

RC: Oh, I don't know; I think Ginsberg probably worked through the same process that Whitman did, of just inspiration and so on. But I think, in reflecting on this, he thought it was a keynote of the Beats. In any case, do you feel there's a connection between Whitman and Miller and some of the Beats?

JK: Absolutely, yes.

RC: How would you characterize it?

JK: What they had in common? That's a very tough question. I'm afraid anything I say is going to sound silly. [Laughs] But I *feel* very strongly the continuity of these guys. By the way, this is just a sidebar anecdote. But at the Horace Mann School, in the same era that I was introduced to "Song of Myself," in French class, I was sitting next to a rather glum person named Jack Kerouac. This was a French class, and he never said anything. Can you guess why?

RC: Why?

JK: Because French was his first language. So he just sat there and endured the explication of French grammar.

He was being seasoned at Horace Mann. They held him back for a year, to season him for the Columbia football team. And then he broke a leg.

RC: Was that your only contact with Kerouac?

JK: Yes. As for Ginsberg, I liked him very much.

RC: You had personal contacts with him?

JK: Yes. For several years, every time I saw him, we argued over the same stupid point. You want to hear what it was? I'm quoting him: "You've got to listen to this! There's a letter from John Burroughs, or one of those people, one of those associates of Whitman, saying: 'Last night, I slept with Walt.' And so, doesn't that speak for itself?" [Laughs] And then, my side of the argument was: "Remember, when people visited in, let's say, the 1870s, they didn't have Motel 6."

RC: He was quite a character!

JK: Yes. He and I were part of a crew doing a documentary on Whitman. I don't know what happened to it. Anyhow, the first day of shooting, we were going to open with a scene from "Crossing Brooklyn Ferry." And so, we were all lined up in the back of a ferryboat. The cinematographer was ready, and his camera focuses on Allen. This is to be the opening line of speeches. And he says, "Walt Whitman was America's first mind-blowing poet." [Laughs] And I said, "You just can't do that! Not at the beginning, anyhow."

RC: A friend of mine used to live in an apartment that was catty-corner to Allen's, in that building on East 12th Street. One day I was standing outside, waiting to be buzzed up. I was leaning against the wall reading a big, thick book: Anthony Summers's biography on J. Edgar Hoover. Suddenly, I felt someone staring at me. About fifteen feet away, there was an old guy, ogling me. I went back to my book, but then I realized it was Ginsberg, so I nodded: sort of acknowledging our local poet. He went inside, and then my friend buzzed me up. When I went upstairs, they were standing in the hall, talking. I'd never met Allen before, and he turned and very meekly said, "Oh, do you mind if I ask what book you're reading?" When I showed him the cover, he grew excited and asked, "Oh, is that the one where he talks about Hoover wearing a dress?"

JK: Naturally, yes! [Laughs] He once got rather annoyed at me when I failed to recognize him because he'd just shaved off his beard. And without the beard, he looked a lot like a butter-and-eggs salesman. Whereas with a beard, he was Allen Ginsberg.

RC: I think Ginsberg's best poem is his homage to Walt Whitman, "A Supermarket in California."

JK: Yes.

RC: You agree?

JK: Yeah.

RC: Why do you think so?

JK: It just is very powerful, and even *moving*, when Walt addresses the boy. He calls him "my angel."

RC: On the one hand, it's such a visionary poem, and a poem that is just given to you, in some deep inspiration. And on the other hand, it's such a carefully crafted poem. There's not a misplaced word, or beat, or anything. Which Ginsberg very rarely achieves in his other work.

JK: That's a very good point.

RC: You describe how Swinburne "rhapsodized about

Whitman's affinities with Blake." Do you see a connection between Whitman and Blake?

JK: I don't see too great a contact between them stylistically. They both tend to be, let's say, dithyrambic, at one point or another. Blake, when he got visionary, it became very institutional. That is, he organizes a sort of poetical church. It's something Whitman would never do.

The disaffection of Swinburne for Whitman is a vivid episode of turning on someone you absolutely worshipped and denouncing him in rather vivid invective: "Hottentot woman, drunk on adulterated cantharides."*

RC: You say that, for Walt, "the poet was the shaman of modern society, a master of 'the techniques of ecstasy,'" quoting from Mircea Eliade's classic, *Shamanism: Archaic Techniques of Ecstasy*, a wonderful book.

JK: Yes.

RC: I recently read an article in the *Walt Whitman Review* by George Hutchinson, who explored the parallels between shamanism and the imagery of "The Sleepers."

JK: That is an incredible poem. I never quite got over it.

RC: Hutchinson says that, while Whitman scholars often compare him to the Eastern Vedic tradition, this shamanistic imagery links him more to the Native American tradition. Perhaps you could comment on that and on the importance of "The Sleepers."

JK: To me, "The Sleepers" was important because he's entering another dimension of *being* almost. And it's a notion of ... I can't get over the simple image of the universality of "The Sleepers." It's not in a characteristic Whitman mode either.

RC: You feel it goes in a much different direction than a lot of his other work, yes?

JK: Somehow, it doesn't quite belong in the 1855 *Leaves of Grass*. But that's where it is.

RC: Why do you feel that, Joe? Could you expand on this?

JK: Let's say "The Sleepers" is closer in understanding and in mood to the great section of *Leaves of Grass* with the episode on the grass. But if you look at the 1855 edition, there are all sorts of really disparate elements in it that not only don't belong ... I suppose the explanation is that he was in a terrible hurry to get it together. There's a poem about the rendition of Anthony Burns, where you have a political level. And then, suddenly, you have "The Sleepers," which is certainly not political.

RC: For lack of a better term, there's a deeply introverted quality to "The Sleepers," whereas a lot of the other poems are very out there, in the world.

JK: Yes. It's a great poem, but it's almost overshadowed by "Song of Myself."

RC: Horace Traubel quotes Whitman as saying "Swedenborg was right when he said there was a close connection ... between the state we call religious ecstasy and the desire to copulate."

JK: Yes. [Laughs] That's putting it in a nutshell, yes.

RC: This is a concept that appears throughout the history of religious thought, yet it was lost upon the literary Brahmins of Boston. Walt's friend James Redpath wrote to Walt: "There is a prejudice [against] you here among the 'fine' ladies and gentlemen of the transcendental School. It is believed that you are not ashamed of your reproductive organs." What's really striking about *Leaves* is how Walt focuses on the body, and on the sensual and sensory experience, as being synonymous with spiritual experience. Is it fair to say that, for Walt, physical ecstasy is the instinctual expression of the spirit?

JK: I wouldn't be that exclusive. [Laughs]

RC: But maybe you could talk about the connection he draws between the two. This seems to be a keynote in *Leaves*, doesn't it, that we should not be ashamed of the body?

JK: Well, that's certainly one of the overt messages, if there is a message. You know: the overt message of *Leaves of Grass*, which is to bring the body out in the open, and not be ashamed. And those people who objected, for example, to the "Calamus" poems, on the grounds that it was overphysical, were really getting it all wrong. There's something very comic about it. [Laughs] That is, they're objecting to the explicitness about the body, but they don't seem to realize that this is, in many ways, a very gay poem. But they're so *dumb* that they don't see it.

RC: When we look at it today, it seems so obvious. And yet, back then, there were parts of *Leaves* that people objected to more, for sexual reasons, than to "Calamus," right?

JK: Yes. By the way, this was one of the problems I had writing this book. Because, occasionally, members of the gay community would say, "What the hell business do you have writing about our guy?" And then, straight people would say, "Well, the important question about Whitman was, "Was he or wasn't he?" What a stupid question! [Laughs] I kept telling them that the matter of whether he was or wasn't is so tired and meaningless that there's no point in talking about it. You don't have to prove anything.

RC: In America, there's a tendency to label literature that way. You go to a bookstore and there's a section for "Gay

Writers," and so on. In France, it's quite different. There isn't this concept of gay writers or straight writers. It's just: "Is he a great writer or not?"

JK: Yes. I often think of my exposure to American literature here. By "here," I mean at Harvard. I was just so naive, and really so simple-minded. I mean, this is before the advent of, let's say, "queer theory," or any other stuff like that. We were missing a lot.

RC: Walt was about eight years old when slavery was outlawed in New York. Although he was quite advanced in certain ways in his fight against racial injustice, he also "continued to believe that blacks in general were genetically and psychologically unfitted for 'amalgamation.'" How would you compare Whitman's racial notions to Twain's groundbreaking work against racism in books such as *Huckleberry Finn* and *Puddin'head Wilson*?

JK: When Howells describes Mark Twain as a de-Southernized Southerner, he again was getting it all wrong. Because there are instances in the Mark Twain story where he practically confesses that "I am a child of another era, and I feel very uncomfortable with black people." Which would be condemnatory now. But he's being perfectly honest.

Why does he have a black butler? He says, "Because I don't like the idea of giving orders to a white man." There's a residue of "good old slavery times" in Mark Twain and in Whitman, as well. They both were very reluctant to deal on an equal basis with blacks, especially in New York. Howells calls him a de-Southernized Southerner, but he wasn't. He was always a Southerner.

RC: After reading your Twain biography, I was struck by how much less sympathetic a character he was as compared to Whitman. You show how Twain exhibited a pattern of blaming others for his own faults and misdeeds and attacking many of his closest friends, except those he depended on, such as his wife, Olivia, Henry Rogers, and Andrew Carnegie. Whereas Walt's empathy brought him all the way to the Civil War hospitals.

JK: Yes.

RC: And at the end of his life, Whitman surrounded himself with close supporters and friends such as Horace Traubel. Would you agree that Twain was not as sympathetic a character?

JK: This is going to sound funny. He's not as grown up as Whitman. [Laughs] In many ways, he's sort of an overgrown child, you know, exhibiting himself. Whereas Whitman doesn't have that exhibitionism. Well, he does, but not in the same vaguely infantile way.

RC: It's more balanced, isn't it?

JK: Yes.

RC: Although Walt's prophecies weren't always accurate, I thought this quote from *Democratic Vistas* was indeed prescient. He says: "In vain do we march with unprecedented strides to empire so colossal, outvying the antique, beyond Alexander's, beyond the proudest sway of Rome.... It is as if we were somehow being endow'd with a vast and more and more thoroughly appointed body, and then left with little or no soul."

JK: That's a great passage.

RC: What would he think of the direction America has taken today, in its 234th year?

JK: What would he think of what's now known as American imperialism? Well, he's very explicit on that point. Even in that passage from *Democratic Vistas*, there's a reference to extending over to Cuba and Canada as well, isn't there? Extending to Cuba. I wonder how Fidel would feel about Whitman. Anyhow, these are people of their times. And they don't shed the social impress.

RC: Yet, what's interesting about this quote is, he ends it by saying "and then left with little or no soul."

JK: Yes.

RC: I'm confused about this quote because, most of the time, when Whitman talks about the expansion of America, he discusses it in a purely positive way. But in this instance, he ends it with this ambiguous line "and then left with little or no soul." So, is he finally questioning it, or not?

JK: No. I thought this was a reference to what Mark Twain called the Gilded Age, because they were contemporaneous. And big money began to take over the railroads, and the factories, and so on and so forth.

RC: So, he's saying it's OK to be this imperialistic, but we should do it with more soul.

JK: Yes. Because I think, deep down, he believes the United States is the destiny of the entire world. You know, the "gospel of democracy."

RC: Would he be shocked at what's happened to America, in terms of the rightwing direction that we've moved in? And in terms of the kind of empire we've created? Would he be disturbed by it?

JK: I think as it comes with a growing materialism and a growing social fragmentation, he'd be horrified. At the same time, given his feeling about blacks, he might feel that this is not a good thing at all.

RC: You end the biography with two lovely lines: "Almost alone among the major American writers, he achieved in his last years radiance, serenity and generosity of spirit."

"An old man who never married and had no heart's companion now except his books, he rode contentedly at anchor on the waters of the past." How would you compare his final years to those of Mark Twain?

JK: Well, I think that passage speaks for itself. Mark Twain's late years may not have been quite so bitter as ... you know, it's very dramatic to think of Mark Twain as turning completely sour. But he certainly is a much less happy person in his old age than Whitman.

By the way, that passage about being one of the only American writers to achieve wholeness and equanimity in old age: I originally had that passage somewhere at the beginning of my book. And then my dear friend and my editor, your friend Michael Korda, said, "Listen, you've got to warm up this story. And I'll show you how to do it. Take that paragraph, and stick it at the end."

Somewhere in your interview with Michael, you quote him as saying he's always been rather shy and had trouble being verbal. And I've known him for forty years, and I've never found that to be true! [Laughs]

RC: In his memoir, he portrays himself as a shy young man. And I was really shocked, because, when I saw him lecture, he was almost aggressive: it was very powerful. The contrast was amazing.

JK: Yes.

RC: It was interesting to compare his portrait of Max Schuster* to yours: the different ways you each described him.

JK: Yes, we've done a lot of trading of anecdotes. We both loved him.

RC: Your portrait was very warm.

JK: I really loved Max. And I felt very bad because, in a way, I betrayed him by resigning to do my own work. He was very angry.

RC: You mention this in *Back Then*. I thought there was real warmth; you had a great sympathy for him.

JK: He was a very sweet man, deep down.

RC: In *Back Then*, you say that your first Freudian analyst wrote an essay that "disposed of *Leaves of Grass* as a product of narcissistic isolation, gnawing loneliness, and homoerotic libido." You devote quite a few pages to describing the enormous sway Freudian ideas held for so many in the 1950s. How can we account for this? Was it due to a kind of mass psychological naiveté?

JK: Yeah, Freud was extremely hot then. For many of us, we had the feeling that if you did not have an exposure to psychoanalysis, it was like never having gone to graduate school. It was obligatory, almost.

RC: The 1950s was such an incredibly different time. If you speak with people who are only twenty years old today, they just can't imagine what life was like in America, back then.

JK: That's the point we were trying to make. That in many ways, the Fifties are as distant from us now as the Gibson Girl* was to the Fifties. An entire shift in culture and in manners.

RC: I recall, years ago, listening to an interview with the fellow who wrote *The Man in the Gray Flannel Suit* ...

JK: I knew him, yes.

RC: He said the idea for the book came as a result of going to work one day in a brown suit, or a blue suit, and he was called into the office and told, "No, you must wear a *gray* flannel suit."

JK: It was true. If you paid a lot of attention to clothes, it was very important if you were wearing, for example, flannel trousers – which we all did – but it was important that the flannel be of the darkest possible shade. And the legs should be very narrow. And it should have a Brooks Brothers label on it. And that was your complete outfit.

RC: It reminds me of what you say in the Whitman biography: how, in the 1850s, you were expected to wear *black* from head to toe!*

JK: Yes.

RC: Joe, thanks for your time; I enjoyed talking with you so much.

JK: I know. It was a lot of fun.

---

* This interview was conducted on 22 December 2010.

* Keats's "Ode to a Nightingale" ends with the lines: "Was it a vision, or a waking dream? / Fled is that music: – Do I wake or sleep?"

* Barney Rosset, the former owner of Grove Press and the first American publisher of Henry Miller, Samuel Beckett, and Jean Genet, led the legal battle to publish D. H. Lawrence's *Lady Chatterley's Lover* and Henry Miller's *Tropic of Cancer*.

* Swinburne wrote: "Mr. Whitman's Eve is a drunken apple-woman, indecently sprawling in the slush and garbage amid the rotten refuse of her overturned fruit stall: but Mr. Whitman's Venus is a hottentot wench under the influence of cantharides and adulterated rum."

* Max Schuster was the co-founder, with Richard L. Simon, of Simon and Schuster. At the inception of their careers, Justin Kaplan and Michael Korda each worked as editors under Max.

* A reference to Charles Dana Gibson's turn-of-the-century illustration of the ideal American woman, known as the Gibson Girl.

* "Black became the predominant color of men's clothes on the Continent of Europe after the third decade of the nineteenth

century. The funereal fashion [...] came from Britain." Luigi Barzini, *The Europeans* (New York: Penguin Books, 1984), p. 35.

An Interview with William Scott, Author of *Troublemakers: Power, Representation, and the Fiction of the Mass Worker**

At the northeastern edge of Zuccotti Park, during the historic Occupy Wall Street demonstration, I encountered a youthful-looking man in his early forties who was sitting on the ground, handing out flyers advertising his book. When I read the title, Troublemakers: Power, Representation, and the Fiction of the Mass Worker, *I sat down and conducted this impromptu interview.*

William Scott is an associate professor of English at the University of Pittsburgh. He's been sleeping in the park beside the other demonstrators since he first arrived on 6 October 2011. A few days after our talk, he began to work at the "People's Library" as a volunteer. Troublemakers, *published by Rutgers University Press, is his first book.*

Rob Couteau: What's your book about?

William Scott: It's about the way novelists portrayed mass-worker movements in the first half of the twentieth century. When I say mass workers, I mean workers in mass-production industries such as auto and steel, on assembly lines.

In part, it's also about a new form of power that mass workers discovered they had: one that didn't depend on union representation or political party representation. It was a power they derived not so much through the power of numbers but through their position at the workplace, on the assembly line. That is, when ten workers discovered that if they stopped work they could shut down a whole factory if they sat down, that was an enormous power that workers discovered.

This new form of power created a crisis for novelists who tried to represent mass-worker movements. What they were trying to do was to show that mass workers in their oppressed conditions on assembly lines actually did have a form of power that was not the conventional form that was popular in the nineteenth century – power through representation, power through political parties in unions – but rather that they had a kind of structural or material power from the workplace itself. And so, my book is about how novelists represented this new kind of worker and this new form of power. I talk about novels that tried to detail sit-down strikes, or acts of spontaneous sabotage, or, in general, direct action: direct democracy movements in mass-industrial settings.

RC: How long have you been teaching?

WS: For about eight years. I was at New Mexico University at Las Cruces for about two years, in the English department there. I've been at Pittsburgh for six years.

RC: How long did you work on the book?

WS: On and off, for about ten years.

RC: Who are the writers that you focus on? What's the main group?

WS: The most well known writers that I discuss are people like Upton Sinclair, Jack London, and Dalton Trumbo: those are some of the better-known writers. The rest of them have fallen into obscurity. When their books were initially published though, many of them were bestsellers. Some of the novels I talk about from the progressive era – the period of World War One – were bestsellers and were well known but have fallen into obscurity since then. One of the purposes of the book is to revive attention on these forgotten novels.

RC: You mentioned Dalton Trumbo …

WS: Trumbo's novel, *Johnny Got His Gun*, was a controversial, famous antiwar novel from 1939, and I talk about that in the book.

RC: I forgive myself for not recognizing his name at first, because it's one of those examples of where the book title is more famous than the author.

WS: It is. They made of film of it, as well.* It was a very popular book, used for a sort of peace propaganda: an antiwar, pacifist propaganda novel.

RC: Maybe you could mention some of the books and authors that have fallen into obscurity that you're trying to highlight.

WS: One terrific novel from 1939 that's out of print is by a woman named Ruth McKenney. It's about the Akron rubber workers, the tire workers, and their sit-down strikes in the 1930s. Cornell University Press reprinted it in the early Nineties, but it's been out of print for about twenty years. I would love to see that book put out again. It's a fantastic novel. I have a lot to say about it.

Then there's Thomas Bell, author of a novel called *Out of This Furnace*, which is actually well-known in Pennsylvania and around the Pittsburgh region. It's about the Pittsburgh Steel workers. That's still in print, but it's not very well known. Then there are a bunch of novels from the progressive era, writers who were affiliated with the Industrial Workers of the World: Leroy Scott, author of *The Walking Delegate*; another book by a guy named Ernest Poole, called *The Harbor*, about dock workers and harbor workers in the New York harbor. A wonderful book. Then a book by a guy named Arthur Bullard called *Comrade*

Yetta, from 1913, about textile workers in New York: shirtwaist workers and that kind of stuff. Those are a few of them. The list goes on, and there are other novels that I could mention.

RC: How did the idea for this generate? Where did you get the idea?

WS: My doctoral dissertation and research was about leftist writers from the Great Depression. In the course of doing this research, I discovered there was a broader tradition of radical literature in this country. So, I wanted to do something that would be broader than just a focus on the 1930s. That's pretty much the origin of it.

RC: What gave you the idea of doing the dissertation originally?

WS: When I was in graduate school, I was interested in the history of U.S. social movements. I was in a comparative lit program, so I started off studying German literature and German philosophy, that sort of thing. Then I discovered there was a movement of radical writers, leftist writers, in the Depression. I had no idea who these authors were. The only writers I ever knew from the 1930s were people like Hemingway, Steinbeck, *The Grapes of Wrath*. But to learn that there was a whole movement that was organized, that had conferences, journals, magazines, and published all sorts of stories, poems, plays, and novels from this era: that just blew my mind. I decided I wanted to learn more about it and that it would be a good topic: an under-researched field, which needed to be looked at again.

RC: You discuss major authors, such as Upton Sinclair, who explore this theme as a focal point in their work. But do you also mention writers that we don't necessarily associate with this theme but who were, nonetheless, affected by it and who dramatized it to some extent?

WS: Pretty much all the novelists I discuss were authors who had a commitment to writing about class issues and the situation of the working class. So, it's hard for me to think of writers who took up that intent as a sort of peripheral or secondary kind of thing. John Steinbeck would be a good example. I don't write about him in the book. But he's a good example of someone who has a sort of side interest in workers' movements in this country, and he addressed it in some of his novels. *The Grapes of Wrath* is the most famous one. Maybe Dalton Trumbo is the most famous example of somebody. *Johnny Got His Gun* is not typically thought of as a book about workers. But in the novel, it's clear that the main character is there to be a typical example of a modern mass-industrial worker. Jack London is another writer who was personally a socialist and was involved with the Socialist Party. He didn't write a lot about workers, though, except in a few of his books. Maybe he's another good example of somebody like that.

RC: Jack London brings a lot of those issues to the fore in his quasi-autobiographical novel, *Martin Eden*.

WS: Oh, *Martin Eden*! Absolutely!

RC: That's an amazing book, isn't it?

WS: Yes! I don't write about it in my book; I write about *The Iron Heel* a little bit, which was a very popular book. And *Martin Eden* was, too; they were both popular books with progressives and with labor activists in the progressive era. For example, he was one of the favorite authors of the Wobblies: the IWW. In many ways, *The Iron Heel* was a prophetic book. It's a fantastic novel.

RC: You could say that many of his tales and stories that have to do with going to exotic places – such as to Alaska, for the Gold Rush – are about people who are *working*, trying to make money.

WS: Absolutely. Then there are his allegorical stories, as well. Even the stories about animals are often allegorical tales about human society.

Historians and sociologists will tell you that this era we're living in now, of big corporate capital, most resembles the period of the 1890s in America: the Gilded Age, the creation of monopoly capital. Big trusts, and things like that. It's the kind of capitalism that Jack London was trying to describe in his books. For that reason, I think he's a very contemporary writer, and the things he says are relevant to many of the struggles that people are having today.

RC: I recently interviewed Justin Kaplan, who won a Pulitzer Prize for his biography on Mark Twain. We were talking about Twain, Whitman, and the Gilded Age, and we touched on the fact that, yes, there really is a connection from that period to this period. Especially when I read about Whitman's life, I see some amazing connections. The 1850s was a decade that one could easily compare to the 1960s: a time of eccentric personal fashion and culture. And then, proceeding into the 1890s, there's a palpable disgust with the growing power of corporations and how the law was no longer equally applied between a citizen and a plutocrat.

WS: Yes.

RC: So, there's certainly a parallel. Which leads us to the fact that there are *cycles* that we see throughout history.

WS: Oh, yes, that's true. In part, one of the reasons there are cycles is because, relatively speaking, Americans are less history conscious as compared with people in Europe. I studied in Germany; I lived there for a while, and I followed the German news. On historical memorial days when they have these milestones, these anniversaries, they're presented as major news stories. We rarely see that in our news here. You can grow up watching the news – if you even watch the news in this country – and never learn about American history. In this country, the news usually focuses on the present.

In general, with Americans, part of their identity is to be always forward looking: gazing into the future and not looking back. This goes part and parcel with the ideology of American identity.

RC: There's a reason for that, because this country attracted immigrants from other places.

WS: Exactly.

RC: At that time, in the nineteenth century, to take a big boat trip like that, you certainly had to have a lot of optimism about the future. You had to be a gambler; you had to be a bit of an intuitive: to believe in possibilities rather than actualities.

WS: Right.

RC: That's the filter through which the American character has been formed.

WS: Yes, absolutely. But I think the downside is that we do tend to repeat things. In part, there are cycles because of this almost constitutional amnesia.

RC: We forget about the past.

WS: We forget about the past, and then the past repeats itself. Vietnam is a wonderful example, a timely example. I'm a big fan of the history of the Vietnam War; I'm very interested in it. I'm fascinated by the various ways that it was debated and the ways it was resisted: all those kinds of things. Also by the rationale, the motivation that was used to get us in the war and to keep us in the war for all that time.

If you look at the arguments that were made, and the mission of the U.S. military in Vietnam, almost point for point it matches up with Afghanistan. Not so much with Iraq, but with Afghanistan. That is, you have a mountainous region, nomadic peoples, and our mission is to spread not just democracy but to spread a kind of service: a "goodwill mission," right? But it's a war, nonetheless. When you hear pundits denying the similarities between Vietnam and Afghanistan, I think they have to do that to distract attention away from the glaring parallels and similarities.

I grew up watching movies like *The Deer Hunter*, *Apocalypse Now*: all these movies that were critical of U.S. involvement in Vietnam. And I grew up naively thinking, well, with films like this, we'll never have to worry about another Vietnam, because everyone knows why it's wrong and what's wrong with these kinds of wars. With any war, but with these in particular. Yet, it started all over again, ten years ago.

RC: The powers-that-be have a great interest in dumbing down the Americans, and in underfunding education, because they don't want people to know about these things.

WS: Right.

RC: One of the big differences between Vietnam and Afghanistan is that they learned their lesson after allowing the journalists roam free through the jungles of Vietnam. In Iraq and Afghanistan, they created a policy of so-called embedded journalists: reporters were attached to military units and couldn't wander around, unsupervised. Another difference is that it became unlawful for journalists to photograph the coffins coming back, draped in American flags.

WS: From Afghanistan and Iraq, yes.

RC: There's even more control of the media now than there was back then. I grew up in the 1960s, watching the TV every night at the dinner table …

WS: The dead bodies …

RC: Yes. During the news, wherever you were in America, you'd see the names of the boys, often from local neighborhoods, who were killed, and where they were from. Largely, these were body bags that came back to the working- and middle class. And because the middle class was affected, that galvanized the antiwar movement and made it a serious threat to the status quo.

The connection between those protests and this one, which we're sitting in the midst of today, is that the middle class are a significant part of the ninety-nine percent. They're directly affected, even though, now, the issue is the economy.

WS: Yes, I totally agree. The other day, there was a woman at the general assembly meeting who was saying that the thing this generation and this particular protest has in common with the antiwar protests in the Sixties is that, in the Sixties, everyone was worried about being drafted. You stayed in college so you wouldn't get drafted. And the way to protest this was to burn your draft card. Everyone knew that they were at risk for dying; they knew people who were dying; they knew they, themselves, were at risk for being sent over there. It was also clear that it was a war against lower-income Americans and people of color. They were the vast majority of the people who were being put on front lines and being killed.

RC: Especially by 1968, toward the end of the war.

WS: Exactly. We don't have a draft today, and the thing about the war in Iraq and in Afghanistan is that the majority of middle-class Americans don't feel directly affected by this. They don't feel as though they're at risk for being sent over and killed. But what we do have today, which students did not have in the Sixties, is student-loan debt. And the easy availability of credit has made it even worse.

When I was an undergraduate at SUNY Buffalo, during my first year on campus, credit companies gave me credit cards and said, "Here, go out and use this." I didn't even have to apply; they gave them to me on the spot, on campus. They had tables set up, and they were handing out credit cards. So, what did I do? I was like, "Hey, I've never had a credit card before. I'll go and buy some CDs." I go and buy some CDs; I'm into debt immediately. This is twenty years ago. Ever since then, I've been struggling with paying off credit-card debt, student-loan debt. I had to pay for my own tuition through college, so I had to take out student loans. I'm still paying that off. Thank God I have a stable job, a good job, and I can pay it. But the situation this puts the vast majority of people in – younger people especially – is that, now, when you're in college, you're racking up debt. So, college is actually not a safe place to be anymore; it's a dangerous thing.

When people graduate with $100,000 in student loans, they have to take that job at Starbucks, and they have to take that job willingly and obediently. They cannot talk back to their supervisors, because they need to keep the job to pay off debt. If they don't, their credit is going to be screwed up, and their lives are going to be screwed up from that point on, and they won't be able to buy a car or a house.

So, this is an interesting parallel. What that woman was asking students to do was to burn their student-loan paperwork. Which, idealistically, sounds wonderful. But realistically, you're screwing yourself if you do that. I would never have thought to do that myself. But it's true that if every student from today to tomorrow decided to not pay their student loans anymore, and to walk away from it, that would create another kind of crisis.

RC: It may not be the most pragmatic solution, but it's a highly effective dramatic symbolic action, which is very important to have in a movement. I often think of how, in 1967, Abbie Hoffman and the Yippies, and Allen Ginsberg, and so many other groups went down to Washington with the intention of levitating the Pentagon through yoga meditation and by chanting, "Out, demon, out!" [Laughs] The Pentagon building is shaped like a five-pointed star, so they thought it was akin to a black-magic pentagram. And this event still resonates among contemporary historians of this period. Norman Mailer's book, *The Armies of the Night*, is about that same protest. So, these symbolic acts are very important. Burning a draft card is an image that resonates, that stays in people's minds. Back then, people would have seen it in *Life* magazine. It's a provocation, an important provocation.

WS: Absolutely, I agree. If you want to see a parallel between this kind of action and that Pentagon action, you're right to see it in these protests as well. Although, in some ways, the focus of the energy at this event, and at similar events that are happening around the country and springing up spontaneously in different cities, has a kind of focus, in spite of the fact that there are no clear demands or concrete sound-bite demands. The focus on finance capital is something that is extremely powerful and that was missing from the Sixties generation, which was mainly engaged in antiwar protest. To some degree, there was a critique of capitalism in there, as well. The problem in the Sixties was that there were competing leftist ideologies. You had Maoists fighting with communists and this kind of thing. We were still in the Cold War period, so communism became a banner under which people were organized, but it was a controversial one.

What's great about this event is that it's relatively free from limited political or ideological definitions or categories. This is really a bonus. Yet, it doesn't lose its main focus on finance capitalism, on corporate capitalism.

RC: Why are you here today?

WS: I have a sabbatical this semester; I don't have to teach. When I first started hearing about this, I thought: This is really important; I want to support it. Luckily, I don't have to teach classes now, so I'm here supporting it.

RC: Considering what your book is about, this is the perfect question to ask. In America in the Sixties and early Seventies, the unions never aligned with the students.

WS: Right.

RC: A few blocks from this location, an event happened in the early 1970s that was photographed and widely reproduced. Construction workers attacked the youth movement as they were marching in protest: violently attacked them, beat some of them to a pulp. And now, we've got major unions, such as the U.S. Steelworkers and the Transit Workers Union, joining a largely youthful protest movement at the beginning, after just a few weeks. What's the significance of that to you?

WS: That is huge. That is actually the secret of May 1968 in Paris. A short-lived kind of success, but, nevertheless, a significant coalition. This is what we didn't have in the U.S. in '68. Instead, there was a lot of tension between organized labor and the antiwar movement.

That's a complicated issue, which has a lot of factors involved in explaining why that's so. It took forty years for organized labor to realize that they were getting shafted. In the Sixties, that process had just started; it hadn't yet kicked in. Mass workers and unions were incredibly strong and still had a lot to gain. The industrialization and outsourcing hadn't hit home yet to the industrial workers in this country. Forty years later, it's hit home in a major way. We've seen outsourcing and the export of an industrial economy out of this country. So, for many years, unions have been in the doldrums and have, in some ways, needed something like this to give them the sort of push they needed to speak out about it.

RC: It's easy to understand why, in May '68, the unions in Paris had an almost instant solidarity with the students, because there's more of a history of that kind of thing there. When there's a strike in France, it often leads to a domino effect.

WS: Yes.

RC: Why do you think it took so long for workers here to understand the need to create this coalition? Why do you think they attacked the students then, and they're not doing it now? What's changed?

WS: I think it's because, in the history of our country, the work ethic is extremely important. In the U.S., we live in culture that worships work for its own sake and that worships work for the sake of upward mobility. The American dream is about working hard and moving up. But there's also a religious element to it: a Puritan work ethic. To be a good American, you have to work hard.

The tension between the student movement and labor existed throughout the 1960s. Hippies were called "bums." They were "lazy bums" and, supposedly, they didn't work. And so, what "hippy" stood for was an antiwork ethic. This made them very unpopular with organized labor.

The reason it took so long is because of the persistence and resilience of the work ethic: this never goes away. Even among the Left and people who are sort of "pro-working class," there's almost a fetishization of working for its own sake: the value of work.

What you're seeing now among working people and organized labor is a convergence of frustration with the economy, with Wall Street, with Congress, and with the outsourcing of jobs. It's a dovetailing of that frustration with the anxiety of the student generation, who can't find work and who need to find work to pay off student-loan debt. These two things are coming together, and it's happening right now. That's one theory I would have to explain why, now, there's a compatibility. And organized labor has finally woken up to realize that it's OK to be critical of the American work ethic in some ways.

RC: We're each a little older than many of the people in this crowd. Especially with the teenagers that I speak to, they really believe in their hearts that something fundamental is about to change. But you and I know how deeply corrupt this country is, and all governments in the world are, and what a dark network exists between governments, major corporations, organized crime, international narco-traffickers: all of that. That's the real "worldwide web." Bearing this in mind, where do you think this is going to go? Where's it going to be a year from now? How are people going to look back on this, twenty or thirty years from now? Are these kids going to be disappointed when the fundamentals don't instantly transform?

WS: Honestly, I can't tell yet. I would be uncomfortable making predictions about that. One side of me, the cynical side, sees all this getting burned out as soon as the weather gets cold and everyone goes home. Then it will be a blip on the radar of the popular cultural history of the United States, and nothing more. But another part of me, the less cynical, more optimistic, hopeful side, thinks that even if the momentum of this particular action trails away, others will take its place. That it will start a domino effect that we haven't seen in our country for a long time. That could be really positive. So, I don't know.

A year from now, what I would love to see is for politicians to actually try to respond to these kinds of demands. Just in the last two years, you've seen the political response, directly, to the Tea Party actions around the country. A very organized movement, and they were directly responded to. They had leverage in the last election, and they will have leverage in the next election. If a similar kind of thing from a progressive point of view could have the same kind of leverage, that could help to balance the scales a bit.

Because of the direction this country's been moving in the last few years, and particularly with the rise of the Tea Party, I've been really frightened, you know? When I hear the Republican nominees, it's really frightening, the kinds of things I hear them say and the kind of things I know they would be supporting. So, if nothing else, even if this fizzled out next week, it could still have the potential to exert some influence in electoral politics.

A lot of people that you'll speak to here are against electoral politics completely. They think the whole system is completely corrupt. And that's a valid position to have. Representational democracy *is* incredibly corrupt, especially when corporations are considered people and they can vote, and they can donate as much as they want to campaigns. This makes everyone here very skeptical.

RC: Talk about a symbolically significant image – a corporation as a person!

WS: Absolutely. That captures the essence of something that's so upsetting to people here.

RC: In fact, corporations *have* become people, because the government's allowed for it. I mean, they have become people in the sense of having personal rights. Even more than people: like "superpeople."

WS: Yes. That's why I think it's valid for a lot of people here not to want to participate in electoral politics. That's fine, but if Sarah Palin is our next president because they didn't go out and vote, they'll only have themselves to blame!* So, I think it's right to critique the system of electoral representation and democracy, but you work with what you've got.

RC: Both things are important: voting, as well as taking to the streets. And right now, taking to the streets is a very meaningful thing to do.

WS: Yes. About a hundred years ago, there was a very similar debate in this country about the value of electoral representation. The Socialist Party was pushing for Eugene Debs to get a lot of votes and to become president. Campaign after campaign, he kept running for president, and he kept getting more and more votes. Upton Sinclair talks about it in *The Jungle*. But there was another sphere of labor people and activists who said this was all a waste of time. The Industrial Workers of the World were competing against that system of democracy. They felt we needed a direct democracy or a worker's democracy. A democracy that would become a reality through the direct action of workers.

In many ways, the reason why this protest appeals to me so much and interests me so much is that I see this as a version of that. Just people realizing a new form of democracy.

RC: In the decades before television, even for those who weren't necessarily interested in literary things per se, there were often books in the household, as a form of entertainment. But with the advent of television, the novel became less influential in the United States. One of the indications of this is that organizations such as the CIA spent increasingly less time, money, and energy on infiltrating literary magazines and literary groups, and on keeping tabs on authors, and things like that. Instead, the film stars and other celebrities were monitored, because they had so much more power. For example, a movie star could call a press conference and draw instant headlines.

In some interview, there's an apt quote by the playwright Arthur Miller. Just before he was due to testify at the House Un-American Activities Committee, he received a message from the one of the congressmen in charge of the hearings. He told Miller: If Marilyn Monroe would just pose in a photo with me, I'd be willing to drop the whole thing. Miller later said that it resembled the cathartic moment in a play: the emotional focal point in which everything is symbolized in one quintessential gesture. He added that the significance of this was that they weren't calling lowly secretaries and bureaucrats from the American Communist Party to testify; they were calling Hollywood celebrities, because that was the only way to maintain headlines.

Bearing all this in mind, what is the political role of the novelist today?

WS: I would hesitate to spell out any particular criteria for things that writers ought to be writing about. In part, I say this as a result of my own research in looking at the debate around the role of the writer in the Thirties, during the Great Depression. There were huge debates about what writers should be doing during this crisis.

RC: That's a good point; let me rephrase the question. What is the role of a politically motivated writer, such as Upton Sinclair and those other well-known novelists that you talk about? What role could they play today? I'm not necessarily asking, "What role *should* they play?" but I'm asking "What role *can* they play," in the context of the background I just gave you?

WS: It's important for people to be aware of them for a number of reasons, and to be aware of the way that politics gets worked out through literature in this country: with all it's mistakes, with all its blind spots. It's important to see how this process works and unfolds, and for people to understand that it's possible to be a writer, and do very creative work, and still have political convictions, and to not see an incompatibility between these two things. John Reed, the writer that Warren Beatty portrayed in the film *Reds*, was also very famous for one of the last statements he made, supposedly on his deathbed. He said, "It's a hell of a thing, trying to juggle poetry and politics." You know, the idea that revolution and poetry never go hand-in-hand.

The assumption that there's an inherent conflict between poetry and politics is something that, for a long time, writers have dealt with or have tried to work in the shadow of. I think it's important for writers, and for people today, students of literature, to understand that there's never been a huge conflict between creative work and political work. The two have always gone hand-in-hand, going back to the eighteenth century even. And that you don't have to write an overtly political poem or novel for that to be a valid expression of your politics.

Right now, I see a lot of potential, particularly in poetry and politics. The reason I say this is because poetry – and this has always been true of poetry – has been an easier genre for people to make their lives heard in: for people who are not trained as writers to throw something together. For example, workers have often written poems. With the slam poetry movement, which emerged about ten, fifteen years ago, that had – and still has – a lot of potential to be used for consciousness raising and for political awareness. Hip-hop has obviously gotten a lot of attention for its political potential. Talib Kweli, a contemporary hip-hop artist, was here a couple of nights ago as a guest, and he did some songs. It was obvious to everyone why he wanted to be here, and why he wanted to perform for us. It was really profound, the kind of message he was providing.

RC: You brought up an interesting point just now about the fact that the two don't have to contradict each other. Jim Feast, who's a critic for the *Evergreen Review*, has been doing an ongoing series about how the most significant writers are never writing out of a vacuum. They're not just portraying themselves in a kind of cerebral cubicle, cut off from the rest of society. Instead, the really great writers are always portraying something that reflects the larger society, the major currents, the historical trend, the overall picture of the moment. Do you agree?

WS: I do, although I don't think they're always conscious of doing that. A very well known Marxist literary critic who teaches at Duke University, Fredric Jameson, wrote an influential book in the early 1980s called *The Political Unconscious*. His argument is that writers, whether they know it or not, are always responding to the political and social issues of their time. The work that they're doing is shaped by this, and it's always a response, whether it's conscious or unconscious. He uses the analogy of dreams, Freud's theory of dreams, that our dreams are always a wish fulfillment. Jameson thought that we should see literature as expressing a kind of wish fulfillment for some type of political solution or change in our society. I think there's a lot to be said for this type of approach.

RC: Of course, if dreams were wish fulfillment, we'd never have nightmares! But that's a long discussion.

WS: Freud actually has a lot to say about nightmares.

RC: I know, he's got an excuse for everything!

WS: [Laughs]

RC: On the opposite side of the spectrum, we also have authors such as John Reed who are so one-sidedly obsessed with the notion of changing the world, and obsessed with their own political advocacy role, that, sometimes, we have to question whether there's something more personal at work that's being projected upon this whole screen. For instance, in *Reds*, a marvelous film that touches on a lot of these things, the director Warren Beatty features several interviews with Henry Miller. There's a classic quote where Miller says: "Yeah, John Reed, he was a real rabble-rouser, a troublemaker. The problem with him was that he wanted to change the world. And nobody can change the world, not even Jesus Christ. Look at what they did to him; they crucified the poor bastard!" Then he ends the quote by saying: "When you're that obsessed with wanting to change the world, we have to question whether there's really something inside yourself that needs change." A valid point?

WS: Well, yes, that's a valid point. But it doesn't invalidate the kinds of commitments and values that somebody like John Reed had, and the things he was trying to do. There's always a psychopathological or neurotic explanation for what everybody does.

RC: We're motivated by many things ...

WS: Yes.

RC: Most of them beyond the analysis of a Freud or a Jung anyway.

WS: Yes. And apart from college debt, one thing that probably the majority of the people here have in common is that their mothers didn't love them enough! [Laughs] I mean, you could probably make that prediction. Or they had some other familial issue that made them turn to issues of social justice and see a lot of hope in that. But that doesn't discount or discredit the fact that they're still trying to do something positive to make the world a better place.

RC: Yes, indeed. Thanks so much for talking with me today.

WS: Thank you!

---

* This interview was conducted on 8 October 2011.

* In 1971, *Johnny Got His Gun* was made into a film directed by Dalton Trumbo. It was remade in 2008 and directed by Rowan Joseph.

* In 2008, Sarah Palin ran as the Republican vice-presidential candidate.

The Miracle of Unity. How Peace Mediator
Robert De Sena Offers Gang Members a Way Out

"Everything is Possible" was one of the most intriguing battle cries of the 1960s. Perhaps it's no coincidence that Robert De Sena, a former gang member who later became an English teacher at Brooklyn's John Dewey High School, was shaped by this era. In the various documentaries that chronicle his ground-breaking work with the Council for Unity, an organization he founded to offer an alternative to gang violence, "possibility" is a phrase that often crops up in his impassioned, heartfelt discourse. One of the impossible things he accomplished was to create peace among rabidly violent gang members by offering them a viable alternative to joining such groups. This he accomplished by applying the work of Carl Jung and Joseph Campbell – themselves innovators in exploring the archetypal structures of the psyche – to the hardscrabble streets of Bensonhurst and Gravesend.

De Sena's background in mythology and Romantic literature also inspired him to create Chrysallia, *a mythopoetic tale about attaining social unity.*

Rob Couteau: When I read through the various interviews and articles about you, I sense the strong influence of literature and art lurking in the background. I know from our recent conversations that William Blake as well as the Lake poets, Wordsworth and Coleridge, who led the Romantic Movement in England, were some of your major literary influences. These men were reacting against the supremacy of reason to the detriment of feeling and intuition.

How did all this shape you, and what drew you to their work?

Robert De Sena: At an early age, I had a level of sensitivity that was very different from a lot of my friends. Being in a really tough, violent neighborhood, sometimes I overcompensated by being much more aggressive and violent to hide that. But my escape was always through literature. And when you have that predisposition to emotion ... I think you have it too, Rob. Without us being aware of it, we married our inner woman at a relatively early age. And with that came a balance that a lot of other people didn't have.

I remember, and I never forgot this, a friend of mine was plagued by this girl we all warned him about. He couldn't express his grief and his sense of betrayal. And, as so many other guys do, he got drunk, then he punched out the side-view mirror of a car and lost the feeling in his hand. If he could have articulated his grief, he wouldn't have done this. And that always struck me: that I was not going to be one of these repressed, corked guys that will store up rage and anger and then just explode.

So, when I was in high school, I took Latin, and that brought me in touch with mythology and the classics. I was predisposed to the Romantic Movement, to Coleridge, Wordsworth, Keats, Shelly. Byron was one of my heroes, an absolute madman, and I was very comfortable there. I celebrated their disdain for structure to some extent, and also their fascination with the creative force. Keats especially had a big influence on me. You know, he boxed, he was a nurse, he got TB, he had this frustrating relationship with this lover that didn't turn out the way he'd hoped, and he ended up dying in Italy. I think I was just drawn to that, and it stayed with me.

All this led me into the world of myth, which opened a template for inner harmony, and harmony with everything outside of yourself. And that became my preoccupying thought when I was teaching in John Dewey High School. And then, of course, I found Jung, who gave me a sense of spirituality that took me right out of any parochialism that lingered from my past, and all of a sudden I was on fire. And Joseph Campbell also had an incredible influence on me.

When I look back, I see four streams in my life that I believe were not orchestrated by me. With these four streams came the possibility of a Council for Unity. One was my background with wise guys, which I still have, with some people from my past. My passion for myth. Group dynamics. And organizational development. Those four streams, if one of them were missing, there wouldn't be a Council for Unity.

RC: It's fascinating that "wise guys" is one of the streams. Tell me about that.

RD: I would see a close friend from high school who was connected, and he would always say to me, "Listen, if anybody ever has any problems with you; you call me, you understand?" When I was younger, my crew got into a real, serious beef with another crew, which was one of the most violent gangs in Brooklyn. And it was going to be Armageddon. So we had this big meeting. We can't not go to this social event, it was a dance, because they would have hunted us down. So we had to go, and basically we were going to catch it. We were discussing what we were going to do; it was like a war council.

"You know," I said, "I got this connection, a 'bad guy,' who always told me that if I ever needed help, I should call."

So they were like: "What are you waiting for? Call him! Otherwise, we're going to get killed!"

I got to thinking: you know, I don't want to get *him* killed. But I called him and told him the problem. He pulled up in a big black Cadillac with five other guys, and let's just say they made that problem go away. Then I started hanging out with him and his crew and, at one point, I really thought about the possibility of getting into that lifestyle. One of the great expressions that comes out of their mouths is: "Hey. We're crime. And crime don't pay." Basically, the translation is: They don't pay for anything. They don't pay for drinks, they don't pay for ... I mean, that's the way it was. Plus, all the women you could imagine, and power. They took crime and raised it to an art form. They kill somebody: no gun, no motive, no body. Huge political influence back in the day. And I mean, for a kid like me, that was a green light. But the more I got involved, the more I saw it was more about money than honor. And I went through a betrayal that I never really recovered from.

Then a guy that I idolized, who was about ten years older, who knew he was going to go, for some reason – Rob, why he picked me out of a crew of fifty guys, I will never know – but he basically made me a project: to get me out before he died. He would introduce me to ex-offenders who were in their mid-thirties, and they all looked like they were seventy. *Done.* Done time, every other tooth missing, unemployable, dealing drugs. That was my mirror. So, this was pretty horrifying.

RC: He gave you a vision of what the future held as a gang member.

RD: Absolutely. Like in *A Christmas Carol*, but with a different application. So, when he passed, I made a promise to him that I'd take his lead.

RC: The influence of the wise guys was to show you what *not* to do.

RD: Absolutely. When we created the Council, we looked at what drew us to criminal lifestyles and to … well, with me, the Mob. And with them, street gangs. You know, there's a fifty-percent divorce rate in this country. When I saw group dynamics, I realized: the overwhelming majority of kids in this country have holes in them the size of craters. And nothing is addressing them. They're surrounded by impersonality, rampant materialism: you are what you wear; money's more important than people; sex is more important than love. They either explode and fuck people up, or they implode and get self-destructive.

So, the need for family, and for being connected to something, was a driving force. That's what wise guys do; that's what gangs do. If I didn't have that awareness, and if I didn't go through the same sort of betrayals that they did, there wouldn't have been any connection there. So, this idea that we joined something that forced us to commit a criminal act to get the benefit of a family, and that robbed us of our free will, was something that had to be experienced viscerally. The fact that I could articulate what this was like, and then have them share this same disappointment, was profound.

The other thing we wanted was to be safe. We wanted security, which is the main reason why I got hooked up. But the reality is, you're not guaranteed safety; you're guaranteed *retaliation*. The engine of violence is fueled by strike and counterstrike, so it never ends. Ultimately we realized that, in this lifestyle, not only were we not safe; we were paranoid. You don't know if you're going home today.

Plus, there's this idea of: if you're really going to be hardcore, you can't live for tomorrow. Otherwise, you won't be a gangster. If you're going to carry a gun, you can't fear death. In fact, in a lot of ways, you have to be in *love* with death. Because, number one, death frees you. And number two, if you don't fear death, you're a very dangerous person. I've heard guys say, "I don't give a fuck if I live or die; I'll come back here, I will kill you, your fucking family ..." I mean, that's the mentality. So, we realized that the other item in the brochure, "Hey, come and join us; you'll be safe," was a crock of shit.

RC: You realized that a choice needed to be made between belonging to something negative, or belonging to something positive. One of the things I was going to discuss with you is how the *unity* of what the Romantics called "cosmic consciousness," and the individual's link with something grander and more transcendent, are all quintessential Romantic themes ...

RD: Yes!

RC: And so, I found it interesting that "unity" also appears in the title of your project, which is about bringing an end to those things that separate us.

RD: Yes, I got that from Keats! They actually had this thing called necessitarianism, negative capability, but one of the things they believed in was an evolutionary consciousness that was afoot in the world. And that the French Revolution and the American Revolution were applications of that. And Blake portrayed this in his own mythology. I once wrote a paper on his *Four Zoas*, which, my God, if that didn't anticipate Jung, I don't know what did.

RC: You could see how Jung took his entire theory of the four psychological types right out of the *Four Zoas*.

RD: Right out of the *Four Zoas*, yes! [Naming all four Zoas:] Urizen, Urthona, Luvah, Tharmas.

RC: Before Jung, there were many other people besides Blake that had a fourfold ...

RD: The *quaternity!** I mean, it's right there.

RC: Yes, that had a fourfold psychological system or *quaternity*. But what Blake also anticipated, besides this fourfoldedness, was that when one psychological function – like, for example, thinking, which Blake calls Urizen, or "your reason" – usurps the psychic energy from the other functions, there is a revolt against it.

RD: There is a crumbling.

RC: Yes, a crumbling or a reversal to the opposite. And I'm convinced that Jung stole this directly from Blake, you know? [Laughs]

RD: Oh, without a doubt! And that whole thing, Blake's view of the world as an inversion: where all things anointed by the monarchy, and what the church would call "heaven," were actually evil. He was the first poet to celebrate sexuality as a godly force.* His idea of the fall was that, when God saw that his material creation was something separate from himself, he fell into those four entities, and he basically sees what goes on in the cosmos as being mimicked here. At the end of the *Four Zoas*, when the four energies are uniting with their female selves and then uniting together, he sees the French and American revolutions as moving in exactly the same direction.

I also read *Fearful Symmetry*, by Northrop Frye. It was one of the most profound things I ever read about an interpretation of Blake's vision.

RC: Ah, the great literary critic!

RD: Yes, a really great literary critic. I found him as challenging as Blake. He takes you through the provenience of Blake's thought and through his mythology. As you read this, you're like: "My God! If Carl Jung read this, and I don't know if he did, this totally anticipates his work.

RC: In Jung's *Psychological Types*, there's only one footnote in the book to Blake, but I think it's a red herring footnote, because he simply mentions something about how Blake's work anticipates the notion of introversion and extroversion.* But he doesn't go anywhere near the *Four Zoas*. I know from reading biographies that, whenever the subject of Blake came up, Jung would get into an emotional tizzy, denigrating Blake.

RD: You're kidding!

RC: I've seen this in biographies of other artists as well. When their true influence gets mentioned, they often get upset. They want to steer you away from it; they don't want you to realize how influenced they were.

RD: "Me thinks the lady protests too much"!

RC: Exactly. Picasso had a similar reaction regarding the poet Baudelaire. Baudelaire had an essay on the modern artist, "The Painter of Modern Life," and it was very influential on Picasso, but he'd try to steer people away from it.* So, Jung was certainly aware of Blake, but he had a very peculiar reaction whenever the subject came up.

RD: When I was in graduate school, nobody wanted to go near Blake with a ten-foot pole.

RC: In France, Blake remains virtually unknown, because the culture there still deifies reason.

RD: The French worship Edgar Allen Poe, and you would think Blake would be, you know, ten dimensions beyond that. I don't get it.

RC: The French Enlightenment was largely a deification of reason, and Blake's appreciation of intuition and pure vision, of gnostic vision, goes against this.

RD: Yes, absolutely. There was a fascinating book, another piece of literary criticism by this guy named Erdman called *Blake: Prophet Against Empire*. And Blake really was an amazing gadfly, a real character. One of my professors told me that Blake used to go into his garden with his wife, naked, and read from Milton's *Paradise Lost*, where Adam and Eve are having sex.* I mean, what a character. Plus, his art …

RC: Oh, his art is incredible!

RD: Yes. I mean, I should go back and revisit all this. My friends used to call me "Orc," because Orc was the revolutionary and rebellious force in Blake's mythology. But to see the personality in all its conflicting dynamics and then go from that into the Tao, the I Ching, the Vedas, and all of a sudden you're looking at a kind of cosmic awareness of the direction the human personality has to move to, and how it must be harmonized. And when it isn't … I mean, when I wrote *Chrysallia*, it was basically a response to two thousand years of the supremacy of the obsessive male need for control, for the obsession with intolerance, and with a Darth Vader kind of order to the universe. A motivation of greed, decisions never made from compassion, and the demonization of women. I'm looking at the consequences of those two thousand years, and I had to make Chrysallia into an icon who was the antidote to Darth Veda. There he is with a light saber, and I gave Chrysallia a Buddhist flower.

One of the great things Campbell said was that, when Buddha was trying to illustrate a point, he held up a flower, and his followers *got* it. And the flower is also a major force in *Gilgamesh*, because it contains the secret to eternity. It dies, and it's born again. All these mythological motifs just came, channeled through me, and I wrote it. And the Council for Unity has one of the greatest mythologies of any entity that I know of.

RC: I've often thought that Jung's work with archetypes could be considered as an expression of the Romantic Movement in psychology.

RD: Yes.

RC: But what you do goes beyond mere psychotherapy, because you've created an alternative social structure that offers direct initiatory experience.

RD: Yes. Even in prisons.

RC: It verges more on the teaching of Joseph Campbell, who believed that the new message would be found neither in traditional psychology nor in organized religion but in creative, artistic expression. The Council is a cultural creation that offers practical coaching and support rather than mere psychiatric indoctrination.

RD: Absolutely. But the Council also, in very subtle ways, takes our participants on a therapeutic journey. The precursor to *Chrysallia* is a six-page dragon-slayer myth that every kid in the Council identifies with. I made the hero just like them: abandoned, negatively conceived …

RC: And you do that through the ritual you've created, rather than sitting them in front of a psychiatrist once a week.

RD: Myth and ritual: that's a tandem you really can't separate. And if a ritual doesn't emanate from a myth, the myth will have limited power. So, each kid goes through seven steps to become a dragon slayer. In the process, he rises from the lowest rung of the ladder in his society to becoming a prince. Those seven things that he does are crystallized in the myth on only six pages. Whether it's gang members or kids in the third grade, they all have dragons. They all know that if they don't face their dragon, someone else will be driving their bus. And they know they can't kill the dragon by themselves, or that they can't even *see* it, and others can.

So, in this collective sense of conjoining to face your personal dragon with the help of others, and through the skill sets and the mythology of Council, you do that. We've had kids create dragon effigies. And Sheepshead Bay was one of the biggest gang schools we had. They took their dragon to Coney Island and burned it. In facing the dragon, they created visual panels where they were totally overwhelmed and minimized in the first panel. And, as they go through the Council process, in the final panel, they've killed it. Now, they're bigger than the dragon. That's the therapeutic journey.

You don't want to see the thing that controls your life. Then you seek help, and the therapist turns the light on in the cellar of your psyche. You scream like hell, because you're confronting the thing that's ruining your life. If the therapy works, you come back up, and that force no longer controls you. Council's mythology follows that therapeutic journey to a T.

When we have our ritual on May 29, 2015, which reflects the entire network, the Council procession will be led by two individuals: one's carrying a sword, the other's carrying a mask. Those are the two dragon slayer weapons. The mask, because it's so powerful that, when you stare through it, it bears laserlike beams. The hero used the mask to burn out the eyes of the dragon, which petrified everybody else.

When kids see the original dragon slayers of Council leading this procession, their hair stands up. At the end of the myth, there's a dragon slayer who becomes king, who wants to leave a legacy, and he takes all the boys and girls past the boundaries that keep them in, and that kept him in, and he brings them to the cave where he found his sword and mask. And the story ends with: He knew there would be other weapons, with their ability to slay the dragons that the children would surely have to face. All they had to do was pass through the dark entrance, which is what he did.

Picture this: there are fifteen hundred kids from every conceivable culture. It's seeing what the world needs to become tomorrow, today. The two youngest kids in the program, the youngest boy and the youngest girl, come forward in the middle of the dance floor in front of these kids. They all read the story; the myth is alive. They get anointed by the dragon slayers with the sword and the mask, then they hand the sword and mask over to the two kids, who do a four-corner salute. Half the place is in tears. The myth is alive. We've got a myth that works. And it's profound. It affects murderers in prison to kids in the fourth grade. Everybody's got a dragon, and everybody's got to face it.

We also do group dynamics. First, we have them deal with the dragon within themselves; then they have to look at the dragon in the group. The dragon does not want them to form the Council for Unity family. If the family gets created and they learn the behaviors to make that work, the dragon's going to lose his power.

So they realize, in the next phase of this, that the dragon is really the ego, and they must annihilate the ego to get the family that they want. Then they go to social consciousness: the dragon in the school. Now, they're looking at external dragons that render systems ineffective. And then, the dragon in the community.

They are going through – here comes the quaternity again – a four-point process where they transform personally. Then they become activists and advocates for change. It's amazing.

RC: They don't actually annihilate the ego, but they transform the ego, right? They annihilate the old, inadequate ruling values of the ego.

RD: I mean, the minute you stop being a biological egocentric being is the beginning of your maturity: your escape from the prison of the self.

RC: So, it's ego*tism* that's annihilated.

RD: Right. I mean, I could split hairs with them, but they wouldn't get it. But this idea of putting themselves first, to be defensive, to be resisting, to not accepting constructive criticism or apologizing for bad behavior … You're not going to get the family you want if you hold onto that egocentricity. So they know: we have to park our egos, or we're not going to get the family.

When you mention all this stuff, you're really forcing me to revisit it. My kids are not going through the journey that we went through, but they seem to have arrived at the same psychological place, without all the constructs and all the exposure.

As Namaste has it, "The god in me sees the god in you." My kids come from every conceivable background. And when they're together, from Buffalo to Riverhead, their perception of one another reminds me of a comment that Joseph Campbell made to Bill Moyers when Moyers was interviewing him. Moyers says, "How do you experience this thing you call God? I mean, I'm a Southern Baptist, but myth has made me much more tolerant. I see the same questions; I see the same answers. How about you?" And Campbell looks at him and says, "You're looking at it. So am I." I cried for ten minutes. I mean, that's *it*. If that's what you see when you open your eyes, that the same light in you is shining back at you, you inherit a different world.

My kids react to one another like that, because they've gone through the Council mythology. And you know what they realize? That in unity, they're safe. And in unity, nobody's making fun of them anymore. So, instead of a preachy cosmic view of why we should all be connected, to them it's a very practical principle. If we're all together, there's nobody left to fight, and there's nobody left to make fun of. That's the level that they're on.

RC: They're experiencing it directly, through their feeling. It's not a cerebral, detached sort of thing.

RD: Yes, right. Fascinating.

RC: Let's talk about your background. When you and I first met, you were teaching at John Dewey, which was probably the most innovative high school in America at that time; would you agree?

RD: It was, without a doubt. The greatest experiment on the secondary level in the twentieth century.

RC: In my junior or senior year, which would mean 1973 or 1974, I was a student in your mythology class, and you were using Jung's *Man and His Symbols* as one of the textbooks. Even today, I think it would be rare to find that in a high school. I don't think anyone else in any high school in America was teaching *Man and His Symbols*.

RD: I was nuts!

RC: It was a wonderful thing for me to see. I'd already read the book, but until then I'd felt completely isolated in my interest in Jung. Now, of course, things have changed; there are many more people interested in archetypal psychology.

RD: The other thing which was great was his case studies on dreams, and the fact that myths and dreams are twins coming from the same collective unconscious parent. When I was teaching myth, we were looking at the manifestations of the unconscious through dreams. Dreams that anticipate the future, dreams that deal with issues of falling, and flying, and, you know …

RC Universal themes.

RD: Yes. Ultimately, I was trying to get my students to realize: If these messages have this profound information that's available to us, and all we have to do is learn another language – because these things aren't literal, they're symbolic – and we can understand that, then the windows of perception are accessible. And ultimately, I was able to get them to examine the conventional view of God and to see the collective unconscious as the psychological construct for what God supposedly does. That this thing is *in* them, and it's telegraphing every day.

RC: As Blake says, When the doors of perception are cleansed, man will see the world as it is, infinite.

RD: Yes.

RC: Again, a theme of unity.

RD: Yes, a theme of unity.

RC: Another remarkable thing about John Dewey was that, although it was a racially "mixed" institution, there was very little racial tension within the school itself in the early Seventies.

RD: Well, it started in '75. One of my original members saved an article from the high school newspaper, the *Vanguard*, about intruders coming into the building and assaulting students. They were outsiders, but students in Dewey were letting them in.

There was a festering Italian-black conflict that existed in the community. You had the Marlboro Housing Project on one side, and a big organized crime presence on the other side of Stillwell Avenue, from 86th Street. It was right out of *Saturday Night Fever*.*

RC: In 1982, Willie Turks, an African-American transit worker, was beaten to death by a mob of Italian-Americans led by a self-described "unemployed weightlifter" named Gino Bova. Although the judge in Bova's trial said there was a lynch mob that night on Avenue X and that "the only thing missing was a rope and a tree," she sentenced him to only five to fifteen years, of which he served less than eight. In 1989, a sixteen-year old named Yusef Hawkins ...

RD: Yes, Joey Fama killed Yusef Hawkins.

RC: ... was shot twice in the chest and murdered for the same reason: for being black in Bensonhurst. This was the sort of atmosphere you were working with when you decided to become a peace mediator at John Dewey, located at 50 Avenue X. Describe how you managed to turn all that around. This is what I'm really fascinated by. How did you figure all this out? You had experience being in a gang, but you had no experience as a peace mediator between gangs.

RD: Actually, I did, Rob. When I was teaching in East New York Vocational High School in the Sixties, the riots in the aftermath of Dr. King's assassination, the Kennedy assassination, the Civil Rights Movement, led to some really horrific conflicts between and among groups. On the one hand, you had this whole flower-power motif where you could go to Central Park on any given Sunday and hang out with kids from every race, color, and creed. And drink wine, smoke pot, and listen to music. And on the other end of it, you had the Black Panthers, the Young Lords; you had a lot of radical groups on campus.

When I was in East New York High School, the population was Jewish, Italian, Black, and Latino. They were protesting every other day. They went out and rioted; they burned cars. I knew every kid in the building; I loved them, and I knew all the bad boys. And normally, all the bad boys gravitated to me.

One day, the school was surrounded. The principal was going crazy. He was newly appointed; he was on probation, and he realized that if the kids didn't come back in the building, and if this hit the press, he was dead. So, he sent out everybody he could: the dean, the guidance counselors, but the kids ran them back into the school. Finally, the dean said, "Listen, there's only one guy here who can get those kids back in," and it was me.

I had no intention of doing that, because I was with them. They were revolting because it was a vocational school, and the curriculum was antiquated. The student government was made up of handpicked white kids. They felt they were being negatively stereotyped. They were radicalized in a lot of ways, and they wanted to see change.

So he asked me if I could go out and get them back in. And I said, "Why should I?" I said, "I'll tell you what. I'll go out there and get them. But when they come back in, you're going to get a different school, because I know exactly what their demands are." And I went through everything: "I want a new curriculum; I want creativity ..." I mean, we took that antiquated model, and we turned it upside down.

Rob, one of the greatest moments of my life: I walk outside, the school is surrounded. You've got these three guys on bullhorns, a white guy, a black guy, and a Puerto Rican whom everyone called Napoleon. And I walked out, and eighteen hundred fists went straight up in the air with a roar. Because they knew that, if I went out, I would never fuck them. So we met for an hour, then we walked back in.

Then I got a Wall Street firm to donate a brand-new English curriculum. My kids were sitting around in circles, deciphering the dreams in *Siddhartha* and how they reflected some of Jung's archetypes. And of course, we ended up on the front page of the magazine section of the *Sunday News*, which ultimately got me to Dewey.

So, I created the prototype for the Council for Unity in this thing called Students United. And it was glorious. It was like being back in the nineteenth century. And they *wrote!* We had this literary arts magazine called *Renaissance.* If you ever want to learn about the Sixties, you could read those four volumes. It's all personal ...

RC: I was going to say, this could only have happened in the glorious 1960s.

RD: *Only*. Without a doubt. When I came to Dewey in 1970, Students United came there on my second day, ready to kill anybody on campus who broke my balls. [Laughs] I said, "Get out of here! I'm going to lose my job!" you know?

So I created Council as an outgrowth of all this. And an article in the school newspaper, the *Vanguard*, it dates us – it's the only thing we have in writing – as beginning in 1975. It dates the formation of the Council to deal with all this racial discord. I could send you an email from this guy, Gil Ramos, who was representing the Puerto Ricans. All the Italians from across the street and from nearby Lafayette High School came down to Dewey to take out the Puerto Ricans. They almost kicked a kid's eye out. They're going for chains and bats, and they're going to confront the Italians at the gate, in the rear parking lot. I got wind of this, and I rounded up all the Italians that were with me, and with Council for Unity, and everybody else I could get my hands on. And, as Gil tells the story: "We're ready to go, and I hear a voice behind me saying, 'If you fuck with them, you fuck with us.' I turned round, and I saw Mr. De Sena with about fifty Italian kids, and that changed my life forever. When I realized they were willing to go to bat to protect us, I had to join the Council."

And you know where we had the sit-down? A hundred Latino, Italian, and black kids in the back of a restaurant in Bensonhurst that was run by "associated guys." They sponsored a free lunch, and we made the peace. They also sponsored our first induction in there.

RC: The connected guys sponsored the first Council for Unity induction?

RD: Absolutely. And it gets even more interesting. They gave us the back room and the band shell. And the bar was perpendicular to where we were, so they couldn't see all the kids seated, but they could see them, one by one, as they came up to the stage and shared their journey in Council, and what it meant, and how it transformed them, and how they viewed the world differently. And so, as we're having the induction, all these wise guys are listening to this!

RC: How do you go into a jail such as Riverhead, with guys that are totally hardcore, and not only get the trust of somebody like that but also help him to get in touch with his more sensitive side, which is what you've told me you do. How do you accomplish that?

RD: Well, first off, there's a reality here that is unavailable to the public. They are in hell. They've had their humanity ripped out of them. They're in prison, and they've been abandoned by this "thing" of theirs that they gave their loyalty to. Now, nobody's writing to them; nobody's putting any money in their commissary; nobody's helping their family. This is very disconcerting. The other thing is that, as men, they are required to wear a mask: to muffle, suppress, and mask the agony, the disappointment, and the tragedy of their journey.

When I come in and roll out Council, and talk about how we created an antidote to gang culture, when I talk to them about the life, and talk about the thing that we joined and the promise of a family, and then go through the fact that, when somebody forces you to commit a criminal act, that's neither a family nor love – when somebody robs you of your free will, that's not what families do – what are they going to do, argue with me? It's the fucking truth.

Council's based on family, unity, self-esteem, and empowerment. Again, we're back to Jung and the quaternity, but in a different way. I just take the four negatives of that: "You were promised safety, you ended up being paranoid." They're not going to argue with that either. "Council's concept to deal with safety is unity. You're in this prison, you're in hell, and all your enemies are here. And to compound the fact that you've lost your freedom, this environment that you've created, this environment of conflict, just compounds the hell you're in. But if you all join Council, you've got a new ecology in this prison. It won't be one of conflict. Now, you can take advantage of programs, you can take advantage of education, because your other needs are being met." So, as we roll out the Council's ethos and bump it up against the negative world that they're in, the transformation occurs. Now, this is the best part: they're *dying* to take that mask off.

If I take you to prison, you will hear new members being engaged by the Council. Of course, they want to know what's this thing is like. And, to a man, without any prompting from me, the members explain: "This is a place where you can come to take your mask off and be yourself. We're all going through the same shit. As you're going to find out, the Council's a family. And it will help you to grow, to develop, and to change. And you're going to learn a new way of behaving."

So, we've introduced a female value system – and if I ever said this, I'd get popped – into a very hard, cruel world of men. The value system is to be vulnerable, to be sensitive, to be transparent. To be open, to be authentic. I use Joseph Campbell: the most heroic thing the hero ever does in the modern world is to be himself. We get into a whole big thing about what this means, and we assign a heroic quality to it. To give compassion, to seek it. And you know what? They're *starving* for it. It's no great fucking trick. This is what they're starving for.

The founders of the Council for Unity in 2007 were a thousand times more violent than the founders in '75. And in every gang school we've ever had, from Columbus High School to Sheepshead Bay, they all have come over. In that newspaper article that I sent you, you'll see that one of the guys – one of the toughest guys in the prison – is crying. It's the first time he cried in years.

RC: You don't use words like "female value system," but you speak directly to their feeling, using different words, and, in the end, get them there anyway.

RD: Yes. It's the Romantic Era in a lot of ways: acknowledging your emotionality. And we talk about it. I use the metaphor of a pressure cooker. It's like thermodynamics. If you put water in a pressure cooker, turn the heat up, and close the valve, that motherfucker's going to pop. If you're repressed and you can't share your grief or your tragedies, you're going to explode or implode. And so, we're the valve in the pressure cooker, and we're inviting them to be themselves. And they are starving for that to occur. But if you were to exhibit those behaviors on the outside, you would be called a "fucking pussy." Because a "pussy" is sensitive, and vulnerable, and transparent. And, as a result, you're not going to act that way or be that way.

If you look at the guys who come into Council, whether it's a gang school or in prison, and see them day one and then see them two months later, you'd think you were looking at another species. They transform. It's a hard thing to get a grip on unless you see it.

RC: Again, you're able to do something a psychologist can't do, because you offer a holistic myth and ritual.

RD: And a tribe. You know, another thing, again, you talk about literature and its impact: I'm in graduate school, in American lit. I had to read de Tocqueville's *Democracy in America*. And one of the things that became clear in defining us as a culture was this obsession with rugged individualism. It defined the American. He wants to be free to move and to pursue his entrepreneurial goals without any restriction. The American has a basic hatred of government and a basic mistrust of government. And the American sense of freedom is more personal than collective. One of the conclusions he came to, he said that, if they are taken to extreme, this people will have difficulty coming to community and could easily fall into faction. And even worst, to anonymity. And that certainly has occurred. To be in this country is to be anonymous. You go into these huge – even luxury – apartments, you're lucky if you know three people on your floor.

RC: It's the antithesis of unity; it's separation.

RD: It's about leaving the small town, where everybody knows my business, to coming into the anonymity of the city, where I'm free to do whatever I want. But God forbid I have a problem, where do you go? So, the Council is the new tribe.

RC: Joseph Campbell would have loved what you're doing.

RD: I had a conversation with Bill Moyers. I was in San Domenico restaurant, very chichi, a lot of media types hang out in there, right across from Central Park South. I was meeting with my lawyer about getting custody of my son. And who's in there but Bill Moyers, having dinner with a colleague, a woman. Anyway, I paid the bill, and we were getting ready to leave. As I'm walking past his table, I said, "I just want to thank you for the Campbell tapes. And I want you to know that I use mythology to get kids out of gangs." So he says to me, "Sit down."

So now, I'm sitting at his table, and he goes into this whole big thing that, in the *Power of Myth*, Campbell talked about how gangs themselves use mythology. When you look at rituals in primitive societies, a prepubescent male would be circumcised and would have to commit a heroic act of killing an enemy or a dangerous animal. Then he would be tattooed, pierced, or scarred, and he goes back to the tribe physically and psychologically different because of this rite of passage.

And that's what gangs are doing today. You are going to have to get "physical-ed" in, or you're going to slice somebody's face open and give him a hundred and fifty stitches. If it's the Mob, you're going to have to put a cap in somebody. The point is that gangs are subliminally reexperiencing primitive puberty rites, which are imprinted. And that the gang has replaced the father as the medium to bring young men into manhood in our society.

RC: That's a very important point. Speaking of which, tell me about your own father. What did he do for a living?

RD: He was a projectionist. He got me a job working at the 1964 World's Fair. He was at the Bell System Pavilion. None of the guys in the union knew who I was. They had a huge crew there, because they were working all these different animations, and there were a lot of conflicts. They would get into a whole big thing, a big conflict, a big argument. But instead of going to the shop steward, they'd consult with my father. Most of them were Italian. They used to call him *la legge,* which means "the law." Because he would never lie, and he was totally honest.

He had a different experience as an Italian-American, because he was alone, on his own, at sixteen, and he lived with other cultures. He was a lot more open than the typical Italian, who would look at anybody different as a "stranger." His father died and, by the time he was sixteen, he was living in a boarding house in Bensonhurst that was owned by Jews. When he got rheumatic fever, they nursed him back to health. But he had a lonely journey.

RC: He had a broad experience with people.

RD: Yes, but he was all alone! I mean, my father's intolerance for a lack of ambition … He wrote me off, since I'd picked that lifestyle. It was like, "This kid don't want a father, so fuck him; he doesn't get one." And I don't blame him.

RC: Bobby, how does *Zorba the Greek* fit into all this?

RD: Ah! I have so many thing to tell you! I'll tell you how I used *Zorba.* When I was teaching in East New York Vocational and dealing with gangs, and after I'd gotten all those guys to come back into the building, we began to reconstruct the academic portion of the school. So I'm saying to myself, "What am I going to teach these kids to break the power of the group on their behavior?" And then the lights went on: *Zorba!* Because Zorba will not be subsumed by anybody. So, the more they became enamored with Zorba, the more they were flicking the switch away from the need for approval and away from being controlled by the other. Then I took them to see the movie, which blew them away. We did the book, and I had every kid pick an anecdote in the story that they felt touched them and celebrated a man who was totally authentic because he wouldn't allow anybody else to define him.

I had this literary arts class that was charged with one of those demands of changing the school. None of them had ever written before, and I'd never taught creative writing. I said to them, "You know, I'm not going to let you write anything yet." "Hey, what do you mean?" "I'll tell you why. I don't believe that any of you are free and without restrictions based on what your friends think. So, first we're going to do *Zorba*, and then I'll take measure of how far you've come along."

Of course, they saw the end of the movie. They knew the book backwards and forwards. I made them dress up, and I took them to see the play. During the intermission, they were talking with these Upper East Side ladies who thought my kids were from some elite prep school, because they were comparing the novel to the movie to the play. And brilliantly done.

So now, they're like: "OK, so what's the final?" I came in with a record player and the sound track of the film. They're looking at me like, "What the fuck are you doing?" And I said, "Here's your final. I know you know the book backwards and forwards. I know you would ace any test that I gave you. But that's not what I'm looking for. I need to see if you're free, the way Zorba is."

At the end of the movie, after the catastrophe, Kazantzakis says to Zorba, "Teach me to dance, will you?" And Zorba goes, "Come on, my boy." That was the apocalyptic moment. Zorba knew that he had poured what he had to into this man that he loved and had made him free. So I said, "Your final exam is to get up, either alone or with somebody else, and dance. Then I put the music on. Zorba's song.

And one by one, they got up, they formed a circle, and they did Zorba's dance. And I'm screaming at them in Greek, "*Yassou lavendi!*"* They jumped up on desks; it was this barbaric yawp, and that did it for me. They were not afraid. They didn't give a fuck what anybody thought. I was screaming at those kids, because I felt they had reached the point of madness. It's like ... when the demon in you is on fire. And I said, "Now, you can write." And that's how I used *Zorba*.

RC: What an amazing story! There's a great line in there where Zorba tells Kazantzakis: "Ah, if only you could dance all that you've just said, then I'd understand." Remember that?

RD: Yes. And he says, "I look at you, and your chest is mute. So are your arms. They say nothing. I don't believe you." That's the last thing he says: "I like you too much not to tell you. You've got everything but one thing: madness. A man needs a little bit of madness, or he never dares cut the rope and be free."

RC: That's so true.

RD: The kids in my class had Zorba's statements stenciled all around the room. "Life is trouble, only death is not." "A man needs a little madness or he'll never be free." All these statements surrounding them, every one was an encouragement to do what Campbell said you *must* do in a world with a crippling system. You must be *authentic*. And Zorba was an invitation to be authentic. He was in the *now*. And he didn't have to go through a complicated, convoluted protocol to get there.

RC: Which is the antithesis of so many traditional religious systems, which preach all sorts of secret knowledge and convoluted, abstruse dictums. But it's really just about being in the miracle of the moment, being in the stream of life, and nothing more.

RD: Absolutely. Zorba's breakthroughs, philosophically, are as profound as anybody who has studied genius from the classics up to now. He lives in the moment; he sees everything every day as if it's for the first time. That's totally Eastern. That's Zen. He's completely authentic, and he lives his life on his own inner dynamic. He does not make distinctions through the accidents of race or culture. He's arrived at these conclusions, and he's an *illiterate!* I mean, that blew me away.

RC: He lives through his heart; he doesn't need to give names to things.

RD: So there it is. Reflecting those things, then inviting kids to react was, for them, an invitation to be allowed to see things differently.

---

* Jung believed that the elemental structure of the psyche was symbolized by a fourfold structure, especially a quadrated circle or mandala, and that such images signify wholeness and promote healing.

* In his "Proverbs of Hell," Blake writes: "The head Sublime, the heart Pathos, the genitals Beauty, the hands & feet Proportion." Author June Singer refers to this as "Blake's first quaternity of man." June Singer, *The Unholy Bible: A Psychological Interpretation of William Blake* (New York: G.P. Putnam's Sons, 1970), p. 88.

* In paragraph 460 of *Psychological Types* (originally published in 1921), Jung writes, "The English mystic William Blake says: 'These two classes of men are always upon earth ... the Prolific and the Devouring.... Religion is an endeavor to reconcile the two.'" As his source, Jung cites "The Marriage of Heaven and Hell," *The Complete Writings of William Blake* (ed. Keynes), p. 155. According to biographer Frank McLynn, in 1948, "After reading the more difficult Blake texts Jung was prepared to accord him a place in the pantheon along with Dante, Goethe, Wagner and Nietzsche as an artist dealing with true archetypal mythological material." McLynn, *Carl Gustav Jung* (New York: St. Martin's Press, 1997), p. 468. But Jung cites Blake only a handful of times in his later writings, and nowhere in his twenty-volume *Collected Works* is there any mention of the *Four Zoas*. Referencing the Blake scholar Kathleen Raine, McLynn adds: "some critics suggest that in terms of the 'individuation process' Blake's view is more thoroughly Jungian than that of Jung himself." Ibid.

* The renowned Picasso biographer John Richardson has this to say about Baudelaire's influence on Picasso: "Baudelaire's challenge ... would be taken up by the painter of tomorrow, Picasso. Not that the artist ever admitted to doing anything of the sort. The more crucial the source, the more determined he was to divert attention from it. Daix confirms this: whenever Baudelaire's name came up in conversation, Picasso would switch the subject to Matisse, as if the poet were his rival's private property. In my experience strategies of this nature were usually a sign that Picasso had something to hide." John Richardson, *A Life of Picasso. Volume II: 1907-1917* (London: Random House, 1997), p. 14.

* *Saturday Night Fever* (1977), a film directed by John Badham, was set in Brooklyn's Italian-American neighborhoods.

* *Yassou* is a form of greeting or farewell (similar to "aloha") and is etymologically related to *Steen iya sou*, roughly translated as: "To your health." *Lavendi* is a slang term meaning "handsome young man." When used as a greeting between men, it can serve as a compliment regarding one's prowess as a ladies' man or simply to suggest that one's companion is a "good fellow."

'When Feeling is First.' A Conversation with Christopher Sawyer-Lauçanno About E. E. Cummings's Prose Masterpiece, *The Enormous Room*.*

I first met Christopher Sawyer-Lauçanno in the summer of 1990 in Paris, where we conducted an interview about his book, The Continual Pilgrimage. *Since then, he's become a cherished friend and literary mentor, guiding my interest into areas I might not otherwise have explored. The lure has always been his passion and enthusiasm for literature and language: one that a reader finds delightfully infectious. A former creative-writing professor at MIT and a widely published poet, he's also the author of* E. E. Cummings: A Biography, The Continual Pilgrimage: American Writers in Paris, 1944-1960, *and* An Invisible Spectator, A Biography of Paul Bowles. *His translations from the Spanish, French, and ancient Mayan have appeared in numerous publications, including the City Lights editions of* The Destruction of the Jaguar: Poems from the Books of Chilam Balam *and* Concerning the Angels, *a translation of the poems of Rafael Alberti.*

The year 2022 marks the hundredth anniversary of Cummings's avant-garde World War One memoir. Besides remaining enduringly modern, The Enormous Room *continues to pose essential questions about free speech in a post-9/11 world.*

Rob Couteau: Tell us about how you first discovered E. E. Cummings via the grasshopper.

Christopher Sawyer-Lauçanno: I was fourteen, and, at that time, I was living in Mexico. There were three books in English in the school library. One was the Palgrave's anthology, *Palgrave's Golden Treasury*. The other I can't remember: probably Kipling. And the third, for some reason, was the 1938 *Collected Poems* of E. E. Cummings. I'd never heard of them, but it was in English, and I could read English, so I pulled it off the shelf. The first poem I came to was one of the dirty ones: "may i feel said he."

RC: Ah, that's one of my favorite poems by him. It's so *witty*, isn't it?

CSL: [Laughs] Yes, it's great!

RC: Can you imagine publishing that at that time?

CSL: No! I mean, that was it. Actually, there's an entire manuscript of Cummings's erotic poems that were never published. It's still sitting in Harvard Library. Once, Lawrence Ferlinghetti and I talked about publishing it. And then it kind of dropped off the map, and there were complications with trying to get the permissions, because Norton felt they owned everything of Cummings's, and they were going to do it themselves. Finally, Lawrence said he didn't want to bother with it anymore. But it's still sitting there. And it's far more explicit than any of the things he did publish.

Anyway, I read a few of those, and suddenly I was taken with the entire Cummings position. I mean, I'm fourteen, and it's like he was talking to me. Then I get to "r-p-o-p-h-e-s-s-a-g-r," and I'm going, "What the hell is this?" You know, *rpophessagr!* I kept reading it, and then I got to the end where it says "grasshopper." And I still remember that great sense of *dénouement* while I'm looking at this and going: "Ah, this is a *grasshopper*, hopping across the page! Oh, my God!" It was just a pretty extraordinary find. It was one of those great eureka moments. So, that's how it all began. And then, of course, I sat down and read Cummings more seriously.

RC: Only he could have come up with a poem like this at that time.

CSL: Exactly, yeah.

RC: One of your favorite works by Cummings is "a leaf falls." Tell me why; and how would you recite such a piece that relies so heavily on the *visual* impact of the placement of letters on a page?

CSL: From very early on, Cummings was interested in writing poems for both the *eye* and the *ear*. In many ways, that's a poem for the eye . If you take out the parentheses, I would just read it: "A ... leaf ... falls ... one... 1 ... iness ..." That's what the poem is.

RC: Through pausing.

CSL: Just pausing between the letters, so the leaf can actually cascade down the page. Which is exactly what happens in this poem. And the detachment from the branch, if you will, with the parentheses, of the leaf falling through the air. In my opinion, it's a little minor masterpiece. I love many of Cummings's poems. But I think this one indicates a whole way in which Cummings could take the most simple, even trite image, and make it new. He was extraordinarily good at that.

RC: Particularly with revelations spawned by nature.

CSL: Yes. He was really attached to the natural world.

RC: Some have argued that free verse goes back to John Wycliffe's translation of Psalms, in the 1380s. And besides Walt Whitman, there were other Victorian-era poets who experimented with free verse. There's also the *vers libre* tradition in French poetry, and the innovation of Jules Laforgue in his *Derniers vers*. We also find examples of what was later called "concrete" poetry in Greek Alexandria during the second century B.C. What did Cummings do to take all this a step further?

CSL: Great question. What Cummings basically did was to realize that the line itself was somewhat tyrannical, in the sense that, even with some of the examples you cite, everything begins at the far left margin and moves across the page. The images themselves remain within the poem. And while there's some sense of trying to break it open, there's very little attempt to play with the typography itself.

Cummings didn't know about Apollinaire's *Calligrammes* yet. But when he was first starting to write poetry, he did know of Ezra Pound's, "The Return," which Pound published in 1912. And when that hit Cummings, it hit him hard. I mean, it's an incredible poem in and of itself. But there you have, suddenly, the breaking up of the lines. There's still the remnants of *vers libre* in there, but, all of a sudden, the way the words are arranged on the page mirror the moments within that particular poem. It's a very mysterious poem. I think it's essentially about poetry. But Cummings suddenly gets this idea of: "Wow, look. If I just space in five spaces over from the left, look what happens to the line." And so, he begins to play with that whole idea. This is about 1915. From them on, he's a committed poet of both time and space.

One thing that Cummings was exceedingly aware of is the way something *sounds*. His whole idea of music for the ear: those pauses matter; those spaces matter. You're supposed to stop for a moment, then go on. That's the way he read them; that's the way he thought of them. But also, as a *painter*, Cummings is incredibly aware of the visual display of something on a page. And so, that's also part of what he's after at that particular juncture of his life, when he's just sprung his first major poem, if you will: "in Just." It's got that spacing in order to try to convey a sense of motion and movement, and stopping in the puddle, and all the rest of it.

RC: So much of what we take for granted today in poetry was first explored by Cummings.

CSL: Oh, absolutely, yeah.

RC: And I understand he was also the first to use the ampersand in a poem.

CSL: So far as I can tell. Although Apollinaire does it, too. But in English, yes, Cummings is it.

RC: I wasn't going to mention Apollinaire but, when I first read your book, I kept scratching my head and saying: "But what about Apollinaire? Wasn't he doing a lot of this at the same time?" But then I read, in Richard Kennedy's biography, that Cummings had no contact with Apollinaire, which is why Kennedy didn't explore this parallel.

CSL: Yes. Of course, later on, by the time he gets to Paris, he does become aware of Apollinaire, because Apollinaire is everywhere in the air at that point in France. Right after the war, he is *the* avant-garde poet, and everyone is looking toward him. And the people Cummings began to know at that time were also paying attention to Apollinaire. But Cummings had already started off on his own trajectory. Apollinaire simply reinforced what he was thinking and trying to do at that time.

RC: In 1917, while they were serving in the ambulance corps in Noyon, France, Cummings and his pal William Brown ended up in a detention center at La Ferté-Macé for being a bit too indiscreet in their assessment of the war effort in letters that they wrote to their friends and family back home. You convincingly argue that Cummings crafted a still under-appreciated prose masterpiece called *The Enormous Room*, which chronicles his incarceration there from September 22 to December 19, and which was published in 1922. Why do you so admire this work?

CSL: It's one of the great books of all time. It's certainly a World War One novel. And, in the best spirit of World War One novels, it has very little to do with the war itself.

RC: As you say in your biography – and I love this – it's a war book without a gun going off. That's just amazing, you know?

CSL: That's right, yeah. [Laughs] Of course, it's really an autobiography; it's not a novel. It's his first published book. It's his first foray into major literary prominence. And he essentially manages to tell a story of his own imprisonment but without focusing on himself as the main character. It's an extraordinary feat to pull off an autobiography where you, in fact, are not the protagonist. There *is* no protagonist. The protagonist is the *room* in that book. The protagonist are the people incarcerated there, most of whom were arrested simply because they happened to be in the wrong place at the wrong time. They're foreigners. They're people who said something or other that the French authorities decided was seditious. You know, undoubtedly, there were also some German sympathizers there, too; perhaps there were even spies there. But you'd never know it from Cummings.

And so, what he manages to do in this book is to create a record of what it means to be human in adverse circumstances. He does it in a prose style that is absolutely extraordinary. He captures the speech of the individuals. He writes in the vernacular. He has no problem with throwing

French right alongside English and not translating it. He is lyrical. The images are those of a poet. And yet, the actual book is this remarkable testimony to what is involved with retaining your humanity in the face of very adverse circumstance. The portraits he paints of the people in this particular detention center are real, unflinching, and yet they're noble. They have a nobility about them.

To some degree, Cummings, being the son of a minister, and having a good Harvard education, was well aware of Christian allegory. While he was not a particularly good Christian at that time – nor ever; he'd already begun to distance himself from the Church – the remnants of *Pilgrim's Progress*, and of the allegorical narratives that are so common in Christian literature, are very much a part of that book. And so, what he does is, he creates a modern-day *Pilgrim's Progress*. Although, since it's almost a hundred years old now, it's hard to say "modern day." But at the time, a modern-day *Pilgrim's Progress*. He has the "Delectable Mountains" being four of the outstanding inmates there. "Monsieur le Directeur" is Cummings's name for Bunyan's beast, Apollyon. He talks about himself as a pilgrim. It's all very fun, very humorous at times, and yet there's a very deep story. It's just the total effect of that book, which I first read, I guess, in the late 1960s.

RC: Interesting time to read it.

CSL: Yeah. And it hit me as being one of the great, important books. It's an antiwar book, for sure; and I was antiwar, so it fit perfectly well with that. But it also knocked me out because this was a style I hadn't ever read before. You know, I was pretty naive; I was pretty young. Later on, I discovered all sorts of other writers who did fabulous things with language. And the rhythms in that book are amazing. The way in which he presents these portraits, these scenes of life, absolutely stirred me, because I'd never read anyone who talked about the way life went on in quite this way. There was a realism there, but at the same time he's totally influenced by the Romantics; he's influenced by the Symbolists. And there's a whole way of describing the world that's an Impressionist painting in many, many ways.

RC: The play with language, the stylistic innovation, is unique and far ahead of its time.

CSL: It is. And I think it's totally unappreciated. It's one of the great World War One novels, but I think it's also just one of the great ... I just said "novels," which it's not! It reads like a novel, but it's really an autobiography.

RC: Apparently, Ernest Hemingway also called it one of the great books.

CSL: Yes.

RC: A hard man to please.

CSL: A *very* hard man to please. A very critical man. [Laughs]

RC: Have you a favorite character from *The Enormous Room*?

CSL: Oh, God, it's so hard. I think Jean le Nègre was probably my favorite.

RC: "The Mecca of all female eyes"!

CSL: Yes. I love him. I love his quiet beauty, his serenity. You know, for Cummings, he's kind of a *saint*. He really does an enormous portrayal of him in that book. He becomes this almost otherworldly character who is somehow here on this earth. And it's hard to know exactly what he's in there for; we have no idea. That's one of the great things about this book. We have no idea why anyone is imprisoned. Except for "C" and "B": Cummings and Brown. They're the only ones that we have a back story to.

RC: Jean le Nègre is certainly the warmest character. And I think it's the most engaging chapter in the book.

CSL: Yeah, me too.

RC: He flies so beautifully in the face of all that hyper-rational French Cartesianism that's practiced by his jailers. He remains at one with his emotions and instinctive self, no matter what. He's also a personification of Cummings's notion that we must unlearn everything and attack reality in a pure state of "IS-ness" …

CSL: Definitely, yes.

RC: … unfettered by intellect, and so overflowing with imagination. Cummings says: "He was never perfectly happy unless exercising his inexhaustible imagination."

CSL: Right, exactly! [Laughs] Yeah, I love Jean le Nègre. There are some wonderful characters in that book. I mean, C and B are pretty wonderful in their own regard; Monsieur Auguste; all these folks are just extraordinary.

RC: It's rare that Cummings unleashes any kind of bald, roaring, untamed emotion in his work, but about halfway through the book, on page 117, he becomes so enraged at the despicable Monsieur le Directeur that he says: "never in my life before had I wanted to kill to thoroughly extinguish and to entirely murder. Perhaps some day. Unto God I hope so." A really beautiful outburst, which for me anchors the book with a very necessary bit of spleen.

CSL: Yes.

RC: Because Cummings can often be bit detached and cerebral, no?

CSL: Oh, absolutely. And, you know, when they're first incarcerated there, Brown says: "This is the greatest place on earth." And Cummings says: "Oh, yeah, it's the most wonderful place on earth."

RC: Cummings says, "The stink was sublime."

CSL: Yes, exactly. [Laughs] And yet, the conditions there are *rough*.

RC: Oh, absolutely! Buckets filled with urine and feces, instead of having toilets and so on.

CSL: Yes. And the food is minimal; exercise is minimal. The room is dark, because the windows have been boarded up. I mean, this is no paradise, by any means.

RC: Cummings gets a bit ill, but his friend develops *scurvy*.

CSL: Exactly, yeah. I mean, it's a serious condition. And the director is, you know, your typical … Nazi.

RC: Of which there were many in France at that time.

CSL: There were *many* in France at that time. And they continued on for a good while. [Laughs]

RC: To this day! *Ooh la la!*

CSL: Absolutely. You know, Cummings is an *honest* guy. Always.

RC: His honesty got him locked up there, in France, right? For saying that he didn't hate the Germans, but he loved the French. [Laughs]

CSL: That's right, exactly. So, there's the whole conundrum. And this is why I say that it's an autobiography without being autobiographical. But when Cummings says that? Yes, you know it's a true emotion. And suddenly, you say: "Ah, ha. Yes. He is human." You know, he's not attempting to be the saint of the prison camp.

RC: I bring it up with a sense of admiration, and also just in terms of technically analyzing the book. I felt it gave it an anchor, an emotional anchor.

CSL: Yes. Very perceptive.

RC: How would you compare *The Enormous Room* to some of the other great war novels that you discuss in your biography?

CSL: It's unique. It is a war novel without being a war novel, but then, so are a lot of the other ones. Dos Passos's *Three Soldiers*, to some degree. There's very little of the war in *Three Soldiers*. There's far more, let's say, in *All Quiet on the Western Front*. Or even in *A Farewell to Arms*. Although, personally, I think *A Farewell to Arms* is a love story, first and foremost.

RC: It's true. With these other books, it's not so much portraits of the battlefield but of the *aftereffect* of being engaged in war that's portrayed.

CSL: Yes. And I think Remarque's book still holds up as one of the true masterpieces of war literature.

RC: I'm glad to hear you say that, because, having recently reread it for the first time since I was sixteen, I was really impressed by the power of this book.

CSL: I think it's also – and I may not be right about this, because I've never done any formal study – one of the first novels to get at Post-Traumatic Stress Syndrome. When Paul's on leave, he goes home, and he can't talk to his father.*

RC: He's psychically alienated, and really destroyed, and he's no longer the same human being he was before.

CSL: Right.

RC: Of course, the really tragic moment in that story is when he looks through the glass case hanging on the wall, and it's the butterfly collection. Symbolizing the innocence he once had …

CSL: Exactly.

RC: And then there's the description of a butterfly on the battlefield, hovering on a skull. I mean, what a powerful metaphor.

CSL: Yes. And he's no longer interested in *any* of the things he was interested in before. It's an extraordinary chronicle of what war really does to one. I think Robert Graves's *Good-bye to All That* is the only other one that completely deals with that notion of what happened to people. Which is also a masterpiece of autobiography about World War One. Yeah, the war did some great things for literature.

RC: Yes. As you say, Hemingway, *A Farewell to Arms*. Dos Passos, *Three Soldiers*. Remarque, *All Quiet on the Western Front*. And then there's *The Enormous Room* and Céline's *Journey to the End of the Night*. The first three of these novels are terribly dark, tragic books, really haunting and despairing. In their desire to achieve a certain goal, the protagonists have largely severed themselves from society, and they're subsequently destroyed.

CSL: Oh, God, yeah.

RC: On the other hand, with *Journey* and *The Enormous Room*, besides portraying horrific events, we also find a great deal of black humor and tragicomedy. And all of which is portrayed with an abundance of literary innovation. Do you feel that Cummings and Céline share these things in common?

CSL: Oh, absolutely. I mean, *Voyage au bout de la nuit* is, clearly, one of the great books of all time.

RC: And one of the *craziest* books of all time, too!

CSL: Yes, and he just gets crazier as he goes along. But there are parallels, actually, between them.

RC: What did Céline think of Cummings?

CSL: We don't know.

RC: Is there any evidence that he was aware of Cummings?

CSL: Céline was aware of Cummings. Whether Cummings was aware of Céline, I don't know, because I've never found any reference anywhere, when I was looking through all that stuff, to Céline. And I would have seized on it, because I would have found that interesting.

They shared a lot in common. They were both stylistic innovators. *Voyage* is, you know, one of the most profound books that anyone ever wrote, anywhere. There's a lot of black humor, but there's also a huge difference between the two. What would have put Cummings off about Céline is that Cummings, for all his Harvard snobbery, loved human beings.

RC: Excellent point.

CSL: And basically, Céline hated human beings.

RC: He verged on sociopathy.

CSL: Oh, yeah, certainly. You know, Céline was complex.

What keeps coming through in *Voyage* is that sense of war itself being a sickness. He continually uses the terms *malaise* and *couchemar*. He's always talking about war as a kind of illness, or war as a nightmare. He's continually seizing on that as part of what this book's about. That's part of the journey into the night.

I know that Céline was aware of Cummings because he was very aware of North American literature. Cummings was widely translated into French. And Céline knew English, to some degree. And he would have sympathized, because Cummings himself was an anti-Semite.

RC: Well, that's true, too; that's another similarity!

CSL: When that big blowup happened with Cummings being sort of outed as an anti-Semite, you could be sure that Céline took notice.

RC: A huge difference in their anti-Semitism, though, wasn't there?

CSL: Oh, yeah, of course.

RC: I mean, Céline was filled with an authentic, visceral hatred.

CSL: Oh, he was outrageous. I mean, if you read his *Bagatelles*, they're just *vile*. And you can't imagine how one of the great prose stylists of French literature could hold such abhorrent views. It's just hard to …

RC: Well, they say that Shakespeare was also an anti-Semite, but that doesn't mean we have to stop reading Shakespeare.

CSL: No. And of course, we haven't stopped reading Céline.

RC: Whereas with Cummings, he had a big mouth, and, quite often, he shot it off without thinking. But when confronted with authentic anti-Semitism, even he was taken aback. For example, with Ezra Pound, right?

CSL: Oh, absolutely, yeah.

RC: He called Ezra Pound an anti-Semite!

CSL: Yeah, right. [Laughs] You know, as much as he and Pound shared all sorts of views.

RC: But I think this tells us something about Cummings, no? That he was shocked by that.

CSL: Yes, it tells us a lot. And you have to remember that anti-Semitism was basically …

RC: It was the *norm* back then.

CSL: It was the norm. And it was particularly the norm among a certain WASP intellect pure group.

RC: As was the norm to be anti-Irish, anti-Italian, and anti everything else.

CSL: That's right. I mean, Harvard didn't let in those folks. They didn't let them in. And that cemented the notion that, somehow, they were inferior and the Harvard boys were superior. That's very much a part of the story.

RC: Most of the prisoners in La Ferté-Macé were complete innocents who were being punished simply for being, as you say, at the wrong place at the wrong time. And for being *étrangers*: foreigners who happened to be living or passing through France during a period of extreme xenophobia and spy mania and who were then scooped up and held without proper trial or due process.

When I first read your Cummings biography, America had suspended habeas corpus and we were holding innocent prisoners at the dreadful Guantanamo Bay detention facility, often for years, even after they were declared not guilty. And now, as a result of terrorism in Paris, dozens of French citizens are being arrested for indiscreet remarks they've posted online. Does *The Enormous Room* present us with a fitting contemporary parable about the dangers of losing free speech?

CSL: Absolutely. And, you know, that's one of Cummings's major issues with everybody, and everywhere: the desire to suppress people's emotions, people's feelings, people's words. Cummings took the First Amendment seriously. He truly believed that free speech should be free speech. He gets into La Ferté-Macé because, essentially, he has written some letters. Brown's the one who's mainly written them, but Cummings has written as well, a couple of things, and he refuses to back down on his right to think what he wants to think. Later on, this is what terrified him about what was going on in the Soviet Union under Stalin. That same exact thing.

But yeah, the parallel is there. If Cummings were around today, he would be signing petitions, leading marches, writing about what's going on in Guantanamo. Because its exactly the same situation for many of those prisoners there as it was for Cummings and Brown, and Jean le Nègre, and who knows how many others. Who simply happened to be on the ground in Afghanistan when the special forces could go in and pick anybody up, and if they were on the ground they must therefore be "evildoers" out to overthrow the United States. So, yeah, there's certainly that.

And France itself has never had a tremendous regard for free speech. They've locked people up for a very, very long time for speaking their minds. I mean, I love France, and they certainly have no issue with erotic literature, with explicit literature. But politics has always been something you could get into trouble for in France, and very quickly.

The recent roundups of all sorts of folks in France because they had something on their Facebook page or because they said something perhaps pro-Muslim, "and therefore they must be a terrorist," parallels very much what happened here. It's the paranoia that overtakes state governments when you have a perceived or – as in this case, with the *Charlie Hebdo* business* – a real, awful, terrible situation. You know, murdering Jews in a kosher grocery store strikes terror in a whole population. And you understand, yeah, why they're going house to house picking up people. You understand why we had NSA, or have NSA, listening in on our conversations, including probably this one. But it wouldn't have sat well with Cummings. And it doesn't necessarily justify the action itself that's been taken. *The Enormous Room* could be read right now by those prisoners at Guantanamo and they'd go, *Whoa!* But there was no water-boarding at La Ferté-Macé.

RC: Well, that's a good point, Chris!

CSL: [Laughs]

RC: That is an excellent point. And may the Bush-Cheney people rot in hell forever for that. You hear that, NSA?

CSL: Yeah, may they ever! [Laughs]

RC: Besides the hell of La Ferté-Macé, Estlin also experienced what he called the "miracle" of Paris. How did the City of Lights help to shape and inspire him?

CSL: Ah, well! He was there at absolutely the moment when modernism broke out.

RC: The lucky boy attended the premiere of *Parade!**

CSL: Right! That's what I mean!

RC: What luck is that?

CSL: Basically, he doesn't need to go any farther! But obviously, you've got to remember where young Estlin came from. He'd grown up Cambridge in a very nice, well-appointed, large house. By today's standards, it would be regarded as a mansion. In fact, now, it's divided into four separate condos. He was privileged. He went to Harvard. He had religion on a weekly basis. He had the tightness of that Harvard-Cambridge society that omitted most of reality in favor of a kind of controlled notion of how young men – because it was all men there – should behave and should live. His big experiences were crossing the bridge over to Boston, to go to a couple of seedier places.

Suddenly, he gets to Paris. And not only is there an *explosion* of art, literature, music – I mean, modernism is in absolute full-swing in terms of art and everything that's happening there – but Paris itself is glorious. There are abundant places to wander as a young man, to get lost, to get yourself into a bit of trouble. He immediately hooks up with a couple of prostitutes, and: "My God, this is so exciting," you know? Life is suddenly possible. He knows French, which is a huge advantage. And he's overwhelmed by everyone he sees. I mean, Cambridge is a nice, neat, drab little community; Paris is this absolutely gorgeous, sprawling, extraordinary, vibrant place. And so, he's just overwhelmed. He's studied French; he's read French writers. He's gotten a little sense of how, suddenly, you might live. And he never quite gets over it.

RC: That's a very fitting way to end that statement. Who among us ever *does* get over Paris?

CSL: Right, you never get over Paris, let's just face it. You never get over Paris! I'm talking to the converted. [Laughs]

RC: One thing that's striking in his biography is the amazingly precious artistic education that he received even when he was just a little boy, at home, largely at the hands of his mother, Rebecca. And I understand Estlin's Uncle George was also a great influence on his creative and literary development.

CSL: Yes. I mean, this boy was a star from the moment he was born, at least in his mother's eyes. She encouraged him to do anything that he possibly wanted to do. She kept – which was wonderful for biographers – every little scrap of paper he drew a doodle on. She kept his little notebooks; she kept his writings. He was enormously precocious.

RC: And some of those precocious poems are *not* bad!

CSL: They're not bad at all! For a seven-year-old kid, they're pretty darn good! And he could already draw incredibly well. So yeah, there's an awful lot to that.

RC: He had a golden childhood.

CSL: Absolutely a golden childhood. He was pampered; he was continually told how wonderful he was. He was continually told by his mother, particularly, that he could be anything he wanted to be, and everything he did was precious and wonderful. You know, as a result, he became quite egotistical, and he remained so for the rest of his life, but …

RC: But never lost his creative spirit.

CSL: He never lost his creative spirit.

RC: Something like Alexander being told that he was fathered by Jupiter.

CSL: Absolutely. And essentially, that's what he *was* told! [Laughs] And Uncle George was also a tremendous …

RC: George was a poet, apparently.

CSL: He was a poet, yes. He was always giving Cummings books that were above his head for him to read. And of course, Cummings read them. He was always encouraging him to write, to think, to read, to go beyond where he was supposed to be at that particular stage in his life.

RC: The first time I read your wonderful biography, I was struck by how supportive Cummings's father was. After all, he even paid Estlin to write *The Enormous Room*. And I was very thrown off by that. I always thought that artists are supposed to have a *contentious* relationship with their fathers! [Laughs]

CSL: Exactly, right!

RC: But the second time I read it, I was impressed by how *controlling* he was. How did Mr. Cummings help to mold Estlin for both better and worse, as a man and as a poet?

CSL: Well, you know, it's a complex business. Both Mom and Dad were enormously supportive of young Estlin. His mother was just a kind of ... Every portrait you get of her – particularly from Cummings, but also from Cummings's sister – she's just this woman who is "absolute unconditional love, all the time." You know, just full of it. And no matter what the children want, she would make sure they have.

Cummings's father is a more severe man, in the sense that he's certainly a patriarch. He runs a house. He's a highly respected member of the Cambridge-Boston community. He's authoritative only in the sense that he's extremely concerned that young Estlin pay attention to certain codes of conduct. You know: right morality, right living. His father is a minister. He was also a Harvard professor at one point. But he's consistently attempting to remind Cummings of what he should or should not be doing. And so, in that sense, he is controlling. And yet, he pays for it: he pays for him to write up his "French Notes" into *The Enormous Room*. He even pays for the typist. He supports his son's literary endeavors in a way that would, in this day and age, be pretty much unthinkable: where you get very little support from your parents unless you want to go to business school or something. But there was a great belief that Cummings was going to be a great writer, or a great artist.

His father didn't quite understand what his painting was about. But he understood the literature. He understood the writing. And his father, by the way, was an extremely literate, well read, scholarly man. When he reads his "French Notes," as *The Enormous Room* was then called, he's just overwhelmed.

RC: He says, "Now I know you are a great writer."

CSL: Yeah! That's what he tells him.

RC: What a wonderful thing to hear from your father.

CSL: Yes! So there is this "double" kind of thing. For Cummings though, his father also represented an impossible being. You know, he didn't worry about trying to be like his mother, because (A), she was a woman; and (B), she was his mother. But young men frequently *are* in the shadow of their father. And here's this man who is basically known by one and all. You walk down the street in Cambridge, and everyone doffs their hat to Reverend Cummings. And he's absolutely upright, moral, has the courage of his convictions, strong, tall, all of those kinds of things. And here's Cummings, who is not particularly tall; he's about five-seven. He's not particularly strong. He's not so interested in being an upright member of society. And there's the shadow, you know? And yet, he loves his father. And his father certainly loved his son. But he realizes, fairly early on – I would say, by late adolescence – that he'll never be his father. And yet, he continually wants to please his father, as he does his mother. But he knows that, no matter what he does, he'll please his mother. She'll understand, somehow.

RC: His father was a preacher, and of course it's impossible to live in the shadow of a saint. For Estlin to carve out a sense of identity, perhaps rebelling and assuming the opposing stance, and becoming a "sinner," was simply a logical conclusion. Also, the son was a product of the Jazz Age, of the Roaring Twenties. How did the latter affect Estlin's personal transformation?

CSL: I think it begins to some degree in the Harvard classroom. And it's an odd place ...

RC: In other words, even before he moved out of the home, just being in the classroom, around his peers?

CSL: I believe so. Because what happens is, he's suddenly exposed to a world of ideas that he'd never known about. He's also exposed to an awful lot of great minds and intellect, but it's not the teachers that are all that important for Cummings; it's his peers. By the time he joins the *Harvard Monthly*, which is the literary magazine at Harvard, and meets up with people like Scofield Thayer, John Dos Passos, Foster Damon – there's a whole group of them – suddenly, they're thinking big. They've been to Europe; they've already been thinking about how art should be made, how literature should be written. They're aware of the latest currents in everything from the cinema, to music, to poetry, to the novel, to art. So suddenly, Cummings is swept up in this. And there's a desire on his part to break with the stodginess, with the purely Victorian mentality. It's not necessarily a bad one, but it's still very much a Victorian mentality that possesses his father, his father's peers, and Cambridge society in general.

It's hard to realize now how extremely stratified Cambridge society was. And particularly where Cummings lived. Basically, it was a place where everyone is upper-crust and white, and "white" being Anglo-Saxon protestant. Not Irish: the Irish lived on the other side. Certainly not Jewish. And certainly not Italian or any other ethnic group. And so, suddenly, here he is at Harvard, with the same kind of kids, incidentally, with the exception of the Portuguese

Dos Passos. But most of them are breaking out from where they'd been. So I think the rebellion begins with the classroom. He's beginning to read beyond ...

RC: Beyond what his Uncle George was giving him.

CSL: *Way* beyond. And his friends are bringing him this and that and having these all-night discussions. And, of course, there's drinking, which he'd never been able to do at home, because his father was part of the temperance society. So, suddenly, it's a huge world.

And you have to "kill" your father. You know, no matter what, you've got to do that in order to become your own person. Even though you may end up *being* your father, later on. But, at that moment, it's very important to overthrow your father. And you don't have to get too Freudian about it, but, essentially, that's what he's really trying to do there: to become his own person.

RC: And he also had the courage to do that.

CSL: Yes. But it's easier for him to do it than it would've been for his father, because, at the time, the currents were moving in that direction. Everything is about to change.

RC: The Twenties was the Sixties.

CSL: The Twenties was the Sixties, that's right. It wasn't the Nineties, of either century.

RC: All of which brings us to a story that Susan Cheever tells in her memoir, *Home Before Dark*:

> "Hey sweetie! Hey! Hey!" the whores in the old Women's House of Detention on Greenwich Avenue would call through the barred windows when his tall, patrician figure appeared walking out of Patchin Place toward Sixth. He knew them all by name.

Isn't that lovely? What a great little anecdote!

CSL: Yeah, it is! It's one of my favorite parts of Susan's memoir. [Laughs]

RC: I love the way she ends her Cummings biography with a description of Patchin Place.

CSL: Yes! And I was really envious, because I never got into the house; she did.

RC: It was a charming way to end the book, where she describes the family that's living in Cummings's old flat.

CSL: Yes, it's really quite wonderful.

RC: Another product of the Flapper Age was Estlin's cherished partner, Marion Morehouse, who would have been seventeen years old in 1920.* Edward Steichen, who photographed her as early as 1924 and made her famous in *Vogue*, considered Marion to be one of his favorite models. "The greatest fashion model I ever photographed," he said. Tell us about Marion's relationship with Estlin, and how they supported each other emotionally and artistically.

CSL: That story begins with two other relationships before that. You can't go to Marion without …

RC: Before Marion, he had a golden childhood, but what bad luck he had with the women he selected!

CSL: With the women! Exactly! The first woman he falls in love with is Elaine Thayer, who's married to his friend Scofield Thayer. And Scofield, as we know now, and as I'm sure Cummings knew at the time, was, if not "bi," gay.

RC: And very much in the closet for a while.

CSL: Yes, in the closet. An esthete, but not particularly interested in his wife sexually. And Cummings falls head over heels in love with Elaine, with Scofield's wife. And Elaine herself is upper-crust. She's not the easiest person in the world to get along with; nor was, I think, Estlin himself.

But basically, they have an affair, and she gets pregnant with Cummings's child. Thayer, being Cummings's best friend, knows what's going on, but he adopts the child – or rather, he allows it to be born as if it's his daughter.

Eventually, Elaine and Thayer are divorced. Elaine marries Cummings, and it does not last very long. There are just too many differences between them. The daughter doesn't realize at the time that she's his child: that Cummings is her real father. They part ways; Elaine goes off to Ireland, and Cummings is bereft. I mean, he's absolutely bereft that Elaine has fallen in love with someone else and left him after he was hoping that this was going to be the love of his life.

For all of Cummings's "sexual identity" as a poet – because he certainly has one because of all the erotic poems, and being one of the first to write poems that were unabashedly not just about love, but about sex – people think he must have had a million women. Well, he didn't. He had only three principal women. And they were each enormously important to him. He was a very tender, very sentimental, and, in that way, a very "son of his father," old-fashioned man. Then he hooks up with Anne Barton, who is a flapper and totally unfaithful from the moment they get together, and this kills Cummings as well.

He loves women as women, and I'll try to clarify what I mean by this. He enjoyed being in women's company. Probably among his closest friends was Hildegarde Watson, who was married to his friend James Watson. I don't believe there was ever a sexual attraction on either's part, but he absolutely adored being in her company. He adored women. He enjoyed who they were. He enjoyed the way they smelled [Laughs]. He enjoyed the way they looked, the way they walked. And so, in a pretty tough period for Cummings – financially, he's not doing well; he never did well, and his mother generally supported him most of his life – but here he is, a "two-time loser" if you will, and suddenly here comes this angel out of the fog, Marion Morehouse. She is young. She is, unlike Elaine or Anne, really interested in being with Cummings.

RC: And not a gold digger, like Anne.

CSL: Not a gold digger like Anne was, certainly. And so, she is gorgeous, and she makes it pretty clear, pretty early on, that what she wants to do is take care of this great man. And, *wow!* [Laughs] He's finally found the love of his life.

Who knows what takes place in those kinds of circumstances? But clearly, there was a tremendous attraction. I didn't write this, because I didn't have enough evidence, but, from the little that I could glean, he was attracted to her initially because she was so gorgeous. It was certainly a major physical attraction. I think it took a while for him to let his guard down so that he could see her in a larger way. He kept her at a distance, initially; he wasn't quite sure of what to do.

And so, what we have is hundreds of pages of writing about Elaine, maybe a hundred or so pages about Anne, but we have only about twenty pages about Marion. Why? Because he doesn't have to exorcise the demons. What he's doing with writing about Elaine and about Anne is trying to exorcise those demons. Because he wrote everything down; he was compulsive about trying to think on paper. You could see the guy pacing about the room, smoking endless cigarettes, then writing something down, to help him try to analyze things. Once he meets Marion, it goes away. He writes about other things, but he's not obsessing about his relationship any longer. And, in a way, this tells you how perfectly matched they were.

What happened as they spent more time together ... I would say she became much more of a 'gatekeeper' for Cummings. Allen Ginsberg told me a story: He'd gone to Cummings's house and knocked on the door, and no one answered. And he'd written him a letter and sent him a copy of "Howl." He really wanted Cummings's approval; it was enormously important to him for some reason.

RC: Who's house did Ginsberg *not* knock on? What a *schmoozer!*

CSL: Well, of course, that was it! Especially at that point in time. [Laughs] He finally gets to Patchin Place again, on another occasion, and he knocks on the door, and Marion comes down the stairs, takes one look, and says: "*You*. Go *away*. And *never* come back." He tries to explain who he is, and she just ... She was the gatekeeper. And it was very much a part of her function in later years. And with Cummings's blessing, because he became more of a curmudgeon as he got older. And by "older," I mean fifty-five. The man didn't live all that long. And she became "the one you had to get through."

I believe her political views really began to affect Cummings's. She was very much a right-winger. At that time, Lindberg was on the radio, and various other right-wing isolationist, "Keep Out of World War Two" folks. And she would get Cummings to listen to these broadcasts, because these were the ones who were "telling the truth." She absolutely hated Roosevelt. Hard to know why; she was hardly an aristocrat! She had very little money, and she certainly had no reason to be a Republican, but then ... Oh, well!

RC: It's often like that. Again, the shadow.

CSL: Yes.

RC: In 1996, Richard Kennedy, Cummings's previous biographer, published an essay titled "The Elusive Marion Morehouse." Lamenting her evasions and obfuscations, he called her "the principle obstacle" in his attempt to re-create "the story of E. E. Cummings's life." Perhaps you can touch upon how some of the rumors that you heard about Marion's past dovetail with the information I've recently unearthed, thanks to Tony Ungaro's help* and to the rapid expansion of genealogical data on the Internet.

CSL: Well, first of all, your information is staggering! (A), the amount of information that you were able to get; and (B), the depth. And the light it throws on Marion to begin with. You know, we didn't even know how old she was! I totally sympathize with Kennedy, because I read his biography before I started my book, and I'm thinking, "Oh, well; I'll dig up this stuff." But I had no more luck than Kennedy. The advantage I had is, I had access to a lot more papers than he did, so I was able to find more information.

RC: I have a feeling that the genealogical information on the Internet was nowhere as developed then as it is now.

CSL: Not at all. I'm a klutz with the Internet, but I did do a search, and I came up with nothing. I called city halls, and I tried to get documents. But, you know, without the right information to start with, you couldn't get anything.

I think Marion always played fast and loose with how old she was, and I'm not even sure that Cummings knew how old she was. But at this point, thanks to your research, we know that she was born in 1903; and, as you've also uncovered, she was the daughter of a vaudevillian: a working-class guy. So, she's nineteen, twenty years old, she's stunningly gorgeous, and then suddenly she gets these bit parts in theatrical productions. And she's in so *many* shows. I think you have her down for over four hundred performances.

RC: Right. So far as I know, she was in five plays that we know the titles of, but they went on for dozens and sometimes even hundreds of shows.

CSL: The Playbills that you sent me were fascinating, showing her there. And her sister, who apparently was also a performer.

So, she's a model. She's in *Vogue*. And she's an *artist's* model: Steichen. At about the time she meets Cummings, it's likely that she was also trying to achieve more in the theater. But suddenly, she moves from being a sort of career woman – because she was certainly building a career – to being Cummings's protector and supporter.

RC: Knowing what we *now* know about her, do any of the rumors that you heard – which you didn't include in your book because you felt you couldn't back them up – make more sense?

CSL: Yes. We're pretty sure that she fabricated her early life, to Cummings as well as to anyone else. There are some letters that went back and forth at the time between Edmund Wilson and various other people. Now, keep in mind, Wilson didn't like her. He felt she was just after Cummings because he was famous. And he didn't trust her past; he felt something was *shady*. He felt Cummings was just head over heels ...

RC: Being taken in?

CSL: Yes. He thought she would eventually do something against him; there was that spirit of things. But obviously, she didn't. She was actually devoted. There's no evidence that she had affairs during the time she was with Cummings. I mean, she did have one affair, but everyone knew about it. She was hardly running around on him. Nor Cummings on her. I mean, he had little affairs ... well, with a graduate that he met at Bennington.

RC: But it wasn't a typical part of his pattern.

CSL: Right. They were very devoted to each other. But the fact that she wanted to just "spring whole"* as Steichen's model, and actress, and didn't want to ever admit anything about her past, even how old she was ...

RC: Here's another interesting thing. As you know, I tracked her parents down to being remarried in the Bronx ...

CSL: Right! And I had no idea even who her parents were, so this was amazing! They were married twice, right?

RC: Yes. In the 1910 census report, they're listed as married, and then, thanks to Tony Ungaro's help, I learned of another nuptial ceremony performed in 1918, at the Church of St. Francis de Sales, on East 96th Street, in the Bronx. When I contacted the church, lo and behold, there was the marriage certificate. I never would have found that without Mr. Ungaro's help. Who's going to be looking for a marriage certificate after all those years, when the children were already teenagers? So, this might be the first clue we have that they're in New York in 1918. And Marion would have been fifteen then.

This is purely speculative, but this is the hunch that I wanted to share with you. Marion supposedly met Cummings backstage after a play that she'd performed in, in 1932. But the Playbill Archive, which lists five other Broadway plays in which she had minor parts, doesn't have a record of her acting at this time. In addition, the source for this incident is Marion herself, in an interview with Richard Kennedy. Now, I find it highly suspicious that Marion never mentions the name of this play. I think it's more likely that Marion and Estlin met at a *Ziegfeld Follies*-type of venue where, according to Kennedy, she often worked as a "showgirl." Apparently, she had trouble getting theatrical parts because of her tall, thin, lanky figure, which made her the perfect showgirl and model for Steichen, because his whole thing was portraying the gown as a fine-art image. And of course, Cummings loved the burlesque, and he used it as a theme in his poetry and even impersonated the dialogue of the showgirls in his work. What do you think? Isn't that a possibility?

CSL: I think that's much more likely. Although Cummings also loved the theater, and he'd written "Him" for the theater.

RC: The stark antiwar message of *The Enormous Room* and of those other novels that we discussed provides another link between the Twenties and Sixties, as does Cummings's unconventional lifestyle. Yet, as he aged, he grew more politically conservative. Isn't it ironic that two of the most celebrated authors of the Sixties – Cummings and Kerouac – were both right of center, anti-Democratic Party, anti-Semites, and financially supported by their *mothers* all throughout their lives? I mean, perhaps this is a silly question, but it just struck me …

CSL: No, it's a great question! And I hadn't even added it all up until you asked me. There are so many parallels, it's ridiculous! [Laughs]

RC: Many people today don't realize this, but they were literary *icons* in the Sixties, weren't they?

CSL: Yes, they were. You know, obviously, there are some differences. I mean, Cummings became increasingly right-wing really because he'd observed the Soviet Union up front, close, and personal. And he went to the Soviet Union as a leftie. He went through Aragon and Elsa Triolet in Paris. Louis Aragon, a big-time member of the Communist Party, is a great friend of Cummings. He goes because they help arrange for him to go, as a writer. And what happens is, he almost immediately sees that this is a police state. And he sees what Stalin has perpetrated. He's totally stunned by it. For him, that's the crucial moment when he gives up on the left.

And yet, just to caricature Cummings as a right-winger isn't quite right either. I mean, if anything, he's a libertarian, in the sense that he believes in freedom of everything. But by this point, he's also fervently anti-Communist. With Dos Passos, the same thing happens to him. Dos Passos becomes a right-winger by the end of his life. And the same kind of conversion, because of that observance of what Stalin had done. For Dos Passos, it's really the later Thirties that convinces him. You know, when you're starting to round up the great writers, artists, and composers, and shooting them, then Dos Passos turns against the left. Initially, against Stalin, and then against Communism in general. Although Dos Passos thinks it through more thoroughly than Cummings does. But for Cummings, it's definitely that particular moment.

Marion certainly contributed to Cummings's anti-Semitism and to his notion of the right. Although, you know, you have to remember that Cummings had no use for war. Cummings is one of the great antiwar poets, ever, in American literature, and so, he doesn't want to go into

World War Two. Remember, the war starts in '38; we don't get into it until Pearl Harbor gets bombed, in '41. There was a pretty strong "this isn't our fight" sort of thing going on in this country, and Cummings was very much a part of it. But I think that, while he didn't have much to do with the left, he also didn't have much to do with the right, either. Although he defended McCarthy at one point, and that was stupid; and so did Kerouac.

With Kerouac, Burroughs told me that it was "all Spengler's fault." But with Burroughs, often, he …

RC: Imagined things?

CSL: He certainly did that. [Laughs] But he also liked to play jokes on people.

RC: He was mischievous.

CSL: He was mischievous, yes. You know, "You asked a question as complex as why did Kerouac become a right-winger? Well, I'll give you a silly answer."

RC: There's an amusing story about some celebrity who goes to visit Burroughs on his ranch, and Burroughs hands him a pistol and takes him shooting. Right after they shoot, the man dropped it because the barrel became red hot. He says to Burroughs, "Oh, my God, I almost burnt my hand on that thing!" And in that very dry intonation, Burroughs replies, "Well, that's why I don't like to use that particular gun."

CSL: That's definitely Burroughs! [Laughs]

RC: He was very much a trickster!

CSL: Oh, yeah, absolutely. And so, he claims it was "all because of Spengler" that Kerouac became a right-winger. But I don't think so.

RC: I also have a quirky theory about Kerouac, although it's not really a serious one. But when you look back on it now, and you realize that the FBI was opening enormous files on all these people who spoke out against the war, and against the government, and so on, Kerouac might have been a lot smarter than we thought he was for keeping his trap shut and hanging out with Bill Buckley.

CSL: Exactly.

RC: I mean, they never bothered him, did they?

CSL: No, that's right. Whereas they were after Allen; they were after Ferlinghetti; they were after just about everybody else. Gary Snyder, certainly. That whole group was being hounded at that point. Yeah, there may have just been that.

It's really complex, but I heard a whole lot more about what people *thought* happened. Ginsberg, who was probably as close to Kerouac as anyone, was somewhat mystified by that turn. But he felt it was because Jack had become disillusioned with just about everything. And yet, Ginsberg continually affirmed that, essentially, Jack had *always* been a sort of patriotic American. This had never *not* been part of who he was. It was *patriotic* to get into an automobile made in Detroit and drive across the country …

RC: That's a good point.

CSL: And see it. And write about your country.

RC: Kerouac had a sort of patriotism with a capital "P" that was almost like a Platonic ideal. You'd have to go back to Walt Whitman to find something similar. They each regarded America as a sort of transcendental, spiritual potentiality.

CSL: Yes. And I think that Allen, as well, was a patriot in that same way: in the way that Whitman was a patriot. I think, for Allen – and he would have loved being in the same sentence with Whitman – it's very much the case that he had that same sense of loving this country. It doesn't mean that you like every thing it does. It means that you fight like hell to put it back on its course. Or what *you* think, at least, should be its course.

Whereas, I think, from what Burroughs told me, and what Allen told me, and what other people told me, essentially, when Jack grew older, he just became more disillusioned with everything. He became disillusioned with politics; he became disillusioned with writing. He became disillusioned with fame. The only thing he doesn't become disillusioned with is alcohol. And that continues until it kills him.

RC: He even said, "As a Roman Catholic, I can't commit suicide, so I'm drinking myself to death."

CSL: Right. That's what I'm referring to, yeah.

RC: That's a great point that you bring up. Ginsberg, God bless him, who constantly put his ass on the line to try to effect change in the country, was really just as patriotic as Kerouac. Yet, they had a completely different *definition* of what America should be.

CSL: Absolutely, yes.

RC: Although he'd already passed away by 1962, one of the things that endeared Cummings to the Sixties generation was his innovative literary style, his disregard for authority, and his unbridled awe when thrust before the numinous dimension of life and the wonder of nature. What was it like to read Cummings in the Sixties, and how did the Beats take to his poetry?

CSL: For me, reading Cummings in the Sixties was like reading someone who was talking directly to me about what was going on. I had friends who were being hauled away to prison for being antiwar. I had friends who were refusing to enlist, who decided they would go to jail as a protest rather than enlist or leave the country, because they loved their country. And you're suddenly reading those Cummings poems about war, and he's talking to you at that very moment. At least, that's the way I felt at the time.

At one of the first California moratoriums against the war, which I think was probably in '68, or maybe '67, I got up to the mike along with everyone else, and I read Cummings. And Cummings hit people in a way that all the rhetoric and everything else that other people were doing … I didn't do anything, I just read Cummings. I got to "i sing of Olaf," finished off with that, and people burnt their draft cards. I mean, that was the *power* of the guy at that time. Everybody's backpack had a couple of different books in it. It had *The Enormous Room* or his poems. It had *On the Road*. It had *Coney Island of the Mind*. It had "Howl." Those were the backpacks.

RC: The textbooks of the generation.

CSL: The textbooks of the generation, right! And if we were lucky, a little Rimbaud, just for good measure. [Laughs] And so, of course, Cummings sounded like a contemporary. I don't think that any of us knew that he'd become a right-winger in his old age. We hadn't read any biographies. Or actually, we didn't care. We knew what he was talking about in those books. And we also knew what he was talking about when he was talking about love and sex. I mean, all of the stuff that he stood for was, in a sense, what the Sixties was trying to emulate, trying to break out with. I remember Kenneth Rexroth, who actually liked Cummings quite a lot, describing him as "that old bohemian dinosaur." He said, "Now, the dinosaur walks again." [Laughs] You know, that was Rexroth.

He was important for Ginsberg because he was very willing to write about the way it was. For Gary Snyder, he mattered because he was the first environmentalist as a poet, at least in Snyder's view. I don't think he was, by any means; I think the Romantics were way ahead of him. But for Snyder, Cummings hit him as an environmentalist. And Bukowski, of course, wrote that wonderful poem about Cummings, "What A Writer."

RC: Cummings's style alternates between a cerebral sort of satiric wit and an immediate, deep-felt celebration of the importance of love: another vital Sixties theme. In one poem, he writes:

> i carry your heart with me(i carry it in
> my heart)i am never without it(anywhere
> i go you go,my dear; and whatever is done
> by only me is your doing,my darling)

Maybe you could talk about the duality of his style.

CSL: Cummings is actually a poet of many styles. You'll see, in his notebooks, that he'll dash off something. Personally, I think he published a little *too* much. But, you know, he *was* sentimental, and he didn't care. It was already becoming *old-fashioned* to be sentimental. Certainly, Eliot did his best to wreck that tradition. And Stevens did his best to put cerebral poetry above all else. And it continued on down the line. Whereas Williams was still interested in body and soul, and what was going on in front; and Williams and Cummings, incidentally, were good friends.

But what you get there is this sort of direct lyrical statement. You know: "I carry your heart with me; I carry it in my heart." Well, what's more trite than that? And yet, it all kind of works together, because you feel like he's telling you the *truth*. And the way it's laid out on the page: the spacing gets close together, the parentheses, the movement of the lines, the very rhythm of them: "I *carry* your *heart* with *me*; I *carry* it *in* my *heart*." There's all that rhythm that you're playing with all the time. It's a melding of, truly, a master craftsman with this very simple, almost trite, sentimental statement.

RC: But deeply authentic.

CSL: But deeply authentic, yes.

RC: I thought this particular stanza was reminiscent of Whitman's opening line from the "Leaves": "and what I assume you shall assume, for every atom belonging to me as good belongs to you."

CSL: There's certainly that, yeah.

RC: What did he think of Whitman?

CSL: There's a page or two in the Harvard archive where Cummings takes a poem from "Leaves of Grass" and rewrites it in his own typography. He was interested in Whitman. He was really interested in what he was doing with breath.

RC: As were the Beats.

CSL: As were the Beats, exactly; there's another parallel there. But at the same time, he's trying to read *everybody*. And he moves on from Whitman pretty quickly. As far as we can tell, those couple of pages are from around 1915, 1914, something like that. By 1916, he's already embracing the *new* in the sense that he's looking at Pound, he's reading Cocteau, he's reading Laforgue. Rimbaud, of course, has already come around. Baudelaire. He's read the Symbolists; he commits Verlaine to memory. So, suddenly, he's off on a whole other trajectory that is more European, that is France.

Eliot, of course, is huge for Cummings. Even though he and Eliot never particularly liked one another. But Eliot is huge for everybody, just because he was huge! I mean, "Wasteland" is not ignorable. Nor is "Prufrock." Cummings actually reviewed Eliot's first book. But Cummings clearly didn't know how to write a review or to write about poetry very well, and, fortunately, he gave it up. But he clearly has appreciation. He also reviewed Joyce's *Ulysses*, although his review was rejected. But that's what he was reading at that point.

So, Whitman kind of drops out. But I believe Whitman never goes away. Because what happens is, by the time you get to the more mature Cummings, he's coming back to that kind of celebration of life, of liberty, of standing in your own space on earth. You know, Cummings is always playing around with the way words lie on the page. But if you think about it, so was Whitman. I mean, those lines really *matter*, the way they're written. Except for those early experiments – and he was experimenting with everything at that time – I don't think he was overtly in debt to Whitman. But I think it's hard to be a poet in America without having Whitman standing over you.

RC: And with Whitman spending his entire life reediting and reediting and changing and adding and subtracting to that poem, who could possibly have spent more time and consideration over how the line appears on the page, right?

CSL: Exactly, yeah.

RC: What do you carry in your heart from Cummings? And how did you apply it to your verse, as you came of age as a poet? Because, obviously, you read him at quite an early age.

CSL: What's interesting is that, when I first read Cummings, what appealed to me were the easy poems. The ones like "i carry your heart with me," or "my father moved through dooms of love," or "if there are any heavens my mother will all by herself have," or "may I feel said he." You know, the more accessible poems: the ones with a direct statement.

There was probably a good twenty years that went by between my reading Cummings and not reading Cummings again. I was off on so many other trajectories. And then, I have to totally credit Richard Kostelanetz for my rediscovery of Cummings. Kostelanetz put out a book called *AnOther E. E. Cummings*. And I get the book, thinking: first of all, Richard's always interesting; and secondly, what's he doing with Cummings? I wouldn't have put Kostelanetz and Cummings together. But then, all of a sudden, I'm putting Kostelanetz and Cummings together. Richard is suddenly educating me, and showing me this whole other dimension of Cummings that I would otherwise have missed. Cummings as the master craftsman, but also as a poet who's really attempting to change the way poetry gets read and gets written. And that was a revelation. Actually, I had the great honor of doing a presentation with Richard on Cummings at one point, about his visual-verbal pyrotechnics. It was quite wonderful.

What I carry around now are all those poems. "Plato told him": it just keeps coming back to me, with all these wars. So, the antiwar poems are still very much alive in my memory. But also, those extraordinary experiments with language. And those leaps. There was a reason that Gertrude Stein liked Cummings so much. She *got* that he was pushing language out. You know, Stein's marvelous;

Stein's doing stuff with the English language that nobody knew you could do. But Cummings was also doing it in his own quieter American way.

RC: In his more introverted, New England manner.

CSL: Yes, his introverted New England way, yeah. And it's fascinating. So I carry that around. Quite a lot. And the whole notion that it matters how words look on a page. It matters where you begin the line on the page. It matters how you jamb the line, because it's going to change the whole effect if you're really paying attention. So, I guess that's where Cummings comes across my radar screen these days.

---

* This interview was conducted on February 2, 2015 and first appeared online at tygersofwrath.com on May 26, 2015.

* As just one example:

> Albert expresses it: 'The war has ruined us for everything.'
> He is right. We are not youth any longer. We don't want to take the world by storm. We are fleeing. We fly from ourselves. From our life. We were eighteen and had begun to love life and the world; and we had to shoot it to pieces. The first bomb, the first explosion, burst in our hearts. We are cut off from activity, from striving, from progress. We believe in such things no longer, we believe in the war.

Erich Remarque, *All Quiet on the Western Front*, trans. A. W. Wheen (New York: Fawcett Columbine, 1966), pp. 87-88.

* On January 7, 2015, the office of *Charlie Hebdo*, a French satirical magazine, was attacked by Islamic terrorists, resulting in the deaths of twelve people, including several journalists.

* Referring to the pivotal 1917 performance of *Parade* by Diaghilev's Ballets Russes in Paris. "Though pursued by ill luck in later performances, and rarely seen, *Parade* had done its work. More than any single event at that time, it set the tone for the postwar years – the tone defined by Jarry, promoted by the Rousseau banquet, and now offered to a wider public. It was a serious-humorous exploitation of popular elements in art, a turning to jazz and music hall and to all the paraphernalia of modern life, not in a spirit of realism, but with a sense of exhilaration in the absurd." Roger Shattuck, *The Banquet Years: The Arts in France, 1885 to 1918* (Garden City, NY: Doubleday & Company, 1961), pp. 154.

* Although she claimed to have been born in 1903. See my essay, "On the Trail of the 'Elusive' Lillian and Marion Morehouse."

* Tony Ungaro was acquainted with Lillian Morehouse, Marion's sister. After Lillian bequeathed her papers to Tony, he then discovered her connection to E. E. Cummings's wife. In July 2014, I came across some genealogical data posted by Mr. Ungaro online, and I subsequently interviewed him. For more on this, see my essay, "On the Trail of the 'Elusive' Lillian and Marion Morehouse."

* This *sui generis* sense of having "sprung up out of nowhere" is also reflected in Marion's one book of photographs, *Adventures in Value*, which contains neither a preface nor an introduction and instead relies on Cummings's intentionally ambiguous poetic captions. According to Richard Kennedy, Marion learned the photographic craft from Edward Steichen: something that might have made for a fascinating narrative, yet the reader remains completely in the dark about how or where she first apprenticed.

Paying Attention. Christopher Sawyer-Lauçanno Talks About His New Book of Poems, *Mussoorie-Montague Miscellany*.*

Rob Couteau: You've recently published a powerful poetry book called *Mussoorie-Montague Miscellany*. Tell us about its gestation, the problems you pose for yourself, and how you attempt to resolve them.

Christopher Sawyer-Lauçanno: You never know what you're doing when you're writing poetry. In 2007, I had the tremendous good fortune to be invited to the first Mussoorie International Writer's Festival in Mussoorie, India. I'd always been enormously intrigued by India, by its traditions, its culture, its food: just about everything. And so, it was a tremendous experience for me to be able to go there. Mussoorie's up in the north, at the foothills of the Himalayas. It's an extraordinarily beautiful place. You walk outside, you look up, and your can see Nanda Devi. Everest is not far off. Mallory's base camp was in Mussoorie.

So anyway, what are you going to do when you're at a writer's festival? I met so many writers I never knew existed, because we don't get a lot of those folks over here. And suddenly I'm finding all these people that are doing this wonderful work from all these different places in the world. It was remarkably stimulating, and the place itself was pretty fantastic. There are paths that cut through the forest and go down to the town eventually, or don't, and lots of dead ends. And so, I just wandered around. And of course, coming off of the stimulus of listening to all this wonderful language – in several languages, by the way – just kind of got me going.

The festival was about a week long, and then I stayed on for a while, after that. I thought, well, I'll write some poems about this particular place, because it was fairly overwhelming. Originally, I thought I'd write a sequence that would be a record of Mussoorie itself and of that part of India. But it didn't turn out like that.

After I returned to Montague, Connecticut, the poems wouldn't go away; the book wouldn't go away; the experience wouldn't go away. And yet, everything began to change as well, because I was no longer looking at the Himalayas. Now, I was looking at the Connecticut River. I was taking my little dog there for walks, and wandering around in this very beautiful part of the world that is Western Massachusetts. So there were a lot of the same sort of things going on, but now I was transplanted back home. My original thought was to create a "Mussoorie Notebook," but it soon became a kind of back and forth. I was still writing poems about India, but it became a "you get taken over by where you are, and the concerns of what's going on in your own life." Eventually, it became "Mussoorie-Montague": a nice alliteration. And then "Miscellany," because I felt I was throwing all sorts of stuff in there that really didn't have a whole lot to do with any discernable record of events in the course of a single day.

RC: It's a wonderful potpourri, and I noticed many literary and spiritual traditions lingering in the background, some of which you pay homage to, or look at obliquely. One that first came to mind was that of the great Austrian novelist and poet, Thomas Bernhard. Tell me about you and Bernhard. I know he's a writer you admire.

CSL: Bernhard is absolutely infuriating.

RC: A great adjective with which to describe him!

CSL: You read Bernhard, and you go: "Why am I spending my time doing this? I've spent now, the last eighty pages, walking across a room. Recording every little detail about this and that: every little thought that's come into his head as he's crossing that room." And then, all of a sudden, it just works. It's amazing. It's about paying attention.

I absolutely adore him. I could say he's infuriating, but I had the same reaction when I watched Fassbinder movies, back in the Sixties and Seventies. I'd watch those films and go: "Oh, *my God.*" But then, afterward, I never could forget them. And it took me a while to realize why I kept going back to see the newest Fassbinder film, who was, at that time in Paris, enormously popular, and so you went to see Fassbinder because it was the cool thing to do. Which is why I went initially. But then, I began to have the same kind of feeling: This man is *paying attention.* And Bernhard, above all, knows how to pace his language. Knows how to observe what's going on. Knows the interconnection between what's in front of his face, or in front of his protagonist's face, if you will, and a whole mental set of calculations that goes on. It's fascinating when you begin to realize what Bernhard is really up to. As a stylist, he's remarkable, but also as an incredibly deep thinker. He's always provoking you to go beyond what's there in the text, what's there in front of you at that very minute, and begin to take in a *larger reality* that, to me, is continually an opening. I mean, you could reread Bernhard and you would get something different each time you look at him. It's no coincidence that he was a great fan of Wittgenstein. In fact, he even wrote a novel ...

RC: *Wittgenstein's Nephew.*

CSL: Exactly, yes. Because that was what Wittgenstein was doing. I mean, Bernhard understood, as Wittgenstein used to try to get across to us, that the meaning of words is best understood in the kind of a *game* that you play. In *Philosophical Investigations*, Wittgenstein talks about that whole way in which language loops back on itself. And yet, it's always in a kind of box. You think it's a referent to a larger reality in the world, but what's really happening is, it's looping back on itself. And Bernhard consistently does that in his work. And it's really amazing.

RC: It's fascinating that you say that, because, as a writer, he's such a remarkable, pyromaniacal stylist; and there's just so much going on that you could just stop *there* and be amazed. But your analysis takes it to a deeper level. And, just like Céline, Bernhard's humor is so dark that you're either overwhelmed by it or forced to laugh convulsively at it.

CSL: Yeah, right!

RC: You could almost divide the world into two types of people. One type which is so pessimistic that they'll read Bernhard and say, "Ah, he *understands*," and then get even more depressed. And the other, more euphoric perhaps, who read him and laugh. Because, as bad as life might seem to you, it's never quite a bad as the way he describes it.

CSL: No, exactly! [Laughs] And you know, the thing you love about Bernhard is that half of his conundrums are self-made, and they're absolutely delightful, because you finally go, "*Argh!*" No, he's hilarious. And I think there are a lot of writers … I mean, Beckett is one of the funniest writers around. Bernhard is enormously humorous. Céline.

And people *miss* that! Burroughs is another example of one of the great original humorists.

RC: A dry, Midwestern carnival-type humor.

CSL: Exactly! Burroughs has nothing to lose over those guys. It's a different sort of humor, but it's very much a part of the human comedy, if you will.

RC: But again, you can say that, or I can say that, because we're both a bit more on the euphoric side of the equation. But to a really depressed nihilistic existentialist, it could possibly push him completely over the edge.

CSL: Oh, yeah; that's true, yes. [Laughs] At the same time, it's totally *misery*, *spleen*.

RC: How did Octavio Paz's poem "Blanco," with its vertical division of the page, each side playing off the other – which is a very mysterious process to enact – influence or inspire your work?

CSL: Paz has been a great hero of mine for a really long time. "Blanco" particularly means a lot to me personally. I heard him read it in Mexico City in 1968, at a really tough time in Mexican history. And the words just kind of hung out there in the air in the midst of everything going on. It was this extraordinary moment where Paz was asserting that art *matters*. And of course, later on, I read it in all sorts of different ways. But I've always been intrigued by that notion of the way the words sit on a page. I'd originally thought I would use that kind of "double vertical" with *Mussoorie-Montague*, but it didn't work.

RC: It might have removed some of the free-flowing quality and made it more rigid.

CSL: Yes, it would have. What I did take away from Paz though, and from a whole lot of other writers – Mallarmé, to begin with, but Cummings certainly, Apollinaire,

Michaux, Paz – is this notion of the importance of how you lay out a word on a page: what the spacing is. Paz has this notion of *garabato*, which basically means a scrawl or a doodle, just translated directly. But Paz talks about language itself as a kind of *garabato*. And poetry as a *hieroglyph*. He really translates *garabato* ... not that he translates, but, when he's talking about it, he uses the notion of a *hieroglyph*. Which is essentially a sign, for Paz at least, that's only translatable to the extent that it's not literal. It carries its own response within itself. In "Blanco," he's playing with that whole notion of the glyph, which comes right out of the Mexican culture.

You know, we think of glyphs as Egyptian. Well, they are, but they're also Mayan; they're also Aztec. And so, he's playing with that notion of the word sitting alone on the page. I once wrote a piece about Paz being Mallarmé's true Spanish disciple, because I think he really is. He brings into Spanish a lot of what Mallarmé was trying to do – and did – a century before. If I remember correctly, one of the epigrams in "Blanco" is a quote by Mallarmé. I mean, he's always aware of that sense of how language lies on the page, the sense of nothingness, the sense of white space, of absence itself having a kind of existence. It's enormously important. So, for me, I think I took away from Paz – not just from that poem, but from a lot of them – this whole notion that, essentially, the illusory nature of reality *is* reality itself. Which is what Paz is always trying to get at.

And of course, Paz spent time in India, so he kind of worked himself into *Mussoorie-Montague* all over the place. You know, when I was writing this, I wasn't thinking necessarily about any of these people. But they were always hanging around in my head. And so, they came popping in from time to time.

RC: I'm glad you said that, because I don't mean to imply that these were direct inspirations to the poem.

CSL: No, but I can't outgrow my learning, either.

RC: It's just interesting to compare your work to other people's work, even when there is no direct influence.

CSL: Yeah! And I'm honored to be in that company – Bernhard, Paz, et cetera! [Laughs]

RC: Another poet you pay homage to is John High and his book, *Here*. I see he's one of the people that you dedicated your book to. In this collection of poems, you and John strike me as *flaneurs* of nature rather than flaneurs of the city. There's also the related theme of exploration: "Better to pack your bags / and hop on the next train rattling / across the twin rails that traverse / the churning river."

CSL: Right. I first began reading John back in 2003. His work was being published in *Talisman* magazine, and I liked what he was doing. Then we became acquainted over time. *Here* had just come out in 2006, and I got it right before I headed off to India. It was the only book I took with me. I figured, I'm going to be running into writers; I'll have a lot to read out there, and I can always raid somebody's bookshelf. So I just took *Here*. And somehow, it worked its way into my consciousness very quickly. It's one of those great seminal pieces of work that begins to open up everything from feeling to being to language. Not too many books do that. Not too many writers are able to do that. And so, it was certainly there.

But yes, absolutely, *flaneurs* of nature. And it's funny, because John lives in Brooklyn, but he does have a little garden attached to his apartment.

RC: The archetypal Brooklyn backyard.

CSL: Exactly!

RC: In many ways, I often think that us Brooklyn boys have a greater appreciation of nature, since we're so utterly deprived of it for the first few decades of our lives.

CSL: Yes! But John is always going off to other places. And you know, before I moved to Western Massachusetts, I'd also been a city boy.

RC: In what cities?

CSL: All sorts of places. Mexico City, San Francisco, Tokyo, Boston, Cambridge. And then Paris. The great cities! [Laughs] I'd always thought of myself as a city boy. But then, in '91, Patricia and I bought this house in Western Massachusetts. And we live overlooking the Connecticut River. It's just extraordinary out here; it's beautiful. After all these years of living here – twenty-four years – I still find it remarkable. Every day, when I walk down the stairs in the morning and look out the double doors at the river, it never fails to do something for me.

RC: Like a great work of art, nature is something we can continually return to, and never tire of, and always see new things.

CSL: Yes, exactly. And what's funny is, I never particularly liked nature poetry; I was never into any of that stuff.

RC: You were a city snob!

CSL: I was! I mean, give me Baudelaire over Tennyson or Wordsworth or whatever. But all of a sudden, I find myself paying a lot of attention to nature. I still don't think that I quite like nature poems, but I'm probably moving in that direction. By the time I'm, you know, ninety, I'll just be writing about the way the trees look. [Laughs] But there's also a sense of exploration. And one of the things I used to feel when I was younger ... This is probably just what happens to most people as they get older: you realize that exploration can happen anywhere. I used to think I had to go somewhere exotic. And I love going to places that are exotic – I still do – to explore. But I also found that an awful lot of exploration can take place if you just look at what's in front of you. To some extent, that whole book is really about paying attention. About looking.

RC: It reminds me of something that Albert Hofmann said in an interview in 1978. He was responding to the vast emigration in the Sixties of all the hippies to India, and Timothy Leary and so on. And Hofmann said, Why are they going all the way to India? Why aren't they simply tending to the gardens in their own backyards?

CSL: Right. Boy, Hofmann had it.

RC: He says something like: You can hold the flower right where you're standing, and see everything you need to see. That sort of thing.*

CSL: Particularly if you drop acid. [Laughs]

RC: Well, that's the ultimate example of not having to move anywhere!

CSL: Right!

RC: Other literary presences that hover in your poem include Dogen and his *Moon in a Dewdrop*, the Upanishads, the Hindu Manusmriti, Wittgenstein's *Tractatus Logico-Philosophicus*, and various Zen texts.

CSL: I've been reading Zen texts for a really long time, and I guess Zen's been a big part of helping me learn how to think. Or *not* think.

RC: That might be more appropriate, yes!

CSL: Dogen is difficult. For Dogen, it's not about koans. He wasn't a great fan of koans, actually. But he makes these statements that you have to kind of think about. And I've been thinking about Dogen for a long time.

RC: He felt that the practitioners were wasting so much time on koans when they should have been directly studying the sutras. He was a sutra man.

CSL: Yes, he was much more into all that. But in fact, what he presents to you, particularly in a book like *Moon in a Dewdrop*, is that the entire text, in a certain way, is a koan. He has this notion called *Uji*. It's always been something that I rattle around against, and I don't know what to do with it. But essentially, it's that time itself is *being*, and all being is in *time*. I still don't know what that means. I probably never will. But this poem is also about that. It doesn't mean you have to know what you're writing about to write. [Laughs]

RC: Dogen's notion of *time* and *being* is one of the reasons that so many students of Western philosophy have been drawn to him.

CSL: Yes. Heidegger has a slightly different take on the whole thing. For Heidegger, it's a much more rational way of looking at things. Essentially, *Dasein* itself, *being*, is for those who rest in being. He brings it into a more logical tradition; he looks at it from the Greeks. Dogen doesn't worry about that.

I turn this stuff over every once in a while, and I think it certainly hit me when I was there. As I say at the beginning of the thing, I'm sitting on a rock, and it was all kind of happening at once. I wasn't specifically thinking of Dogen. But the first poem I wrote in Mussoorie was the absolute first poem in the book. Which is not the way I usually work. And I just wrote it down in this little notebook:

For the time

BEING
BEING in time
but also in place.

Being is singular and plural
severally and in abundance.

That was the way this book started. The rest of it is not linear. I rewrote, and culled, and winnowed, and dumped, and everything else. But that first poem in there was actually the way this book started. And it was really the experience of sitting on a rock and attempting to figure out what I was doing. And I say, somewhere close to the beginning: "Which beings me to the clearing / and the rock. / I will sit here until / just before sunset / try not to give a name to where I am." And so, naturally, I think Dogen is there somewhere. Again, I'm not sitting there with Dogen and writing something off of it; it's just kind of hanging around.

Let's see: Wittgenstein. Oh, well, Wittgenstein has been important to me for about forty-five years. I read him as a young person; I read him as a student. Then I taught Wittgenstein when I was at MIT, and I never quite got it all. But Wittgenstein is also one of the great Zen masters. Well, that would kill him if he heard that. But essentially, it's the whole relationship between language and the world that he's concerned about. That the limits of language really are the limits of philosophy. Which is not to say the limits of thinking, because we think beyond language. And he's always trying to figure out that conundrum of how to say the unsayable. The only way we have to express what we know in an absolute direct fashion is in writing: is in the word itself. But is that word treacherous? Probably, it is. How do we know what we're doing?

And so, that was a part of it. You know, I was a semiotician for a long time, and spent a lot of time exploring. But I was never a doctrinaire semiotician. I came more out of the philosophical side, I guess.

RC: The philosophical-surrealistic side, I would imagine.

CSL: Yes, absolutely.

RC: Because Wittgenstein often strikes me that way. He's so hyperintellectual that he almost transforms into a surrealist before your eyes.

CSL: Oh, yeah, sure! And, again, the Upanishads, because in the Sixties we were all supposed to …

RC: That was a necessary book to have in the backpack.

CSL: Yes. Recently I reread them, and now they're really striking me as pretty amazing. And the Manusmriti. When I was an undergraduate, I took a class in the philosophy of religion and read Nietzsche. And Nietzsche says somewhere, I can't remember what book it was, I think it's probably in *Ecce Homo* where he says that the Hindu Manusmriti is a much better guide to life than the Bible.

RC: Leave it to Nietzsche to slip that in.

CSL: It's Nietzsche! So, being the young eager-beaver undergraduate, I decided: "Oh, I've got to read that!" [Laughs] So I remember digging the Manusmriti out in '68, or something like that. And being sort of like: "What the hell is this? Basically, it's a book of instructions." And it didn't do much for me. I thought, "Well, OK, Nietzsche gave me a bum steer." But when I was in India, I came across a 1912 translation of it; and, for some reason, I picked it up, and I made a few notes. And this time, it hit me as a whole different type of book.

RC: Possibly because of the translation?

CSL: No, because I was older and wiser. And when I first read it, I was expecting to have Zarathustra come walking out of the book. Initially, I was approaching it with that expectation.

RC: When we read things before a certain age, if there's not an immediate "peak experience," we're gone; we're out of there, right?

CSL: [Laughs] That's right! Yet, we never really get over those books, although we may *think* that they're lousy.

RC: Of course, with the Upanishads as well, there's a lot of tedious, very linear instruction: morality and ethics, and how to wash your feet and so on. Thus, it could be easy to miss the gems. But maybe that's why there *is* all that stuff. It's only if you're going to sit down, and if you have the fortitude, that you deserve to get to the gems.

CSL: Yeah, you have to work through it. The Upanishads are incredibly beautiful. One of the fellows at the writer's festival was a Sanskrit scholar. And to hear the Upanishads – or any Sanskrit work, including the Manu-smriti – *intoned* is an amazing experience. You have no idea what the words mean, but it doesn't matter.

RC: And we miss all that music in the translation.

CSL: All that music was there, and it was really quite something.

RC: The word *Zen* is rooted to the notion of "quiet consideration" or "quiet *and* consideration" as well as "tranquil contemplation." Although this is also disputed, according to Cicero, the word *religion* is rooted to the word *relegere*:

"to treat carefully, or give careful consideration to." In his "On the Nature of the Gods," he writes: "Those who carefully took in hand all things pertaining to the gods were called *religiosi*, from *relegere*."

CSL: Ah, interesting!

RC: In this sense, your treatise is certainly Zen-like. On page sixty-five, you even say, "Pay attention," which you mentioned before when you were discussing Thomas Bernhard. Now, isn't that a wonderful literary tie-in that we just made?

CSL: I do, huh? Oh, that's right: "Tread softly, pay attention. Find the way back home." [Laughs]

RC: But anyway, bearing all this in mind, it struck me that it's a sort of zen text.

CSL: It is; I wouldn't deny that for a moment. And it's interesting, because a couple of the more doctrinaire Zen people who have read it find it far from that.

RC: Because they're too doctrinaire.

CSL: Yes. John High, on the other hand, who is a Buddhist priest, is enormously fond of the book. And that's what matters to me, because he's not only a Zen priest, but he's also …

RC: He's got good taste, which you can trust.

CSL: Exactly.

RC: I wasn't going to bring this up, but it's perhaps of interest in this context. I believe you begin the first part with a quote from the Upanishads, and the second part with a quote from Gertrude Stein.

CSL: Yes. [Laughs]

RC: Which immediately impressed me, because there's a wonderful quote by Joseph Campbell – and now, I wish I had it in front of me – who says that, in the future, the message will no longer come from the traditional religious institutions; it will come directly from the artist, the poet, the painter.*

CSL: Yes, that's right. I can vaguely remember that.

RC: Therefore, it's no wonder that the traditional religious people would *not* get it, but John High would.

CSL: That's right. Exactly.

RC: Mircea Eliade, the great scholar of comparative religion, once coined the term *hierophany*: a rupture in three-dimensional space and time, a "breakthrough of the sacred into the world," which was often triggered by a natural element. In your poem, rocks, rivers, and monkeys are quite important, grounding the ethereal meditations with solid nature underfoot. The nature that reveals our *own* nature, but that also anchors and nourishes it.

CSL: Eliade was right. It's interesting because Dogen also came close to a kind of animist notion of being: being in *everything*. Rocks, trees, stones, pebbles. The snowfall. You know, I have a sense of constant wonder at the way the world manages to renew itself, no matter what we seem to do to it. How long this will go on, I have no idea. But I'm always astonished by what can happen. There's a certain predictability in the natural world that is comforting.

RC: A cyclical aspect.

CSL: Yes. You know the tree *will* put out its leaves this year ... you're confronted with that whole notion of cyclical motions in time, and all that, as time marches through space. To me, it's a continual source of inspiration – and sometimes even exultation. Yes.

RC: We're also reminded of the constant edgy presence of death in your work: "Embarkations are hard: / disembarkations harder." Sometimes, you accomplish this with just a simple phrase, such as "only dead leaves stirring."

CSL: Yes. I mean, you know, death is real. At the time I was writing this, people that I knew were dying. And have died. My mother was in bad shape. My brother-in-law died before the book came out; my mother did, too. I wasn't necessarily pondering my own death; but, if you don't ponder your own death, there's probably something wrong with you. So, yeah, I was very aware of the temporality of it all. And how do you hang onto it? Well, you hang onto it by being there at that particular moment and giving it your *all*. And letting that "all" give something back to you. But there's definitely that dark side there. Which I don't even know, is maybe ... We have that way of looking at it, "the dark side." There's an awareness of our fleeting existence on the earth that's very much a part of that book. And the whole notion of cycle. In nature, there's death and regeneration. And in our own existence, there's death, and who knows about the regeneration? But at least there's death. We can say that. [Laughs]

RC: Chögyam Trungpa once said, "Life is a good thing, but death can be a good thing, too."

CSL: Oh, yeah, exactly.

RC: You've also managed to take certain ancient traditions and explore the same concepts with a modern voice: "consciousness floating in a where / that isn't here / unconsciousness closing in like a parenthesis." And you explore a playful meditation on spirituality and words themselves: "a modifier dangles from the giant rhododendrons." This seems to be one of the grand themes of the book.

CSL: Yes, absolutely. I love language, but there's a point where you just can't get too serious about it. Which is why

I wasn't a great semiotician. Because, at times, I used to sort of feel: "*Eh!* What a bunch of nonsense!"

RC: Fortunately, you betrayed the dogma.

CSL: All the time! And I'd write stuff that, one day, I would think was profound, and the next day go, "My, what *is* this?"

RC: I once met a retired linguist, an American professor in Paris, and I asked him what he thought of semiotics. He laughed and said, "I call it semi-*idiotics*."

CSL: That's right! [Laughs] Well, you know, that was the great war, featuring linguists and semioticians. For me, Roman Jakobson was the one who got me off on this; and I never got over it. But language has always been important to me, as is obvious from everything I've been saying. Bernhard, Paz, Heidegger, Wittgenstein: they're playing with this whole notion of "What is language, and what can we do with it?" But at the same time, you can't get too tied up in knots about it. You can have an awfully good time.

RC: Especially if you're an artist, you can't afford to do that: to get overwhelmed by the dogma.

CSL: Exactly.

RC: We also have your exploration of the limitations of words. You write:

> Place this right angled Klein jar
> in the left angled slot.
> As in explain to squirrels and blue jays
> why they shouldn't eat the seed
> put out for the wrens and sparrows and finches.
> As in describe luminous motion.
> as in mind crammed with monkeys.

There are the monkeys again!

CSL: That's right!

RC: And I also like this line very much: "To name is to codify / also to destroy. I won't name this feeling: / I do not wish to get to the heart of my mystery." That's very much in opposition to so much of the pointless intellectualizing that we've witnessed in the last two centuries. Western philosophy often strikes me as an elegant way of stating the obvious, or as a convoluted way of groping toward the ineffable. But with Wittgenstein, we at least have a definition of philosophy as something that results in the "clarification of prepositions," or his attempt to do so.

CSL: Yes.

RC: In your book, however, you attempt one step better: into what I would call the poetic clarification of poetic prepositions.

CSL: *Whoa!* I'll buy that one! Thank you very much, Mr. Couteau! [Laughs]

RC: Of course, this is the result if a crash course in Wittgenstein over the last few days! But it struck me, going back and forth from *Tractatus* to your book, that there's a kind of *echo* of that, somehow.

CSL: Yes, absolutely. Years and years ago, I tried writing something poetic off of Wittgenstein. It was a mess; it was terrible, so I gave up. But I knew he wouldn't go away. Eventually, he would come back in the right form. So, it kind of worked it's way onto this one.

RC: You mentioned *feeling* before, and this is another thing I wanted to ask in regard to your work. One of my problems with a lot of European philosophy is the eclipse or the usurpation of the feeling function ...

CSL: Right.

RC: And the overreliance on hyperrational thought that we often find at the root of such inquiries. Yet, we can only *value* things properly with the assistance of our feeling. Your poem bridges these seemingly disparate sensibilities, because you honor logical thought, and you use it to your advantage, but you also make *fun* of it. Which perhaps is the role of the artist.

CSL: Yes. And I think that's the most difficult thing to do, is to remember, as E. E. Cummings said: "Since feeling is first, who pays any attention to the syntax of things that will never wholly kiss you?" That's from his poem, "since feeling is first." [Recites poem] "For life is not a paragraph, and death, I think, is no parentheses."

RC: You quoted the last line in your book.

CSL: It's one of my very favorite Cummings poems. Whenever I get too "in my head," I think about that poem. If you don't, you don't have much left. I mean, I spent so much time in academia with great minds, but empty shells, essentially.

RC: Wittgenstein portrays logic in an almost deified manner. He says logic is "a mirror-image of the world. Logic is transcendental." And he adds that value can exist outside only the world, which I interpret to mean beyond *his* conscious grasp. This is another quote from *Tractatus*: "If there is any value that does have value, it must lie outside the whole sphere of what happens and in the case. For all that happens, and is the case, is accidental." Now, I assume he means by this that something that we might term "acausal meaningful connection" cannot exist either cosmologically or on an interpersonal level. You, however, seem to differ from him in this way, because, in your poem, you assert and assume a value, an inherent value: in consciousness, in creativity, and in the heart.

CSL: Absolutely. Yes, I do. You know, I fully appreciate all of what he's doing there. It's not by any means a small thing. Essentially, *Tractatus*, it's seventy-five pages long, and he's attempting to boil it down. The very first sentence is: "The world is everything, that is the case." He takes seven propositions and attempts to create a whole notion of what logic is in relation to language. At the seventh proposition, after he's gone through all this work – with propositions, propositions, true functions, et cetera – he finally ends up: "What we cannot speak about, we must be silent." And so, ultimately, silence, as Beckett well knew, wins the game. So we have to throw away the ladder.

RC: But obviously, you still take good things from him nonetheless.

CSL: Oh, yeah, certainly. But yes, I do have issues. And I'm hardly a doctrinaire anything. I just kind of make my own way, and keep moving in my own direction. But yeah, very interesting. Very interesting.

RC: Heraclitus has an axiom, which I'm sure you know, which goes: "It is the opposite that is good for you." Which suggests that we're often drawn to our own unconscious polarity: one opposing our native temperament. Bearing this in mind, this is from a book called *Wittgenstein: Conversations 1949-1951*, by O. K. Bouwsma, who says:

> Then we rode to the top of the hill near the library and looked over the town. The moon was in the sky. "If I had planned it[," said Wittgenstein, "]I should never have made the sun at all. See! How beautiful! The sun is too bright and too hot." Later, he said, "And if there were

only the moon[,] there would be no reading and writing."

Now, when I read this, I wondered if Wittgenstein was unwittingly projecting his feeling function and the values it bestows upon that ancient image. And I thought the excerpt itself almost reads like a passage from your poem!

CSL: Yes, it does! [Laughs] I do have that one Wittgenstein quote there, you know: "If the meaning of a word is the private exemplar of the object, then 'I know what I mean by *toothache*.'"

RC: That's a wonderful line, yes! "But no other person can know it."

CSL: Exactly!

RC: It's so interesting that you bring this up, because that's an example of *extreme* feeling, isn't it? I mean, it's not just a sensation; the toothache triggers the emotions.

CSL: Right. What happens with Wittgenstein, though, is that by the time you get to the *Notebooks* and *Philosophical Investigations*, he's running back to feeling as being of significant consequence. You ultimately don't know what to do with it. You know, Chomsky has the same problem. And, well, that's a whole other discussion. We won't get into that one today! [Laughs]

RC: Nietzsche is one of the few Western philosophers of modernity who not only attempts to incorporate feeling into the whole hierarchy of philosophical thought, but who also declares that it's of equivalent value to thought.

CSL: Absolutely. Certainly Nietzsche, and then the whole of phenomenology itself cannot exclude feeling, as much as it wants to focus on mind. Heidegger maybe being the one exception, because he's really centered on the whole notion of mind. And yet, he uses expressions like "clearing," and "care," and all of that, which are expressions of feeling. But Merleau-Ponty and Sartre were extremely aware of the human emotion as playing a part in anything we do.

RC: You write, "Belief is tested / when a jammed infinitive / makes a monkeyclature out of verbs. / So we lean on adjectives decked out / in their Sunday best / and passing nouns / out for their morning constitutional."

CSL: Yeah, I had a good time with that. [Laughs] You know, there is a lot of monkey in that book. In Zen, when you're having a hard time meditating, they talk about the "money mind." And in India, watching all those monkeys everywhere – they were very present, very aggressive – I suddenly got what "monkey mind" really meant. Of course, it comes out of that tradition; that's where Buddha started out. The origin of Buddhism is literally in that part of the world. But with all these monkeys, you suddenly *get* "monkey mind." And so, I was sort of: "*Oh!* What a revelation!" On a terribly ridiculous level! [Laughs] And so, monkeys got in there because of the Zen monkey-mind business. And then, *monkeyclature*: I just couldn't resist that.

RC: It's a wonderful neologism. And monkey business is precisely what you're getting at here.

CSL: Absolutely. You know, it's about the whole failure of language.

RC: In Chinese astrology, the monkey is one of the bestial signs. There, the monkey's role is to climb up on the highest bough, eat his banana, and throw the banana skins down and laugh while the other animals are slipping and tripping and falling over them. He's a kind of harlequin figure, a trickster.

CSL: Exactly.

RC: I thought we would end with a few things about Dogen, especially since he had such an impact on you. He was known for being an innovator both in terms of his approach to Zen as well as his use of poetic language. Like many of your own favorite stylists, he employed neologisms and word play in the great French tradition. This is his description of "Mind-only." "Mind," he says, "is the 'skin-flesh-bones-marrow'" and the "raising-a-flower-and-bursting-into-laughter." All of which he hyphenates like a lengthy Germanic adjectival phrase. But like you, he doesn't just jettison the mind. "Despite all this, it should not be abandoned.... it is the mind in which all things themselves are ultimate reality, and the mind which communicates between a Buddha and a Buddha."

CSL: Yes. And this kind of sums up what my book's about, if there's anything that it's about. But, yeah, I was pretty much working out of that. What a wonderful quote. Dogen was amazing. But my limitation with Dogen is that I have to rely on translations. And the 1912 French translation is nothing like the original. From what you read in the commentaries, he uses this incredibly refined, stylistic, poetic manner of expressing himself. Gary Snyder is probably finished his translation of Dogen by now, which I think might be quite good.

RC: This last quote has a wonderful tie in to what you've succeeded at doing in this poem. Dogen relates the story of a poet named Su Tung-p'o who awoke on a mountaintop and achieved enlightenment upon hearing the sound of a gurgling brook. Just before this occurred, he'd listened, baffled, to his master Chao-chio lecture on "the discourse of *in*-sentient beings" – as you said earlier, rocks, rivers, snowflakes – and how important this was for creativity. "I suspect," Dogen says, "that Chao-chio's talk […], still reverberating, may secretly be intermingled with the nightly sounds of streams." "Ultimately speaking, is it the poet that is enlightened, or is it mountains and waters that are enlightened?"

As Eliade says, we often think of nature inspiring or transporting us, but this view is considerably larger. As you say in your book, "subject is object when object is subject." And so, I get this same sense from your verse: that it's not just a description of what's going on in *your* mind, but it's this very visceral attempt to remove all boundaries between the ego and what's around it.

CSL: Yes, that was the big attempt. Whether I succeeded or not, I don't know. [Laughs] This book took quite a while to write. I began in spring of 2007, and I kept working on it in bits and pieces. I also read from it on a number of occasions. And I finished in Istanbul, in 2012.

I finally felt that I just had to stop; I didn't know what else to do with it. Then I sent it to Ed Foster, at Talisman House. Ed helped me to decide that, you know, it's done. As I say in the last sentence, "Completion is a fiction." And Picasso was absolutely right: A work of art is never finished, you simply stop working on it.

RC: Thank you, Chris.

CSL: Thank you for such great questions and for such extraordinary thinking on your part.

---

* This interview was conducted on February 5, 2015 and featured at tygersofwrath.com on May 26, 2015.
* "I've never been able to understand these people. What I got out of LSD, I carry about inside me. I have to stay in my own daily life. To see the flowers in my own garden is to see all the

mystical wonder of existence, of creation. You don't have to go to India to see it." From "Interview: Albert Hofmann," *Omni* magazine, July 1981, p. 72.

* "And then we have William Blake: 'If the doors of perception were cleansed every thing would appear to man as it is, infinite.' Thus we have the message in our own tradition, where it is known, however, as poetry, not religion, while our religion, actually ... is being radically misinterpreted because it is read differently from a poem or enacted play." Joseph Campbell, "The Interpretation of Symbolic Forms," *The Mythic Dimension: Selected Essays, 1959-1987* (New York: HarperCollins, 1997), pp. 166-167.

James Dempsey Talks About
*The Tortured Life of Scofield Thayer**

The recipient of awards from the Associated Press and United Press International, James Dempsey teaches journalism, writing, and English literature at the Worcester Polytechnic Institute, in Massachusetts. He's also the author of The Court Poetry of Geoffrey Chaucer: A Facing-page Translation in Modern English *and the novels* Zakary's Zombies *and* Murphy's American Dream. *This is his first biography.*

Rob Couteau: I'm in love with your book. You've created something so important, I think.

James Dempsey: It took me a long time, so I'm really gratified to hear you say that.

RC: How many years did it take?

JD: I was working on it for nine years. Not all the time, obviously. It was mostly summers of research, here and there. Mostly at Yale, but there was also plenty of material at New York Public Library, Georgetown University, the Barnes Foundation in Philadelphia, and the Boston Athenaeum.

RC: Good books do take a long time, you know?

JD: Well, this one sure did!

RC: How did you mentor yourself in learning to master the craft of biography? How do you go about assembling a life story?

JD: I had no idea when I started, to be honest. And I just started putting together all the research I had. I put it into a chronological timeline, but, as I went along, I found that little parts of it were starting to cohere, and you begin to see themes coming out of it. And that's what turns into chapters, eventually. When there isn't any theme, you basically just go with the chronology. So, I was trying to emphasize what seemed to me the most important aspects. But, by the same token, when you're a biographer you're at the mercy of your materials, and you can only write about what you have and what you know, and there's so much you don't know. It's kind of a ballsy thing, or a stupid thing, to do a biography, because you're really saying: Well, this is this guy's life. That's a very arrogant thing to do, in some ways.

RC: It's a dirty job, but somebody's got to do it. And I think you did a good job with it.

JD: [Laughs]

RC: One of the things I liked about it, and about your writing, is that I sensed the great empathy you had for this very tormented soul. You've said that Scofield didn't get what he deserved in terms of his accomplishments, and you wanted to "give him his due." Who was Scofield Thayer, and what was his legacy?

JD: I think the two things, really. One is the *Dial*, and the other was his art collection. And the interesting thing is that he didn't regard the *Dial* as his life work. He always felt the *Dial* was getting in the way of his own writing. And it was, because it takes a lot of work to edit a magazine. Somebody once said that we are not who we *think* we are but what we *do* every day, and that's what he did every day. What he produced was really remarkable. Even though it pissed him off to have to do it.

Then there was the art collection, which was also a passion of his. He put together a folio of reproductions called *Living Art* that represented what he thought was the best of modern art at the time, that he sold in this country. He was a real ... "impresario" might be a little too vulgar, but he did believe in spreading art and art's ideas around as much as he could.

RC: The *Dial* was originally founded by Emerson in 1840, I believe, and published as a transcendentalist magazine. Tell us about the history of the *Dial* before it came under Scofield's control.

JD: Well, you're right about that. It lasted about four or five years. Margaret Fuller was the editor of the *Dial* when Emerson was running it. There was an attempt to bring back a magazine called *The Dial* in 1860 that failed, and then another one in 1880, in Chicago, and this is the one that took. Francis Browne was the publisher and the editor. It became a mid-West beacon of culture and aesthetics. It was very well thought of, if a little ...

RC: Stodgy?

JD: Yes, stolid but stodgy. You know, if you read it, you'll find that the literature usually amounts to maybe a review or two. Or something in the letters column about some obscure pronunciation of a Shakespearean word, or something like that. But it wasn't really up to date. And there were one or two pieces poking fun at the rising modernist ideas, such as free verse. And then, of course, they adjoined it while it was in Chicago, and they were part of it when it made the transition to New York City.

RC: Thayer's *Dial* was tremendously successful as a booster and promulgator of modernism in America, yet it also suffered tremendous financial loses. You estimate that Scofield sacrificed about 100,000 dollars a year to keep it afloat. Who were some of the artists and writers, both traditional and avant-garde, that he published? What were the keynotes of the *Dial* during his tenure?

JD: If you'd have asked him at the time, I think he would have said that he wasn't pushing any particular ism: that he just wanted quality material. But because they were willing to look at a lot of avant-garde material and material by young writers and consider it on the same level as that of established writers, it gave more prestige to the modernist movement in a lot of ways. It made Cummings's career; no doubt about that.

RC: Absolutely; Scofield was tremendously helpful to him.

JD: And Marion Moore did well because of it, too. But they also published a lot of the more established folk. The first person to receive the Dial Award was Sherwood Anderson, who was of the generation before. They also published Joseph Conrad, William Butler Yeats. You know, writers that were not modernist or weren't really in the front of the avant-garde, but you couldn't deny that they were important writers.

RC: I understand that he was the first to publish "The Waste Land" in the United States.

JD: He was, yes, but they decided not to go with the notes to the "Waste Land." Thayer probably insisted on it. Of course, as you know, Thayer was not happy with the poem. He thought it was very disappointing.

RC: In some of your other interviews, people have brought up the fact that he had an ambivalent relationship with some of the modernist writing. Yet, at the same time, we could speculate and say, well, perhaps his vision was so forward looking that, to him, things like Joyce's *Ulysses* and the "Waste Land" *were* too traditional. Maybe he saw something more forward moving in the painting of the era, for example. I mean, it's a difficult call to make, right?

JD: It is. For what we think of as modernism, there's no doubt that his taste as regards to art was much more avant-garde than it was regarding literature. But he was up-to-date there, too. I mean, he was a big fan of the German novelist and playwright, Arthur Schnitzler. And Schnitzler is not so well known in that he was one of the first people to use the stream of consciousness. And so, Thayer was very much aware of the various techniques of modernism; he just wasn't impressed by them.

RC: Exactly. And perhaps, to some young writers today, or fifty years from now, looking at *Ulysses*, or the "Waste Land," they may find it a bit stodgy.

JD: Well, I know that some of my students do. "Why does it have to be so difficult?" [Laughs]

RC: There's no record of Scofield attending school until he was ten years old, and you say: "Thayer suffered from some kind of serious sickness or traumatic event in his fourth year, which perhaps affected his education." Do you have any idea what may have happened to him, or do you harbor any sort of speculation that you didn't want to mention in print without more specific evidence?

JD: I would love to know, Rob; I really would. And my speculation might be wholly off key, too. I just wasn't able to find any evidence of his education before then. And considering that he was such a packrat, that he did keep, you know, every paper that he wrote from middle-school on, I would imagine that, had he gone, he would have said something.

RC: I'm actually referring more to what the trauma might have been, rather than the education.

JD: There's only one mention of that, and that comes from him. He talks about *the* incident that took place in his fourth year, and that's all we learn about it. He's frustratingly obtuse, sometimes, in his writing.

RC: It could have been something extremely embarrassing, as well.

JD: Yes, indeed.

RC: Thayer said: "My father's eyes showed *hatred + detestation* of me." And he imagined his "mother's heart as having electric-lighted plate-glass windows in it. Not necessarily intimate." Wonderful understatement there.

JD: [Laughs] Right.

RC: Like many of those who are later diagnosed as schizophrenic, Thayer had an extremely contentious relationship with his parents. What do you think their overall influence on Thayer was, for better or worse?

JD: That's a really good question. He was the only child. So, you know, if anyone was going to carry the flag of the Thayer name forward, it was he, both in terms of producing children and also running his father's empire, which was really extensive. But of course, he showed no interest in that whatsoever. And his father died when he was seventeen, so he really wasn't around to guide him as a young adult. It seems that the mother was somewhat scared of him, and he went around doing more or less what he wanted. He did hide a lot of things from his mother. He would hide the fact that he was buying certain paintings. He didn't speak to her about being in therapy with Freud. So, you know, there was a sensitivity there. But I think, by and large, he was the more dominating one of the two. And so, he did what he wanted.

RC: The death of the father might have been one of the best things that ever happened to him.

JD: It could have been, yes.

RC: You know, based on his descriptions of the father. And also the fact that, if the father was around, he might not have had all that wealth to play with, and to create the *Dial*, I would assume.

JD: Indeed. And the father seems to be very much a kind of engineering man. You know, the classic Dickensian "Mr. Gradgrind," who understand machines beautifully but doesn't get on with people too well.

RC: In another one of his great understatements Thayer said something like: My father had no grasp of human psychology.

JD: Right. Or even when it comes to animals, he said, he's got no sense of psychology.*

RC: We find a very high percentage of childhood sexual abuse in schizophrenia. Did you ever have a sense that something like this may have happened to Thayer?

JD: There's no doubt that his sexual life was ... There was some kind of damage in it somewhere. Exactly what it was I was never able to find out. I'm editing a journal coming out next year; it's called the *Worcester Review*. They're giving me an issue to do a "Scofield Thayer and the *Dial*" thing. And I got a really interesting essay from an Oxford prof, who was looking at a Cummings drawing in the *Dial* and talking about paganism and the pagan poets, which is how many of them were viewed at the time. And how the immature view of the rampant satyr running after the virginal nymph was a classic paradigm for them. She suggests that most men would outgrow that. But for Thayer it seemed to become more and more powerful as he went deeper into his insanity. You know, he did "like them young," as they say.

RC: Thayer was born into a tremendously wealthy family. And you say that, at Harvard, he learned about the "connection ... between money and between sex": "Serial marriages comprised a form of prostitution ... by which a woman could become wealthy in exchange for allowing her body to be enjoyed by more than one man." And, in Scofield's words: "American girls enjoy the distinction of being the only members of the animal kingdom which – thanks to the American system of frequent and advantageous divorces and remarriages – pull themselves up by the cunt." When I read that, I thought: Thayer may have missed his calling as an eccentric social commentator.

JD: [Laughs] It's quite a quotation, isn't that?

RC: It really is. Maybe he should have been writing more nonfiction than poetry, because it's very 1960s, 1970s in diction, that kind of remark, I thought.

JD: Yes, indeed. I read most of his comments for the *Dial*. And most of his poetry, which was OK; it was uneven. But reading his notebooks is just fascinating, because he would touch on people of the time, and he'd be talking about social movements, and social aesthetics, and his opinions were just really interesting.

RC: Some of them are similar to this remark, in that they're intensely subjective but contain an element of truth, a grain of truth quite often, and are bizarrely funny. It would be interesting to publish some of this stuff.

JD: Definitely.

RC: Going back to what we were talking about before, he felt that, in general, women were too much of a pushover for a man of wealth, and he later developed a fetish for women who put up more of a resistance. Was this a key aspect of his attraction to adolescent virgins?

JD: I don't know. And it's conflicted, because just about every woman who was close to him was very, very fond of him. And the affection is really unfeigned.

Alyse Gregory was probably his closest friend. And much, much later, she got into a bit of a fight with Santayana, because Santayana had made a reference to Thayer in a letter that he'd sent to Gregory's husband at the time. This was probably fifteen or twenty years after Thayer had been removed from public life. And she was *furiously* and adamantly defending Thayer. So, it's difficult. At the same time, he talks about not being able to enjoy a woman unless there's resistance that he can overcome. And how that figures in with the younger, maybe even prepubescent girls that he seemed to be attracted to, certainly young girls, I don't really know.

RC: I had the impression that, as a hyperintellectual who was often out of touch with his feeling function, he was only able to safely express his emotions with much younger women. Another way of saying this is that his emotional life was somewhat on the level of a twelve- or thirteen-year old girl. Although inappropriate, his relationships with adolescents may have served an important psychological function in terms of keeping him emotionally grounded. Would you agree?

JD: Yes, it's an interesting point. It reminds me a little bit of the way Humbert Humbert defends himself in *Lolita*.

RC: I was just going to bring that up.

JD: When one reads *Lolita*, one of the chilling things about it is how well you understand where Humbert is coming from. And he's such a smooth talker; he just pulls you right in. And you don't quite see the monstrousness of it.

RC: It's funny because, next week, I'm interviewing my friend Robert Roper, who just published a book called *Nabokov in America: On the Road to Lolita*. So *Lolita*'s been very much on my mind. And it's going to be a very interesting tie-in: from your interview, then to his.

JD: I can't wait to get around to reading that book; it sounds great.

RC: What you just said possibly also applies – not in terms of his overt sexual life, but in terms of his hyperintellectualism – to Nabokov himself. There always has to be a reason why you end up writing a particular novel, and I think it's perhaps not uncommon for someone who's so cerebral on the one hand to be somewhat out of touch with his emotions. And this constellates, somehow, the image of the young, virginal, pure, feminine, vulnerable girl as carrying the symbol of that undeveloped emotional life.

JD: It's a fascinating thing. All kinds of young men go through that period when we think it would be so simple if our partner was, you know … If we could just sexually objectify them and that was the end of it! [Laughs] But you know, life is not like that. It's much more complex.

RC: There's always the other person to consider.

JD: Right. It's a human being, man! [Laughs] But if you've got tons of money, you can get away with much more than you might otherwise.

RC: And also, in this time period, the whole issue of pedophilia in general was less in the forefront of the collective consciousness than it is today. It even went to the other extreme in the 1980s, when teachers who were quite innocent of anything were being arrested and thrown into jail and so on; it was kind of a witch hunt. But in Scofield's time, it was much less in the forefront of people's awareness that older men might be abusing younger girls.

JD: Right. Definitely.

RC: Ever since their years together at university, Scofield was enormously helpful to the poet Edward Estlin Cummings. Maybe you could talk about their relationship, and how he helped Estlin, and the incredibly baroque tale of Nancy.

JD: They met at Harvard. When they first met, it was Thayer who was very much a mentor. Cummings was eager to get on the staff of the *Harvard Monthly* and to start publishing his poetry, and Thayer helped him do that. There seems to have been a pretty real friendship that formed between the two. He seems to be the single male that had the longest, most profound relationship with Thayer. Even though he was certainly not above making fun of Thayer when Thayer wasn't present.

And I think the first time Cummings met Elaine, he realized that he just wanted her. He immediately started writing to her, even at her finishing school. I think that he had a crush on her from the very, very beginning. And that may have been part of what made him want to stay close to Thayer, too. And then, later, of course, when Thayer started the magazine, Cummings boasted to his parents that, with Sibley Watson and Thayer's magazine, he basically had his own publishing house.

RC: He really had the launch of his entire career through the *Dial* magazine, yes?

JD: Yes, indeed.

RC: Thayer also purchased a number of Cummings's paintings. What do you think of Cummings as a painter?

JD: I'm not an art historian, but I rather like some of them, I must say. Especially his figures and some of his landscapes. Others seem derivative of the modernist techniques. But when he goes for the representational stuff, which I much prefer, I rather like his stuff.

RC: What did Thayer think of Cummings as a painter?

JD: I don't know; I'm not sure that he actually wrote that down anywhere. He was fond of his drawings, and he published a lot of them in the *Dial*.

RC: I believe in the first issue that he took control of the *Dial*, there are Cummings's poems along with some of his drawings.

JD: Yes, there was. Six poems and several drawings.

RC: The relationship between Elaine, Estlin, and Scofield is quite interesting and a bit bizarre. When I first read the biography of Estlin Cummings, I had the sense that Scofield was really pushing Elaine and Estlin together. And then, of course, there's the very strange story of Elaine Orr's daughter, Nancy, and how she didn't realize that Cummings was her real father, not Thayer.

JD: Until she found herself getting a crush on him. [Laughs[

RC: Right! As an adult, she befriended Cummings, ended up modeling for him, felt in love with him during the course of posing, and, according to one version of the story, confessed her love, and was only then was told by Cummings that he was her real father. When I first read about this, I thought it resembled an ancient Greek drama. It's a very unusual story, no?

JD: I think Elaine would have been right at home as one of those strong female figures in Greek tragedy, because she was a very powerful woman who controlled the world around her very well and used what she had to get on. You know, the way she dumped Cummings three months after marrying him, and then marrying somebody who was quite wealthy, and then bringing up Nancy with these varying stories about her father. First of all, that her father was dead. Then, that the father wasn't dead but was insane and there was no point in trying to get in touch with him. She was determined to stamp her own version of reality on what was around her. She was a very strong woman in that sense, because it worked a great deal of the time.

RC: Would you say that she became, or was forced to become, a very strong woman as a counterpoint to her earlier life, when she seemed very weak and vulnerable, and even misused a bit by Scofield? I mean, in the descriptions that I read, she's almost like a borderline personality: very unformed, and very much under the control of Scofield until it finally all breaks apart. And then, she becomes a kind of horrific control freak.

JD: Yes. But we really only have her through the vision of Thayer and Cummings, so there's bias, certainly, in how we view her. There's a whole trove of letters at the Beinecke Library that were embargoed until 2012. And I was convinced that these would show me all the secrets of Thayer, you know? Whether he was homosexual; what the incident in Vienna was about; or the young boy in New York.* And when I got to them, it turned out that there were countless letters between Thayer and Elaine going through their whole lives. I mean, right up until the point when Thayer was declared insane. And they were striking in how affectionate they were, on both sides. So, she had a fondness for him. And then she had that quote. I think that quote is actually through Cummings, and it's in a play that is obviously based on this triangle. She says something like: "Thayer taught me the lesson of my life. I owe everything to him." I don't know what that lesson was. Was it: You've got to look out for yourself, and make that the first thing? Or what? What was it?

RC: So many mysteries in this story.

JD: Mm, there certainly are.

RC: Sigmund Freud had much more experience with so-called neurotic patients than he did with schizophrenics; and his approach to art and creativity was rather reductionist and materialistic. Everything was ultimately rooted in sexuality, for example, and any artistic product was merely a sublimation. Conversely, Freud's rival, Jung, cut his teeth in the Burgholzli Psychiatric Hospital working largely with destitute schizophrenics, and he later published a book on schizophrenia and sent it to Freud, which led to their brief but intense friendship. Jung viewed art and creatively in a more spiritual and holistic way, often citing artists and writers as avatars and visionaries who were, as Pound said, the antennae of the race. For all these reasons, I found it somewhat ironic that Thayer ended up with Freud and only seems to mention Jung as a way to draw Freud's jealousy and ire.

JD: Yes, isn't it? I didn't know that Jung had such experience with schizophrenics, but that's really interesting. It would have been fascinating to see what would have happened if Jung had taken him on as a patient rather than Freud.

RC: There's also some reference in your book where you say that one of Thayer's friends was trying to convince him to go to see Jung. So, he was aware of Jung.

JD: He was indeed. He was very up-to-date on the whole movement of psychoanalysis, which was a hot topic at the time for the intellectual. He was right on top of what was going on. He did manage to get an article out of Freud. That didn't get published, and it's uncertain as to what exactly happened. I got the impression that Watson and Kenneth Burke, who was then editing the *Dial*, either didn't like it, didn't want to translate it, or *something*. But it never got in there. It sounds like a very decent article, too.

RC: That's amazing, that they would turn down an article by Freud for the *Dial!*

JD: [Laughs] Indeed.

RC: Especially since the ego structure is so fragile and delicate a membrane in the case of schizophrenia, any sort of tension or stress can easily result in a psychotic episode. And quite often, as a result, schizophrenics are incapable of dealing with criticism or self-critique. As the illness progresses, the fault for any sort of problem becomes increasingly projected upon others in what appears to be an act of self-preservation. But this is also accompanied by increasing paranoia, since it's always "the others" who are to blame rather than oneself. How did this play itself out in Thayer's life?

JD: I don't know if that's something you wrote, or got from somewhere else, but I think that's fascinating.

RC: It's just off the top of my head.

JD: Well, that's wonderful. The paranoia *is* a kind of defense mechanism, in that it puts all the bad stuff outside of oneself. Then all you have to do is fight it. But of course, the paradox is that it's all coming from inside yourself. So, you're fighting yourself, without really knowing what's going on.

You know, Alfred Barnes was the big bogeyman for Thayer. He's the one who crops up again and again in the more paranoid writings we have. And it's a damn shame; although, what little I know of Barnes, it seems that he *was* a bully, and he certainly wasn't above using physicality to get what he wanted. That was something that Thayer was quite timid about. He wasn't a physical guy who would get into a brawl in a bar. You know, he'd send somebody else in to do the fighting for him.

RC: As you say, his wealth really protected him in so many ways. I can think of many incidents that you describe in the book: the way he ran the *Dial* where, if there was any little typo, they'd have a big meeting and find out *who* was to blame. That sort of thing. And Barnes, being probably equally wealthy, and very influential, powerful, pugnacious, and a real bully, would be one of the few who could try to call Scofield to task and create the kind of stress that would really provoke a horrendous psychic tension within him.

JD: Yes. And it got to the point, I think, where, no matter what happened, Barnes was blamed for it. Whether it was the wood creaking at night, or somebody poisoning the water of his home.

RC: How did Scofield's friend and business partner, James Sibley Watson, help to keep him grounded during their time together? And how was Watson's influence felt at the *Dial*, in terms of the art and writing that was published?

JD: Watson was a much quieter fellow and, because of that, he doesn't really get as much credit as he might otherwise. As I mention in the book, he was very much a Francophile. Thayer was much more in favor of the German artists and writers, and they disagreed a great deal. But if it hadn't been for Watson, "The Waste Land" wouldn't have been in the *Dial*; *The Cantos* would not have been in the *Dial*; lots of stuff that we think of as the high points of modernism wouldn't have made it, because it wasn't to Thayer's taste. And of course, he was very much down to earth, and he was very involved with the family when the discussions were going on about what to do with Scofield when Scofield was running and rampaging through Europe, and having breakdowns left, right, and center. And Watson went on to a really interesting career as a filmmaker.

RC: One of the most inspiring and enduring relationships that Thayer experienced was his love affair with Europe itself, and with the art that he adored and collected there. When he left New York for his final trip to the Continent, Marianne Moore said: "I am afraid, Mr. Thayer, you are a spiritual expatriate." I thought this was a very resonant phrase that described him in so many ways. What do you think she meant by that, and how would you interpret it yourself, knowing Thayer as you do?

JD: When he quoted that, he was very pleased; he was very happy to have had that said of him, because he thought it was something admirable. In the beginning, Europe, and especially England, was seen as almost the mother country. That's why he had to go to Oxford: to round out his education. There was also, at the time, the notion of transnationalism, which was a really big idea for Randolph Bourne: his friend who died in the influenza epidemic. The idea of transnationalism was for everyone to rise above a petty nationalism and to see a more global brotherhood of man. I think Thayer very much bought into that, but his preference was certainly for the European Western tradition and canon. Very much so. He wasn't too fond of … He had his orientalism period; there's no doubt about that. He decorated his apartment in a very Asian style, and he had a Japanese valet. But the interest, for example, in African masks that a lot of the modernist painters began to show at the time: he was not interested in that at all.

RC: One of the great tragedies of Thayer's life is that he found such a succoring, fulfilling reality in the world of modern art, and yet he felt completely unmoored and ungrounded in the everyday, mundane world. This is also reflected in the title of your book: *The Tortured Life*. Even well before his illness forced him to withdraw from any active social life, photos of Thayer reveal an incredible tension and intensity in his gaze. Yet, despite these challenges, he made an invaluable contribution to the spiritual world of art and literature. His taste was visionary. Were you also struck by how he managed to accomplish so much despite the pain that he carried in his soul?

JD: Yes. And I'm constantly admiring of the way people with mental illness *get stuff done*. I don't know if it's a distraction from the illness or if they are simply heroic in the effort that they have to overcome it. But he managed to do it; there's no doubt about it. And you know, as he said himself, he was talking with Marianne Moore, and she was mentioning how he seemed bored in social situations. And he said: "Not bored, in torture." I don't know if that meant he was socially awkward. Lots of stories from his younger years show that he was anything but socially awkward; he was very gregarious and sociable. Maybe all that was just a front; maybe he was just putting on a face for the world.

RC: It makes me think of the incredible mind he had, which may have eclipsed some more fundamental emotional sensibility. He seemed to have a difficult time in just relaxing and connecting in a simple emotional way with the people around him. Unless it was a young girl, or unless it was someone equally intellectual. But there seemed to be little middle ground.

JD: Yes. I think sex was a real release for him, because it reduced life to a physical urge. And for somebody whose brain is just going nonstop, there is a certain respite in being able to achieve that.

RC: I thought that this note, which describes Elaine Orr's reaction to a difficult moment during their honeymoon, was unwittingly prophetic of what would befall Thayer's own soul. He says: "Elaine Orr's cry at the Potter [Hotel] was not only the cry of a broken virgin, it was also the cry of the lost soul when, driven backwards, without the strength of backbone to withstand the Devil's push [...] it feels the earth give way and only air beneath it." He adds: "The eyes opened wide like windows to break."

JD: It's kind of a beautiful impressionistic poem about *something*. [Laughs] It seems to be a mixing of the taking of a maidenhead with the fight between the angels up in heaven, when Lucifer gets thrust down to hell. It's an astonishing thing for him to say. The broken back is an image that comes up several times when he describes her after the honeymoon. And this is something that this other academic that I was mentioning noted: That it's as if he was done with her, you know? She was like a snake with a broken back; she was useless. Once he had what he wanted, that was the end of it. But the quote you just read is much more ... There's such great drama in it.

RC: The sense of utter helplessness is sort of what happens to him later on, you know?

JD: Yes; and he becomes an angel, too. When he describes himself after one of his breakdowns in the hospital, he compares himself, I think, to Keats's angel: beating his wings helplessly against the bars.

RC: I remember you quoting that in your book, and it made me flash back to this quote about Elaine. And there's also: "The eyes opened wide like windows to break." Earlier, he described his mother as "plate-glass windows." Again, there's this strange connection with the glass, as a symbol of separation and so on.

JD: Yes, and also the conflation of mother and wife.

RC: Scofield assembled an amazing body of artwork that was later donated to the Metropolitan Museum in New York. Who are some of the artists represented in the Scofield Thayer art collection?

JD: Picasso; Matisse; Chagall; the sculptor, Lachaise ...

RC: Who did a beautiful bust of Thayer.

JD: Yes. Demuth, the American artist, and a *ton* of work by the German, Egon Schiele. A lot of which is very erotic.

RC: Beautiful, sensual figures.

JD: Yes, indeed.

RC: James, thanks so much for your time today; this was just a wonderful talk.

JD: Thank you, Rob. It's always a pleasure to talk with someone as gifted and as knowledgeable as yourself. I think what you're doing is really important, getting stuff and putting it out there for people. Whether they want it or not!

---

* This interview was conducted on 17 July 2015.

* "Despite Edward Thayer's great material success, his son held low opinions of his father's sensitivity and intelligence. His father, he wrote, 'ignored psychology, even the psychology of animals.'" James Dempsey, *The Tortured Life of Scofield Thayer* (Gainesville, FL: University Press of Florida, 2014), p. 13.

* In 1926, a distraught father showed up at the door of E. E. Cummings in Patchin Place, claiming that Thayer had sexually abused his sixteen-year-old son.

A Conversation with Robert Roper,
author of *Nabokov in America: On the Road to Lolita**

Rob Couteau: Congratulations on all the great reviews you've received for the book! You must feel good about that.

Robert Roper: Yeah, I feel good. Writers being miserable specimens of humanity, I guess one could always imagine a more terrific review, a more influential … You know, Barack Obama spotted with one of my books in his hand, getting on an airplane. That kind of thing.

RC: We're going to work on that today, don't worry! [Laughs]

RR: Good. For me, when a book comes out, it's always kind of an anxious time, as well as, you know, you feel happy, gratified, whatever. But I feel pretty good. And I've just been screwing off, really. I should be working on something new.

RC: You worked on this for about three years. It must be a great relief to just let it go and take a break, I would imagine.

RR: That's absolutely true. And also, Nabokov is such a complicated figure, and my own responses to him are so mixed. There's some stuff I love; some stuff I really could do without. I hate his snottiness; I love his this or that. At the end, it was exhausting intellectually. I'd written a big manuscript, and I was following different threads.

RC: It's truly admirable how many different threads you have in the book; this did not go unnoticed. I want to try to follow some of them today. I thought we could begin with your portrait of Nabokov before he arrived in America: "The Nabokovs had been through the historical wringer.

They were Zelig-like figures of twentieth-century catastrophe," "'little' people with a monstrous evil breathing down their necks." What was life like for them before they arrived in the States?

RR: I think the most important thing was how threadbare it was. They were really without much scratch. For years. And they got pretty adept at it. He was not prone to depression or worry particularly. I would say much less so than a lot of struggling artists. She was kind of a worrier; she was the worrywart.

So, it was a life lived without very much. At the same time, he was writing a lot. He was prolific. And she believed in him a hundred-and-fifty percent. There was all kinds of joy surrounding his writing achievements in Russian, and then when they started crossing over into English. But they were always living in scruffy digs. You know, kind of appropriate for a "want to be famous" writer.

RC: Of course, she had to worry more, because all throughout his biography she took care of the basic reality function that he tended to ignore, like any good intuitive writer.

RR: Yeah. And where the hell is that wife for me? Or for you? Really, you know?

RC: [Laughs] I think that wife doesn't exist anymore in 2015.

RR: Right.

RC: You say: "There is beauty and magic all over Nabokov's body of work, but the claim to greatness rests most solidly on the American efforts." And you note that *Lolita* didn't just spring from a Mozartian well of inner genius. How did his American experience transform him as a man and as a writer?

RR: Gosh, that's a very large question. Something that other biographers haven't talked about very much, and that for me seemed really important, was that actually getting to America led to a tremendous burst of relief and hope. Just on the basic level.

RC: He even caught the last ship out of France before the Nazis ran wild.

RR: That's right, yeah. And that same ship, the *Champlain*, after dropping them off in New York, returned to France and was sunk by a mine off the French coast.

RC: The skin of his teeth.

RR: Yeah, really the skin of his teeth. I found his first responses to seeing New York Harbor in some letter or letters. And you can see: he's happy. Just like anybody who gets out of an impossible situation and can finally admit to himself how desperate it was, he was just really kind of overjoyed.

And then, this lifelong obsession with collecting butterflies meant that he was just rubbing his hands, hoping for the first opportunity to get out there, into that big-assed country that he'd been reading about for at least thirty years, since he was a little boy: reading about all these great places to hunt butterflies. He's very unlike all these other émigrés who tended to huddle in little enclaves, mostly in New York. A lot of those people lived their whole lives continuing to speak German, or Russian, or Hungarian to each other. But he very quickly got out into the whole country. And so, that can, in itself, be, if you're of the right temperament, a great accelerant to your hopefulness.

And if you find a way to write about it, it's like, *wow*, that's really, really great. Other very, very talented writers that came over more or less at the same time – Brecht and

Thomas Mann – they couldn't do it. They couldn't get a handle on America. And they *disdained* America. So, they had many reasons not to write about it. Nabokov disdained it in some ways, but he also enjoyed the hell out of it, and he did find ways to write about it.

RC: It's very interesting, what you just said, because you can see that burst of euphoria in between the lines of *Lolita*, particularly in the description of landscape, and the almost carnival-like atmosphere of the goofy things that he found: the roadside attractions and so on. You say he traveled about 200,000 miles by car as he zigzagged across the country. In one of your letters to me from a couple of years ago, you wrote: "There was an interesting concatenation of road-trip books published around the same moment: Kerouac's, *Lolita*, *America Day by Day* by Simone de Beauvoir, *Air-Conditioned Nightmare* by Henry Miller, Clancy Sigal's memoir *Going Away*, and Steinbeck's *Travels with Charley*." In your book, you say: "Other authors of the postwar moment mocked a sanitized America, prominent among them Miller and Kerouac. Kerouac's work of the '40s [and] '50s would seem definingly un-Nabokovian, but *The Dharma Bums* […] stubbornly lays hold of Nabokovian materials and approaches." How do these books resonate beside *Lolita*, and what are the specific correspondences with *The Dharma Bums*?

RR: That's another good question. I'm not as big a fan of *On the Road* as you are, and as many millions of other people are, but *The Dharma Bums* is a great novel.

RC: I actually agree with you on that point. I think *The Dharma Bums*, and one of his last books, *Vanity of Deluoz*, are by far his greatest books. Far beyond *On the Road*.

RR: Yeah. And I found, well, reading them, obviously, they're very, very different. The hero of *The Dharma Bums*, he's on a journey of purification and self-simplification. He's kind of becoming a bit of a saint himself. A saint who lives in this world. And obviously, Humbert Humbert [Laughs] is a more fictionalized character and a much darker, more evil person. But he was also transformed by his travels. Just in his attitude toward his little sex captive, his glee in having access to her body at the beginning turns into this kind of inexhaustible fascination with her. And he loves her; he falls in love with her. At the same time, there's a birth of … You don't want to say that the guy feels guilty, but he does have a consciousness of the enormity of what he's doing to her, and so, there's a tremendous spiritual evolution even in this very evil person.

The books are like each other in that way. And then there's a great joy in the landscape. In *The Dharma Bums*, it's all over it. And also, the hero keeps bursting out into little bits of poetry. And *Lolita*'s full of quotations of poetry, and lines of prose poetry. So, while those two books are written in very different registers, to me they're terrifically relaxing to read. The voices are completely assured, and morally questing, brilliantly observatory, and – I don't want to use fancy words, but – founded in sensoria that are exquisitely attuned to the reality that the characters are living through. You know, just the way we see the colors, and the shapes, and the characteristics of the country registered; there's something very, very similar, to me as a reader, in both of those books.

RC: I found it fascinating that you approach *Lolita* as a road book, in the tradition of these other books that you mentioned.

RR: Yeah. That's an older tradition. It starts with Captain John Smith, and then Bartrum, and Crèvecoeur, and Chateaubriand. They came over and traveled all through America, registering this vast continent as well as they could. So, Nabokov's in that tradition, too. But I think, in the postwar moment, there was a renewed energy to get out into America and report on what it was like. I don't know why, exactly. Maybe it had something to do with the war. And America had come out of the war whole and not destroyed. And in some ways heroic. And people wanted to take its measure.

RC: We can see how far ahead of its time *Lolita* was in capturing the idiom and attitude of America at mid-century if we compare it to certain other works of roughly the same period. Except for a couple of the erotic scenes, Edmund Wilson's *Memoirs of Hecate County*, a very important book in the history of censorship and published only about ten years before, more resembles the work of Henry James in terms of overall style, diction, and sensibility. Whereas with Nabokov, as you say, "A darkly dissident cultural skepticism comes into play with *Lolita*. The extent of it will become clear over the next decade and a half, and tonal similarities abound – in the movies, in productions like Hitchcock's *Psycho* ('61) and Kubrick's *Dr. Strangelove* ('64), and in literature and other cultural domains with the roiling intensity now associated with the term 'The Sixties.' Alert readers pick something up."

RR: For me, all of the changes of the Sixties were almost not possible without *Lolita*. When I first read that – I read *Lolita* when I was still a teenager, a late teenager – I was just *electrified*. I mean, the whole moral dimension of the book went completely over my head. I knew that something bad was happening to a little girl. But the rest of the book was so shockingly true of what I had dimly started to feel, and an awful lot of people had dimly started to feel. And suddenly, these observations were being put into words. So, for me anyway, that awakening started with the way he looked at the country, and the way he talked without apology and made dark hysterical fun of it, while he was doing other things, many other things, too, with his prose.

I wouldn't quite agree with you that *Memoirs of Hecate County* belongs to Henry James. Not that Henry James is some lesser example, but ...

RC: I should have made that clearer. I don't mean in terms of content, necessarily, because he's talking about the 1920s and Thirties. But I mean, if you look at the grammar, and the basic sentence structure, and the sort of tone. Even though Edmund Wilson wasn't an aristocrat, it almost has an aristocratic type of tone; he even mentions his black servant. So, it resonated for me as being closer to a nineteenth-century type of prose than something like *Lolita* or the books that you mentioned that come after *Lolita*.

RR: Yeah, I would agree with that. And Wilson has this kind of grand cathedral organ of a writing style. It's pretty simplified in *Memoirs of Hecate County* but, still, there are echoes of Jamesian paragraphs that are perfectly shaped. Yeah. Of course, *Lolita*'s got a tremendous literary culture in it and behind it.

RC: And the slang. As you point out, Nabokov really studied the slang of teenagers at that time. But you find none of that in *Hecate County*, which was published only ten years before, and which more reflects the way people spoke in the Twenties. I don't mean to pick on that book; it's a marvelous, wonderful novel, but it just struck me that we could take that book, or other novels from around this period and compare them to *Lolita*. You know, as E. M. Forester does in his classic, *Aspects of the Novel*: he's got half a dozen novelists sitting around from different periods. And sometimes, two authors separated by a hundred-and-fifty years sound more alike than two from ten years apart.

RR: Right. I think it's interesting, what you point out. And the idea that an immigrant could make that leap: that tonal leap. I don't think I really can explain it. I have to fall back on just that Nabokov was good and very audacious.

That's the other really big thing that he got from being in America. He got the sense of this vast country. He read very widely in the contemporary literature of the time. And he sensed, he knew the ice jam was breaking up around censorship. He was very afraid of it; he didn't want to end up in jail, or lose whatever money he had. But he could sense there was a change coming. And somehow, being in America, and being kind of joyous about it, and seeing what his contemporaries were daring to do, made him much, much bolder than he'd ever been. When he was writing Russian novels, he would also burn the ears of some of his readers in the 1920s and Thirties, but it was nothing like the leap he felt he could take when he started writing *Lolita*, in the late Forties.

RC: He certainly had the boldness of a great artist.

RR: Yeah. I mean, what defines a great artist? At least, in his case, there was a boldness. Certainly. And he could just go the whole hog in America. Also, it was not lost on him that the hottest and most promising novelists of his time were writing sex books of one form or another. And also the tremendously successful commercial writers, like Grace Metalious, who wrote *Peyton Place*. So, he picked up on that, and this was the direction he wanted to go in, too. I mean, he'd always written sexy books. You know, not pornographic books. That was something that felt very comfortable for him.

RC: Rereading *Lolita*, I was struck by what a mysterious and enchanting story it is. And with each reading, the pedantic allusions seem less important while the emotion of the tale comes more to the fore. As you note, it's a parody of the Romantic confessional novel, and there are all these hermetic references, but it's also much more than that. You quote Nabokov's former student, Alfred Appel, who says: "Nabokov found ways to make parody play for pathos as well as for laughs [...] The novel has it 'both ways, involving the reader ... in a deeply moving yet outrageously comic story.'" Would you agree that the emotional dimension increasingly resonates despite the author's cynicism about all forms of sentiment?

RR: Yeah, absolutely. That's why millions of people have read the book, and it still continues to sell in vast numbers. I mean, on one level, it's a very simple heartbreaking story that ends in terrible tragedy. You know, he didn't leave that out. In other of his books, you see him kind of working at cross-purposes to his own moral impulses. He can't stop mocking them and undercutting them, and simple sentiment is held up to ridicule. That sort of ruins a lot of his books for me, when that happens. And because he falls in love with his own intentions ...

RC: His florid prose?

RR: Well, his prose. But also, he'll have what seems to him a brilliant idea for a novel, and then he executes it. That's really what he's about: showing that he can do that. Very impressive, sometimes. But here, this is the story of a completely believable little girl, and this completely believable pedophile who's also strangely attractive and fascinating to follow.

RC: It makes it a lot different than many of his other books.

RR: Right.

RC: It's pretty clear from biographical data that Nabokov never embarked upon the sort of sexual transgression that *Lolita*'s protagonist was known for. So, what I'm more interested in exploring with you is why his creative process was so focused on this theme and what it reflected for him: personally and psychologically. You say: "He would return to the theme of […] the bodies of young girls in other texts, so that, from one perspective […] his entire body of work can be said to be centrally about this matter."

RR: It's maybe useful to keep in mind that this period when he's writing – let's say, the Thirties through the Sixties – is a period of great sexual awakening. Of bringing sexual material into the scope, the unashamed scope of serious writing. So, he was with that; he was with that enterprise. And, at the time that he started to write about a pedophile, he and some other writers convinced themselves that they were being daring to write about that. Sort of like: If sex had been said to consist of kissing, and fondling, and writing love letters, and suddenly somebody said, "No, it's that, and it's also *fucking*." He felt he was bringing a new species of forbidden sexuality into play, and that was part of the bold enterprise.

Nowadays, a lot of people who hate the novel and still want to ban it say that this kind of thing should never be written about. But back when he was starting to write about it in the late Forties, there was nothing like that agreement:

that this was somehow beyond the pale. So, he was, in a way, doing what he thought was noble work, to write about that. But it was also tremendously promising to him.

A friend of mine is currently reading *Lolita*, and he said he's really digging it, but that it's making him look at little girls differently. [Laughs] You know, it's making him relax his normal way of: "Uh oh, that's a pretty little girl, but we just don't look at her that way, because that's wrong." Well, reading Nabokov on it, he's looking at little girls differently. And for whatever reason, I guess Nabokov found them to be fascinating personally, as a man. That doesn't mean that he ever interfered with them; I don't think he ever did. He had various flirtations when he was a college teacher, and a beautiful co-ed who got very close to him at Wellesley was interviewed years later, and she said he definitely liked girls; he just didn't like little ones. So, I don't think he ever had a personal involvement. OK. But he did look at them and see them. He was sensitive to how they were sexy. And a turn on. And fascinating. And beautiful.

RC: As you and I have spoken about before, art is a mystery; great writing is a mystery. I don't mean to imply that there's a direct causal connection, or just one explanation, for any of this. But there were a couple of other angles I wanted to bring up with you on this theme. In *Speak, Memory*, Nabokov reports that, when he was ten years old, he met a girl named Colette on a beach at Biarritz. For the next two months, he "thought of her constantly." In a phrase reminiscent of *Lolita*, he says: one night, he "lay awake … planning our *flight*." I thought that was an interesting turn of phrase.

Humbert traces his later impulse for pedophilia back to a similar childhood encounter with a girl on a beach. And there are *two* girls in Nabokov's memoir who elicit his early passion, just as there are two key "nymphets" who precede Humbert's encounter with Lolita. How do you interpret all that, and are we to take Nabokov at his word here?

RR: Certain very good writers use their autobiographical material. Most of us writers feel that there's nothing else left to us. If we can't use our autobiographical material somehow – transmogrified quite often – then what do we have? He was definitely close to his own memories and his own … You know, he could recall the intensity of that pre-pubertal fascination with a little girl, with a girl his age. I had romances when I was eleven that were really intense, too. I can't recall them the way he can recall his. But I think, definitely, he's quite obviously drawing on his own material, sure.

RC: In his dream journal, he writes: "I am thinking rather smugly that nobody had ever rendered the name of nostalgia better than I." As you know, and you're touching on this now, nostalgia is often constellated as a result of something not being lived to its fullest: often, something of great emotional import. A scene from our past returns to haunt us, because it contains an emotional complex in need of further development. I'm reminded of one of the final images in *Citizen Kane*, with the close-up of the sleigh named "Rosebud": perhaps, a symbol of lost childhood innocence. Is it possible that the nymphet in Nabokovian literature symbolized a Rosebud complex for Nabokov? That is, a sensibility untainted by his hyperintellectualism and his abundant cerebral cynicism. A counterpoint to his consciousness.

RR: Yeah, that says it very carefully. And I find, throughout his writing, especially with the stuff that I like, he's quick to make himself an object of humor, or to do so with the heroes that are very clearly stand-ins for him. I think it's because, just as you describe, this is a very intellectual, deeply learned guy, a powerful mind, but he's always kind of reminding himself that he's that mug he sees in the mirror. And he's a little fat, and he's bald now, and he's got false teeth. And, you know, something funny happened at the cocktail party last night, where he spilled everything on his lap. He's not ashamed to bring himself in as an object of fun, and to humanize himself. I think that's part of the appeal of Humbert Humbert, too. Humbert is a monster, but he's also making delicious fun of himself.

RC: Oh, he's completely self-effacing in that sense.

RR: Yeah. He's also quite aware of how ridiculous he must seem: a guy with a funny foreign accent in suburban America. But he plays his role: This is who I am. So, somehow, Nabokov, through a lot of work, and great gifts, but mainly through a lot of work, found ways of combining his intellectual power, his pure conceptual power, and a deep learning, and all these different languages, with that simple "in touchness" with his ordinary human feelings of embarrassment, excitement, and self-mockery. Somehow, he put those things together.

RC: I want to see if you can identify the following quote. Tell me who this sounds like to you: "Finally, what I decided I'd do, I decided I'd go away…. I'd start hitchhiking my way out West. What I'd do, I figured, I'd go down to the Holland Tunnel and bum a ride, and then I'd bum another one, and another one, and another one, and in a few days I'd be somewhere out West where it was very pretty and sunny and where nobody'd know me and I'd get a job. I figured I could get a job at a filling station somewhere, putting gas and oil in people's cars."

RR: That sounds like an awful lot of writers. It sounds like James Salter; it sounds like Kerouac; it could be a line from a Norman Mailer novel ...

RC: You mentioned Kerouac. I thought, in terms of tone, diction, and style, it was very reminiscent of Kerouac and *On the Road*. But it's from the final pages of *The Catcher in the Rye* ...

RR: Ah!

RC: Just before Holden Caulfield cracks up. And I thought, from this, one might conclude that *Catcher* strangely anticipates Kerouac's road book.

RR: Yeah.

RC: Maybe you could talk about the parallels that you found between *Lolita* and *The Catcher in the Rye*.

RR: I would say, more generally, there's a parallel between Salinger and Nabokov. As I talk about in the book, how they emerged as writers at the exact same moment. And they were, inevitably, very aware of each other. We know, because Nabokov actually went out of his way and said some praising things about this guy, Salinger. He almost never said anything nice about a contemporary writer. Then there's that beautiful vulnerable little girl who is this radiant source of meaning in both of their most famous works. Phoebe is Holden's little sister. The catcher in the rye is a teenage boy, so he doesn't have anything like Humbert's awareness of his own sexuality. But there's this fascination.

For some reason, postwar, little girls, in their beauty, in their fun, in their goodness, were, I think, very meaningful symbols. Maybe after the war and all the death, and the impossible horrors, to look at a child and see her as this radiant and human reminder of perfection ... And both these writers picked up on that.

RC: Throughout the history of symbolism, the child has always been a symbol of rebirth, hasn't it? Especially the female child: it's the rebirth of the soul.

RR: Yeah, sure, absolutely, in American literature. Think of Pearl in *The Scarlet Letter*. And *Daisy Miller*, a slightly older girl. Yeah, definitely. So, both of them are obsessed with beautiful little girls. The focus of my book was not to try to explain – whether it can ever be explained – why certain tropes appear at a given historical moment, but ...

RC: I thought it was fascinating, the way you brought up the fact that they're both writing contemporaneously, and yet the treatment is so completely different: "Both find a fertile subject in postwar teenagerhood [...] Both invoke an America in which to write about magical young girls is somehow a necessary thing – a key to what is." And yet, as you discuss, there are also vast differences. "Humbert soon does to Dolly something that Holden, in his fragile emotional state, might have found unbearable to hear or even think about."

RR: Right, yeah.

RC: Holden is sexually naïve, at times almost presexual in attitude, whereas Humbert is eclipsed and devoured by his narcissistic fetishism. Holden wants to preserve untainted childhood; he even tries to efface the obscene graffiti scrawled on the wall. Whereas Humbert only cares about his own solipsistic world of self-gratification.

RR: Right. They're sort of like different poles around this. That, to me, is kind of suggestive; I like that pairing for that reason. Yet, when I reread *Catcher in the Rye*, I felt, you know, Holden is just so straightforward, and talks to us on such an intimate level, that we assume he is very sophisticated. But I kept feeling this sexual terror in him. You know, he's going to have a hard time growing up.

RC: That's such a good point. It's something only a really good writer can do, especially with a first-person narrative: to let the reader know, indeed, there's so much else going on that's not being said here. He sort of dramatizes it in that scene where he's in New York, and he tries to get a prostitute to come to his room, but then he doesn't want to do anything with her.

RR: Yeah, right. You know, I've always been puzzled and saddened by how little came of Salinger as a writer after his great period. As we do know, he was kind of caught up in romances with younger women. He didn't have the fully mature wife and saintly amanuensis that Nabokov did. Somehow I felt that, under other circumstances, he would have gone much farther, and written a whole lot of other stuff.

RC: In *Moby-Dick*, the old Manxman, in comparing Pip and Ahab, says: "One daft with strength, the other daft with weakness." By befriending Pip, whom you call an "enchanting child," Ahab is indirectly acknowledging the value of vulnerability. Charles Olson says, "from this moment" Ahab's tone "is richer, quieter, less angry and strident. He even questions his former blasphemies, for a bottomed sadness grows in him." "What Pip wrought in Ahab throws over the end of *Moby-Dick* a veil of grief."* This is reminiscent of Humbert's character-shift at the end of *Lo-*

lita. Perhaps you could talk about your comparison between the two books.

RR: I know Nabokov read *Moby-Dick* and had a period of discussing it intensely with a lab assistant he had at Harvard when he was working in the museum, organizing the butterflies. He was very taken up with the book for a while. And Melville is an unusual figure in the American pantheon in that Nabokov never said anything snotty about him. He praised him. And there are signs of his admiration in *Lolita*.

For me, *Lolita*'s a very sad, dark story. We can't believe, and don't want to believe, that we see the trajectory, but we do sense it well before the end. Humbert's growing love for *Lolita*, for the little girl who's now growing up, and finally for the young woman who's pregnant by another man, whom he sees at the end of the book, doesn't take away what he's done, and the horror of it and so forth. But it makes it much more bearable, and much more moving.

And I think it's the same thing with Captain Ahab. That's even more of a preordained catastrophe; we sense that very, very early. I don't think Melville developed that humanizing of Ahab the way that Nabokov developed Humbert's change. I mean, that wasn't what Melville was principally after. But he had these great instincts, Melville, so he knew he had to do something. He had to put in some other colors. I find all that business with Pip very moving. Those are the parts of *Moby-Dick* that I most remember. Nobody else does, but, for me, they were really important.

RC: Would you agree that Nabokov's sympathetic portrayal of this ghastly figure, Humbert Humbert, is the real genius of the book?

RR: Yeah, sure; it's a great accomplishment. Again, it's something he'd been working on through a lot of other books. He has many other kinds of monstrous, cracked heroes or protagonists or antiheroes. So, he'd been working at that for a long time.

The genius of the book – I'm always nervous about using that word, "genius." [Laughs] But the *greatness* of the book – I feel fine with that – is in its encounter with America, too. Just the fact that he found America enticing, and very beautiful, and he was able to respond to the great open door that America shows to people, you know? "Come on, look at all of me. Come down and explore." He could respond to that but also sense mystery and doom in the landscape. I mean, that was an act of extraordinary receptivity or creativity; I don't know exactly what.

RC: And also, the goofiness of the landscape, as well.

RR: Yeah, right, completely: in all the wonderful vulgar touches. So, I wouldn't just say it's Humbert. I mean, Humbert's voice is inseparable from what's great about the novel. It's superb. But it's not just that. And I would say the moral evolution is also unexpected – and unexpectedly moving.

RC: In another one of your letters written to me while you were working on *Nabokov in America*, you say: "Still haven't figured out how to interrogate Nabokov over his finicky self-adoring 'I am a genius' body of work, nor over his savage attacks on all signs of honest creativity in other writers of his time, Henry Miller certainly among the targets of his loathing (and also Faulkner and Mann and Malraux and Pasternak and Hemingway and all the women authors and just about everybody except that equally finicky young New Yorker writer, Updike, who kissed the

master's ass and therefore won words of praise). The reading about him has led me down some interesting by-
roads. He is a 'large' writer I discover, all the issues of
modernism present in him, not to mention all of twentieth-
century political history, and some issues of science relat-
ing to his butterflies. But while 'large,' many of his books
seem small to me. That's not bad necessarily. But maybe it
explains some of his viciousness toward other writers, who,
in their non-Mandarin prose, touched regions of the soul he
intuited but couldn't visit." And in your book, you add:
Knut Hamsun "joins Dostoyevsky, Turgenev, Leskov, and
dozens of other writers of authentic power on Nabokov's
list of little or no respect."

Did Nabokov suffer from an unconscious doubt about his
own value? Or was he just blind to the emotional power of
these writers because of his own emotional shortcomings?

RR: Gosh, that's a good question. I think, yes, there was
some great doubt in him. I mean, otherwise, why do you
keep insisting that the world acknowledge you as a genius?
I mean, even in your last decade, your last years of life, you
know, he's still insisting that people recognize that he's a
genius at creating chess problems of the *solus rex* type; that
he's a genius of Russian poetry; the list goes on and on.
And the accomplishments were fully acknowledged by the
world by the time he was sixty-five. And yet, he still
needed it. There must be some kind of … I don't know.

To be a great and gifted writer at the time of modernism
is a very big problem, because basically the modernist task
was to write hateful and disturbing and disruptive novels
that would give avid normal novel readers a terrible head-
ache. So, it doesn't begin with *Ulysses*, but *Ulysses* is a
great example. I mean, you really need to read it in a col-

lege class with an inspiring professor who can tell you: "Don't be bored by this chapter, it's really wonderful!" [Laughs] I think somebody once said of it: "It's a demonstration of how *not* to write a novel." So anyway, Nabokov's fully sensitive to his times, and he's not going to write straightforward, middlebrow novels. Not *him*, by God! And so, he accepts the modernist task. But, at the same time, he's a guy who loves to be in intimate contact with his readers. He loves to move them. He loves to fascinate and enchant them. And so, somehow, by an almost impossible contortion, he arrives, eventually, when he's in America, at an opportunity to write in a way that almost anybody can read that isn't a giving up of his modernist task. So, that was a tremendous struggle.

I see a lot of his unhappiness, and the vicious things he said about other writers, as a reflection of just how impossible it felt to him. Through most of his career. You know, it's amazing that he was as productive, as continually productive, as he was. And you only have to compare a really boring, failed novel like *Bend Sinister*, which he finished in 1946, to *Lolita*, which he started writing in '47, which was phenomenally readable, and moving, and deeply complex but openhearted. Whereas the other one is none of those things. You see what a tremendous load he was carrying, and he had to find a way to put it off his back, and yet not disrespect it and move on. And I think, at least to me, a lot of his strange behavior reflects that.

RC: Fascinating. You also document the tragic loss of friendship between Nabokov and Edmund Wilson. You call it "a savage, ultra-public bloodletting." Although intellectual disagreements were the supposed cause of the rupture, there's also the fact that Wilson went out of his way to help and support so many other writers, while Nabokov went out of his way to disparage them. How did Wilson feel about Nabokov's loathing of past and present literary figures, some of whom Wilson was promulgating in his critical essays?

RR: I think that was really the straw that broke the camel's back for Wilson. He was never comfortable with that, and they had arguments about that. And finally, when various other wounds to the ego on both sides had mounted up to a certain level – which happens with a deep friendship, where people are perhaps obsessively frank with each other – when Nabokov went off like a madman against Pasternak, you could see Wilson saying to himself: "I just cannot fucking understand this guy."

RC: He even called him *sadistic* at one point.

RR: Yeah, that's right. You know, there's a level of saying nasty things about other writers that goes along with the literary life; it's not unknown, of course. But this was way over the top, and I think Wilson finally couldn't explain it away himself. And so, that was very important to their breaking up.

To me, it seemed very, very sad, because they had a truly wonderful friendship and deeply enjoyed each other's company. Their letters are maybe the most fun literary correspondence of the twentieth century. I mean, I haven't read all the famous correspondences, but I've read a lot of them. They're tremendously witty, and you can see how inspired they are by each other's letters. And then, when they got together, they would swap dirty books. Wilson gives Nabokov a copy of the *Story of O*, and they get together quickly, so they can talk about it. And Vera's nose is out of joint, because she knows they're talking about some dirty subject and snickering. You know, they're just having a good time. And to see that all sacrificed, that's kind of sad.

RC: You call *Pale Fire* "esoteric and spiritualistic." "It makes a case for a higher realm. The existence of such a dimension is implied by anomalies of this world we inhabit; the Great Mind that decrees a world of doubles, riddling coincidences, and secret correspondences is, by a curious coincidence, the very model of the mind that can understand it. This spiritual project is an old one in American letters. Emerson, Hawthorne, Whitman, and Dickinson, along with many lesser-known authors, make up one cohort of spirit-seekers." But "by the end of the nineteenth century metaphysical speculation had fallen somewhat out of favor."

I'm intrigued by how, unlike these other spirit-seekers, with most of his work, Nabokov approaches this realm more through an archly cerebral mind-game rather than through a feeling-toned intuition. With him, it's more of an intellectualized intuition, such as you'd find in a Sherlock Holmes story. Would you agree?

RR: I would say that he started with the same intimations that maybe a lot of us have, you know: materialism doesn't explain the whole kit and caboodle, that there are unexplained coincidences that are so suggestive. And things happen in every life, if you're paying attention, that are just eerie. I think he had all of those usual sensations and experiences. And, in *Speak, Memory*, he talks about them, and elsewhere too. And then, being himself, of course he had to try to get *rigorous* about it. I mean, he was always very careful, because he didn't want people to mock him. He didn't want to be seen as a new Arthur Conan Doyle, who spent many years around Ouija boards. But he had, I think, the ordinary sensations of sensitivity to ... spirits. I don't know how else to talk about it.

RC: To the whole nonrational world.

RR: Yeah, right. And, at the same time, he's this hyper-intellectual writer and also this serious scientist, a lepidopterist. I mean, in that area too, you see him just barely restraining himself, because he doesn't really believe in Darwinism. He's like a creationist a lot of times: This world is too fabulous, too full of strange suggestions and eerie, magnificent complexities, to have evolved through something as corny and stolid as evolution. He doesn't really believe it.

A number of modern Nabokov scholars are quickly trying to brush all that under the rug and say: "Well, we misunderstood how brilliant are his insights into evolution. It's not that he rejects it; it's that he's talking about it on a whole higher realm than we are." But no, I think he was like an "intelligent design" believer.

RC: You just mentioned Nabokov scholars. In your book, you write: "The scholars of Nabokov [...] rejoice in discovering what is complexly hidden." "Nuggets of hidden reference are everywhere," but "There is an esoteric and ever-narrowing quality to the hunt, and an undistinguished reader such as myself feels at times a quiet dismay: when will the picking over be complete, can we not get back to saying more obvious, possibly more urgent, things about the curious author?" How did you attempt to "borrow Nabokov back from the experts"?

RR: I'm sure that the experts don't think that I've done it adequately, but I did read all of what they wrote. I think I mention in the book that I sat around for a couple of years reading nothing but Nabokov criticism. And it was really a lot of fun, basically. I mean, some of the stuff is head-bangingly boring, but a lot of it's really good. So, I at least had to be familiar with their lines of analysis.

I think part of the scholarly enterprise is to be, in some ways, very modest. To look for unfound little factoids or allusions in texts, and to bring them forth, and to talk about them in a rigorous way, and make as much as you can out of them. And, in this book, anyway, I tried to be very specific about the few texts that I talk about – you know, in these American texts – but I'm talking about the guy's whole life. So I couldn't – and I didn't want to – talk about an allusion to Dos Passos that's hidden on page 129 of *Lolita* that nobody's ever seen before. That's not the kind of writing I want to do.

RC: As I mentioned before, I reread it twice in the last couple of years, preparing for our talk today, and I happened to have *The Annotated Lolita*. It's got all the allusions you could possibly want, and it was apparently crafted with Nabokov's approval. But in the rereading of it, all those things seemed so much less important to me than the pure, raw feeling and emotion of the characters.

RR: Yeah, me too. And yet, there are moments when it's great fun to crawl up with Appel's *Annotated Lolita*. He was a smart guy who did a lot of hard work, and he brings in things that I never would have thought of. By the same token, Brian Boyd, who wrote the big, double volume of Nabokov has just completed an annotated *Ada* – you know, Nabokov's supposed masterwork – and I have zero interest in reading that, because the book itself doesn't move me and kind of bores me. No doubt, every text of Nabokov's can give employment to a number of smart scholars. But that's not, finally, the most important thing about it, about his books.

RC: To be perfectly honest, I find him very, very difficult to read. I've picked up so many of his books and put them right down again, because of this intellectual approach he has, and for the other reasons that you've mentioned.

RR: Yeah.

RC: Whereas *Lolita* isn't like that; there's a completely different dimension in *Lolita*. By the way, I enjoyed your inclusion of the famous Groucho Marx quote: "I've put off reading *Lolita* for six years, till she's eighteen."

RR: [Laughs]

RC: *Lolita* really impacted the culture rather widely. Was it his greatest work?

RR: I guess so. Let's see. Is it my favorite Nabokov work? I think so. I've gotten a whole lot of pleasure out of *Pale Fire*, which not everybody likes. And *Speak, Memory*; I love that book.

He considered *Lolita* to be his greatest work. And that says a lot, because, after all, he's a very self-defending writer, so he's essentially saying, "My most popular book, my easiest-to-read novel that even a smart eleven- or twelve-year-old can read, I think it's my greatest work." And so, I go with him in that judgment.

RC: Is it because his usual intellectualism gets a bit eclipsed by the emotion in the book, and because of the presence of that magical child and the way that he portrays her?

RR: Yeah, that's part of it. Although, again, I would go back to the book itself and its language. For me, it's just fucking funny, line by line. And so perceptive. And also tremendously touching. He talks about how, when they were deep in their travels, they had reached a point where he would fake going to sleep, and then he would hear her wait a little bit and then start crying. Every night. Every night. I'm hard-pressed to come up with something in American literature that has moved me that much. You know, as much as that little report. Very simple language.

RC: And the usual cerebral tone of his prose is, in *Lolita*, put off onto Humbert Humbert. So he sort of uses Humbert to make fun of Nabokov's own archly intellectual quality.

RR: Yeah. I think it's good to remember that although Nabokov had big struggles in his life – he lost his money, they were kicked out of Russia, his father was murdered, you know, a lot of trouble – and despite his doubts about himself, still, he saw himself as, and was, a tremendous winner. He could carry almost any room on his charisma and his verbal brilliance. And he was not shy; he threw his weight around. There were always some people who were very irritated and frightened by him. And then there were people who just adored him; they just loved him. And so, he was a guy who could find his way and get over in almost every situation.

I think pretty early in his life, probably in his thirties, he also started seeing how there were aspects of his personal behavior that were monstrous. That he had been very cruel to his younger brothers, for example. And that he had this impulse to say shitty things about other writers. He knew he went too far, but he didn't stop it; he didn't want to stop it. And so, his larger personal enterprise in his writing was to be more and more honest about what could be monstrous and very, very cruel about somebody who was brilliant. And *Lolita* is where it comes out maybe the strongest. He's doing the same thing in *Ada*, but it's just tiresome at that point.

So, that's good, that's great. He's not just congratulating himself on how brilliant he is; he's starting to see other dimensions: darker sides of it.

RC: Nabokov rather cunningly tells us that Lolita lost her virginity to a boy she meets at summer camp. When Humbert finally has her alone to himself, it's Lolita who proposes that they engage in an act of eroticism that she considers to be merely a game: one that, in her mind, has no connection with childbirth. Was this an ingenious way of making the story slightly more palatable as well as complex: by avoiding the deflowering of an adolescent by Humbert and making the girl herself initiate a physical seduction?

RR: That's hard to answer, but I think it came out of his research about teenager sexuality. He read all kinds of books about it before he really started writing. You know: average age of onset of menstruation; how often teenage girls masturbated; all of this stuff. It's in his notes. And I think he came upon the fact that, hmm, something like twenty-seven percent of girls of fifteen had already had intercourse: something like that. So, in a way, he thought he was being accurate when he did that. But of course, I think he's conscious of the fact that this throws an interesting complexity into the situation, and we do avoid that situation of a big hairy brute, you know, sticking his cock into a little squirming twelve-year-old.

RC: Well said, Robert!

RR: [Laughs]

RC: You said that he and Edmund Wilson had many a chuckle over the *Story of O*. Was it Maurice Girodias's

English translation that they were looking at together? Nabokov's archenemy, I should say, Maurice Girodias. That's kind of ironic.

RR: It might not be, because they both read French.

RC: Girodias was a great thorn in the side of Nabokov even though he helped him quite a bit by publishing *Lolita* in France. *Lolita* even had the honor of being briefly banned in France, as a result of pressure from British censors, while it was being openly published in America. This was also a very ironic and bizarre twist.

RR: Yes, it was. The way it all worked out for him ... I mean, he could not have scripted it any better.

RC: It's amazing. And as you say somewhere in your book, "Without Wilson's stewardship, the road would have been different – there might not have been a road."

RR: Yeah, that's right. I mean, he could have been like so many other gifted writers: "Yes, I'm proud to say I published three stories in the *New Yorker* fourteen years ago, and now I'm working hard at Cornell," you know? "I've got tenure, and I'm looking forward to my retirement when I can back to my writing." I mean, really, that could have been it. That could have been his path.

When I say it was really fortunate how it worked out, I mean, about *Lolita*, the fact that everybody said *no* in America. He got it to all the good and important publishers. Then it comes out in the Olympia Press edition, and that allows word of mouth to build to a frenzied point, especially after Graham Greene somehow gets his hands on a copy in 1955 and writes, at the end of the year, he says: The three best books I read last year were A, B, and C: C being a book called *Lolita* that you've never heard of. Then this drumbeat starts to build, and people start sneaking the book into the country: in small numbers, but to influential people. And then, all the turmoil over *Lady Chatterley's Lover* and *Tropic of Cancer* is going on, and there are court cases, and finally it's getting to the point where the defenders of decency are being recognized as being completely ridiculous. Just as that logjam breaks, Putnam says, OK, we'll bring it out. It was the first world success of a sex book after the break of that logjam.

RC: Even the way it came into Putnam's hands is absolutely hysterical. Do you want to mention that?

RR: Yeah, I thought that was great. [Laughs] It was some "questionable" woman – well, I don't know if she was questionable, but she was …

RC: She was sort of what we might today call an "exotic dancer," no?

RR: Yeah, that's right. And obviously, a good reader, too! And here's a sexy book, somebody gave it to her, and then she shows it to Minton, Putnam's editor-in-chief, and they're conducting an affair at the same time or a little later.

I didn't think they were going to let me tell that story about Nabokov's son, Dmitri, getting it on with Mrs. Minton, Polly Minton. It's in the Berg Archive, buried deep in a page-a-day diary. Other people have read it, but nobody's been allowed to put it into a book. Or has tried to. Maybe I'm the first one who thought it was a great story and wanted to. But when I submitted all my quotations … you have to list everything you want to quote from a Nabokov source that's at the Berg Collection. And this really gave me the heebie-jeebies. You have to submit that to Andrew Wylie's agency, too. The Wylie Agency now administers the Nabokov Estate, and it's the most powerful literary agency in America, and Wylie is known for sometimes highhanded professional behavior and for militantly protecting his brands. So I had to ask permission of them and also of the Berg Collection. I had this long, long, long list of stuff. And some of it was to quote three words – "It was 'a pretty day'" – but then there's this long quotation from Vera's diary: of when Dmitri and the distraught wife have a little fling. And somehow, they all signed off on it. I don't know if they didn't notice or what.

RC: That's an interesting back story; I didn't realize that.

RR: I was very grateful that they did sign off. It was generous of them – very open-minded.

RC: I just reread some of John de St. Jorre's *Venus Bound*, the history of the Olympia Press. And, in there, he says that this woman not only tipped Minton off to the book and received a generous finder's fee for it, but it wasn't the Olympia Press edition that she'd read; she'd read excerpts of *Lolita* in a *literary magazine!* Isn't that hysterical?

RR: She must have read it in the *Anchor Review*. I didn't know that; I'd always assumed it was the Olympia.

RC: So, she *was* a very well read person.

RR: Yeah!

RC: Well, thanks so much for penciling me in and spending some time on together. This has been a great talk; I really appreciate it.

RR: Yeah, really fun. Needless to say, yours was the best prepared and most intelligent interview I've had, so I want to thank you for that.

---

* This interview was conducted on 23 July 2015.

* Charles Olson, *Call Me Ishmael* (New York: Grove Press, 1947), p. 60.

ALSO BY ROB COUTEAU:

The Sleeping Mermaid, *with an Introduction by Christopher Sawyer-Lauçanno*

Novelist and literary enthusiast Rob Couteau brings readers part of his love with *The Sleeping Mermaid*, a book of flowing poetry and thought that asks plenty of questions and offers plenty of answers. *The Sleeping Mermaid* is a poetry collection well worth considering.
– Midwest Book Review

Had Henry Miller written poetry it might have resembled the poems of Robert Couteau you are about to read (or have read, and have come to me afterwards, as you probably should). This is not to imply that Couteau is a Miller knock-off. He's not. He's an American original, as was Miller. What I mean is simply that Couteau, with his painter's eye (another Miller similarity), addresses quite directly themes and subjects that Miller was also enamored by: Paris, women, the quotidian surprises life throws us, an acute understanding of mythology and folktale, of tradition and revolution, and finally, the chance encounters that, if we are wise enough to embrace them, help to make us more human.

In Couteau's work there is no phoniness, no artifice for the sake of artifice – though in the great French tradition this poet knows so well, there is some art for the sake of art. Couteau does not venture into realms of obscurity where meaning is confined to the interior of a Klein bottle; his poems all have direct force, subjects, even verbs. He is intent on having his readers share in his observations, whether it be his artful retelling and reinterpretations of Native American story and song, or his appraisal of how a woman parades across the avenue. He does not ever sacrifice ordinary sense for an extra-ordinary significance. Instead, he speaks with fervor, with something to say, with something he wants us to hang onto and in the process come to an understanding of why it matters not just to him but should matter to us.

In other words: he knows what he wants to say, and says it.

Couteau's poetic material is as vast as his learning and imagination. And yet he does not seem overly concerned with making tidy themes, or buttoning his knowledge into a small sphere. Indeed, I often sense that he hasn't really selected his material; rather his material seems to have selected him. But obedient to the muse and his own gifts, he records for us with clear-eyed insight the spectrum of his collisions between subject and object, the real and imagined, the read and reread and then reinvented, himself and the perceived, the distillate of being always awake and attentive to what confronts him. Indeed. Couteau is not conditional in his probing of the human condition, even to the point of exposing his own condition in face of what he is examining. He steps right in, and in turn allows us the gift of his informed vision. What we see is not always pretty, nor dressed up for the photo-op. But he never panders. He sees what he sees and puts it down on the page with grace and often beauty. And we, as readers, benefit enormously for his willingness to go the distance with what matters.

I think it was William Carlos Williams who said that poetry is belief. Couteau believes in belief, believes that poetic worth is measured in faithfulness to what is, what has been, and what could be. These are his talismans; these are the points where he begins and ends. His poetic excursions take us to many places: to the Paris of Rimbaud and Picasso, to the Native North Americans, to mythology and history and how the woman he is encountering is seducing him as he seduces her (and us), and finally, how alone, the cosmos plays itself out at 3 a.m. when the only lap dog is memory.

– A former creative-writing teacher at MIT, Christopher Sawyer-Lauçanno is the author of *The Continual Pilgrimage: American Writers in Paris, 1944-1960, E. E. Cummings*, and *An Invisible Spectator, A Biography of Paul Bowles*.

Doctor Pluss, with an Afterward by Jim Feast

Amazingly beautiful, haunting prose. It's a great book.
– **Christopher Sawyer-Lauçanno**

Reading *Doctor Pluss*, Rob Couteau's intense, dramatic story of a psychologist who works at the Walt Whitman Asylum for Adults, one might think, especially since there is no authorial information given on the book, that Couteau is a psychiatrist of some sort. How else could he write with such assurance about this milieu?

However, turning to his book of essays, poems, reviews and interviews, *Collected Couteau*, though it, too, contains no authorial information, one begins to see that he is a well-informed layman, who has thought deeply about psychological issues. Not only has he thought, but he has also forged a coherent philosophy through both the direct study of the subject and a close reading of literature.

Part of his philosophy is revealed in the interpretation of schizophrenia in a review of a book by John Perry. He notes that "Perry's work in traditional psychiatric settings led him to conclude that those in the thrall of an acute psychotic episode are rarely listened to or met on the level of their visionary state of consciousness." If care providers paid heed to what the patients were trying to show in their symptoms and musings, they would often find that "forced to live an emotionally impoverished life, the psyche had reacted by provoking a transformation in the form of a 'compensating' psychosis, during which a drama in depth was enacted, forcing the initiate to undergo certain developmental processes."

Couteau quotes Perry concerning this state: "The individual [patient] finds himself living in a psychic modality quite different from his surroundings. He is immersed in a myth world." This modality may seem to be regressive, but it is far from unfruitful. "Although the [myth] imagery is of a general, archetypal nature," writes Couteau, "it also symbolizes the key issues of the individual undergoing the crisis. Therefore, once lived through on this mythic plane, and once the process of withdrawal nears its end, the images must be linked to specific problems of daily life." This leads, in the best cases, to a healing whereby the patient is now able to face and cope with problems that caused the flight into illness.

Perry's work is not that well known, but readers may be more familiar with the once-celebrated theories of R. D. Laing. While not finding archetypes in his patients' thoughts, Laing agreed with Perry in treating the schizophrenics' attempts to communicate as valid efforts to reach out, and in finding that their psychological difficulties were often rooted in their untenable lives.

This is not to say that Couteau wholeheartedly endorses these ideas of Perry's. That's not the point. Rather, Dr. Pluss, the staff psychiatrist in the novel named after him, does. Instead of coldly and clinically assessing his schizophrenic patients (as dominant psychiatric norms dictate he should), Pluss befriends them, sharing his own passions, such as his love of modernist art, particularly of Paul Klee, in a workshop where the inmates learn to appreciate art as a form of therapy. Further, he listens carefully to them as they exhaustively recount their life views. He may criticize these patients' sometimes-outrageous ideas, but he takes them seriously.

The description on the back of the novel states that the book is "based on actual dialogues with schizophrenic patients," something evident from the stories told to Pluss. With a fantasy akin to Freud's famous Rat Man case, one woman thinks a ravenous cat lives in her midsection. That's why she constantly has to eat. Otherwise, the beast, in its craving for food, will begin consuming her internal organs. (In Freud's story, the patient imagines rats gnawing on his friends' buttocks.)

The most significant patient is Jonah, who believes his own mental problems are so tremendously fascinating that, when he engages in a self-analysis (talking to himself), somehow the Viennese master himself comes back to life to eavesdrop. As Jonah tells Dr. Pluss, "And Freud listened to the analysis, glued to his television. He wouldn't eat; he wouldn't sleep; he wouldn't anything." Ironically enough, Jonah's psychoanalysis simply consists of enumerating, without explaining, his own situation. "I'm a patient; this is a hospital. Why am I in a cage?" While this fantasy may not seem terrifically engaging, when not raving Jonah presents thoughtful and provocative comments on religion, other patients, and even on Dr. Pluss, who is himself undergoing a nervous breakdown.

Pluss had been a painter but gave up the arts to devote himself to helping people. Now, as he is increasingly enthralled by some of his patients' mythic visions, he begins painting again. Using notes of his talks with schizophrenics, he recasts their ideas as art. He creates, for instance, a series of paintings on Jonah, who sometimes thinks of his mind as a clockwork. Pluss depicts "Jonah being cured of paranoia at the Bulova Watch Repair School and leaving behind his persecution complex in the grim milieu of the Bulova assembly line."

Couteau has some misgivings about the sympathetic ear approach of Perry. This is suggested by the fact that Pluss goes beyond listening to his patients' stores, gets caught up by them, and eventually seems to go a little mad himself when he quits the sanitarium and disappears. I say "seems" because, mirroring Pluss's dissolution, the narrative strands of the book, which had been tightly wound in the first section that focused closely on Pluss, begin to unravel, with Jonah taking over much of the narrative and becoming a new focal point. This shift of gears can be a bit disorienting as the realism of the opening is partially abandoned, but it does give the reader a chance to see the schizophrenia developing as it gains hold of Pluss's thought processes. Pluss is like the psychiatrist Dr. Dysart in Peter Shaffer's play *Equus*, who begins to doubt his profession, since when a cure succeeded, it often converted a passionate, inspired, if addled person into a normal but dull zombie. Pluss is attracted by the crazed creativity of so many of his charges. Unlike Dysart, though, who confines his admiration to rueful ruminations, Pluss mimics his patients, becoming psychotic in the process.

I mentioned previously that Couteau obtained psychological knowledge not only from studying and from thinking about books on the mind but also by reading literature. Indeed, it is important to note that while Pluss took the ultimately dangerous path of learning from his patients, Couteau has deepened his insights by interviewing great writers, such as Ray Bradbury and Hubert Selby Jr.

These interviews are not simple Q&A's but are interactions with a lot of give and take. The interview with Selby (done for *Rain Taxi*) delves deeply into spirituality and ethics. In a notable passage, Selby remarks, "What we seem to be taught, at least in the Western world [is]: we're born with a blank slate, and we have to learn how to get and get.... But no one ever seems to train us in methods of finding out that we already have within us all the things that are valuable: all the treasures. But it's only in the process of giving them away, to somebody else, that we become aware of having them."

This thought seems to follow up on insights brought to bear in *Doctor Pluss*. One reason for the immobilization of so many in psychiatric offices or institutions (according to Couteau and the Shaffer of *Equus*) is that conventional education does not provide tools for people to deal with stress or act in a humanitarian, giving manner, only instructing them on how to get ahead.

I can't help, though, but note that Selby, like Couteau, suggests he has learned from unique individuals, pointing to none other than *Evergreen Review's* own editor, Barney Rosset, for special commendation. In discussing his first novel, *Last Exit to Brooklyn*, which Rosset published, Selby engages in an interchange, beginning with Couteau's question:

> Why was *Last Exit* allowed to be published in the United States in 1964, while *Tropic of Cancer*, which was a much less obscene book – by the classical definition – was banned until just a few years before this?

Selby: I think because … it [*Tropic*] had been banned for many years. You could only smuggle it in and all that sort of stuff. So, it had a different resistance and a different procedure to go through.

Couteau: It had an already-established weight, a history that it had to deal with.

Selby: Right. Yeah. And, of course, Barney Rosset took care of business and made it possible for a lot of things to happen.

It's nice to see that old debts – Rosset's discovery and championing of Selby's work – are here being repaid, but this also brings me to a final thought on history. Some readers may find Couteau out of date, in that Laing and the anti-psychiatry movement to which he belonged are not the household names they were in the 1960s, but they (as represented by Perry) seem to orient and spur the author's fictional and nonfictional excursions. While some may say this current of psychology has been superseded, Couteau has a gone a long way toward showing that it still possesses validity and staying power. How else account for the intellectual freshness, richness, and potency of his novel and essays?

– Jim Feast is the author of *Neo-Phobe* (with Ron Kolm) and the former assistant editor of the *Evergreen Review*.